r

Accountability:
Curricular Applications

Arthur V. Olson

Professor
Georgia State University

Joe Richardson

Associate Professor
Georgia State University

Foreword by Leon M. Lessinger

INTEXT Educational Publishers

College Division of Intext
Scranton   San Francisco   Toronto   London

The **Intext** series in
Foundations of Education

Consulting editor

Herbert M. Kliebard
The University of Wisconsin

Library of Congress Catalog Card Number 78–183719
ISBN 0–7002–2392–4

Copyright ©, 1972, by
International Textbook Company

To

our wives: Aila and Nora

and

our children: Robert, Virginia, Randolph, Danny,
and Anne

Leon M. Lessinger

Foreword

Performance based accountability as educational policy marks a qualitative change in educational practice, content, and support. It may well be described as the harbinger of radical reform.

Why is this so?

Performance-based accountability addresses the three-way relationship between results intended as communicated through objects, resources allocated to achieve the objectives and the results actually achieved. Further, it undergirds the oversight of the three-way relationship described through the use of independent review and public reports.

Like the emperor without any clothes, education under the spotlight of accountability stands naked and exposed. Nakedness infers neither praise nor blame; it does suggest honesty. What one "sees" in the naked form is as much a product of the viewer as of the object viewed.

Accountability as a mind-set offers an alternative to the traditional view of education. As a performance-based phenomenon it focuses on:

1. Learning rather than teaching,
2. Effectiveness rather than efficiency,
3. Outcomes rather than ingredients or process.

The assembly of written documents in an emerging, professed anxiety-creating field is difficult and fraught with potential error. This is so because the people in the field (like ancient Gaul) are divided into three sectors: those on the cutting edge doing things in the name of accountability, those observing what is happening, and those who are critical of what is going on. In the latter sector, there are two groups: those critical on the basis of what is going on and those who are critical but not fully cognizant of what is happening.

History is the documentation of what happened. We are not yet ready for a history of accountability nor is it possible to tell what accountability is.

Professors Olson and Richardson have assembled here an interesting selection of articles which taken together afford the serious reader a good insight into the accountability phenomena as it is emerging. Further, they have begun the process of articulating some of the key characteristics of the concept especially as it relates to curriculum both by their selection of articles and the "bridges" they have constructed between them. The happy result is a book of readings which is neither partisan nor hostile but seeks clarity and balance.

I am pleased that my two colleagues at Georgia State University have afforded me the privilege of writing this brief foreward. We have entered an age of accountability in education. Works like this will professionally shape the course of that age for good by helping the serious student both with knowledge and perspective.

L. M. L.

Atlanta, Ga.

October, 1971

Contents

Accountability as a Concept

Application to the Curriculum

Programs in Action

section **III**

Accountability as a Concept

section **I**

Introduction

WHY ACCOUNTABILITY?

> . . . all over the world, the school has an antieducational effect on society
> . . . we need the constitutional disestablishment of the monopoly of the
> school, and thereby of a system which legally combines prejudice with
> discrimination . . . we need a law forbidding discrimination in hiring, voting,
> or admissions to centers of learning based on previous attendance at some
> curriculum. This guarantee would not exclude performance tests of compe-
> tence for a function or role, but would remove the present absurd discrimi-
> nation in favor of the person who learns a given skill with the largest
> expenditure of public funds—or what is equally likely—has been able to
> obtain a diploma which has no relation to any useful skill or job . . . Free
> and competing drill instructions is a subverse blasphemy to the orthodox
> educator. It disassociates the acquisition of skills from 'human' education
> which schools package together, and thus it promotes unlicensed learning
> and no less than unlicensed teaching for unpredictable purposes.[1]
>
> *Ivan Illich*

It is becoming only too apparent that the absolute faith in public schools,
so typical of past eras, is fast coming to an end. From both the ghettos and
the suburbs comes the cry for schools to defend their actions . . . and too often
the indictment is "failure." This broad range of discontent is clearly manifes-
ted in the waning of financial support for schools. Referenda and bond issues
are being soundly defeated, a unique situation for many school systems which
in the past have prided themselves on providing their schools with whatever
financial support was requested. Educators are now facing a solid, organized
array of parents, students, and taxpayers who are making demands in place
of providing unlimited support. Accountability, a common term in the busi-

[1] Ivan Illich, "Why We Must Abolish Schooling," *The New York Review of Books,* Vol. XV,
No. 1 (July 2, 1970), p. 11.

ness community, is now being applied at least verbally to the educational community.

   It appears that accountability is going to be a dominant theme in education for some years to come. It is becoming the battle cry from poverty areas where parents are demanding more than statistical verification that the longer their children stay in school, the further ahead they get. Add to this, the simple and very serious fact that schools have failed to teach their children to read or to provide them with basic mathematics skills! These same parents are asking why schools should be supported for wasting the potential productivity of students who are alienated by an educational system which insults and confuses them. For the first time, parents of minority group children are demanding to know who directed the schools to indoctrinate their children with the precepts of this country's dominant culture. Educators tend to understand too little of what their pupils bring with them from their homes and neighborhoods and therefore they tend to ignore or devalue what they discover. The "victims" of this "cultural deficiency" are made to feel like failures, and their school experience seems negative and pointless to them.

   Discontent with our schools is not restricted to minority and disadvantaged groups. There is mounting evidence that many of our affluent suburbs are disenchanted with their schools also. This is to some extent a more perplexing problem inasmuch as these parents have long assumed that the community is very much involved in deciding what their schools shall teach and to a very large extent how it will be taught. Yet, there is growing support through boards of education that teachers' requests for higher salaries and more facilities be matched by some proof of educational productivity.

   Another dimension of the problems of affluent school districts is the rather clear case of dissatisfied students. Parents and boards of education are correctly or incorrectly holding the schools accountable for student disaffection. They are demanding to know what small classes, advanced laboratories, new teaching strategies, and tailored curricula have to do with the fact that many of their children are turning their backs on college.

   From a distance, it might appear that minority groups and parents from low-income areas are claiming that their children are not being trained to manage skills necessary to participate in today's world, and at the same time are being indoctrinated with a foreign culture. Parents in more middle-class communities may be claiming quite the opposite: their children come to school with many of the necessary skills, but are not being educated to appreciate their own culture. This may be a gross oversimplification, but in both instances, the schools are being asked to justify what is happening to their children.

   Responsible educators agree that schools have responded to community needs in many instances with less than sound practices. For example, numerous schools and school systems have attempted to provide individualized programs by initiating "ability grouping." There is no evidence to support the contentions of promoters of this system; in fact, statistical studies show that differences among patterns of varying ability tend to favor the broad range. It is possible to cite too many other responses by educators that are less than enlightened.

Although Ivan Illich is read much more closely today than ten years ago, even the strictest proponents of educational accountability stop quite short of his proposal to abolish public schools. Whether or not one agrees with him, educators are having to give some thought to what today's schools are about.

SCHOOLS FOR CHILDREN

> . . . first, it is impossible; but where conjoint action for precise goals is required—for example, in designing a humanistic school curriculum—emotion by itself is not precise or effective enough, even in its most exquisite form. To speak about the 'child-centered curriculum' may make you feel warm all over, but it just won't do, unless it is also accompanied by the necessary system of precise evaluation which would make such sweet feelings relevant in a hard, dynamic world.[2]
>
> *Robert Pimack*

Accountability does not mean the absence of humanism in schools. Quite the contrary. The basic imperative of humanism is to discover and develop the full potential of each and every individual human being. The most general directive that can be applied to schools is the necessity to create an environment where the individual is able to develop his promise without the barriers of social class, race or any other factor that leads to psychological damage. The school must be a supportive, nuturing environment, a place where the child is held to be of supreme moral worth and each individual child is loved for his own sake.

The community must be recognized as the source of learning experiences that cannot be denied the child. A child must be free to plot his own experiences. Only this freedom can lead to the development of attitudes and values that belong to the child. Our job as teachers is not to indoctrinate children with our own attitudes. A free and open environment, which supports inquiry and problem-solving, based upon concerns, needs, and interests of children, where children are free to try and fail and reconstruct, will do more to develop positive attitudes, values and behavior than the traditional structured environment.

But humanism must not be translated into a cult where the mere mention

---

[2] Robert Pimack, "Accountability for Humanists." *Phi Delta Kappan,* Vol. LII, No. 10 (June, 1970), p. 621.

of objectives, goals, evaluation, and assessment are unquestionably antihumanistic. It is the essence of humanism to develop human potential in place of offering excuses and reinforcing failure. The task of instruction, therefore, must be approached with intelligence and scholarship.

On a more basic level, schools must attend to tasks that in and of themselves may not seem very glamorous. To teach a child to read and to master basic arithmetic skills may not be considered by some to be a very creative task. Yet, to not provide these tools is to keep the door locked to the vital kinds of experience that lead to strong ego development.

The argument that learning to read will rob a child of his spontaneity or will decrease his natural curiosity and autonomy is simply fallacious. The right to read is not a negotiable item; it is every child's right. Schools cannot back off from this mandate. But those who teach reading must create the learning environment which will insure that the child maintains his own sense of initiative and constructiveness. The learning process becomes one of accomplishment rather than obligation, and the successful reader discovers a key to his own further achievement.

Few people will dispute the fact that schools will continue to be one of the major institutions of our society. However, our schools must redefine their role to meet the needs of the modern era. Teachers must join their students in setting new priorities and finding new solutions for the problems of the local as well as the international community.

PERFORMANCE CONTRACTS

The particular desire of many communities to be provided with some assurance that their children will be taught the basic skills had led to the operation of performance contracting. James Mecklenburger and John Wilson describe a performance contract, similar to the Gary, Indiana model, as follows:

> A school board prepares a 'request for proposals' (RFP) which specifies the board's purposes, standards, funds available, constraints, and preferences for entering, then evaluating, then terminating a contract. Frequently a management consultant assists in the preparation; often teachers, parents, and community leaders assist also. Finally, the RFP is published, requesting potential bidders to submit proposals; bids are received and bidders chosen to receive contracts.[3]

Examples of performance contracts will be explored in a subsequent section of this book. However, for purposes of this discussion, it seems interesting

---

[3]James A. Mecklenburger and John A. Wilson, "The Performance Contract in Gary." *Phi Delta Kappan.* Vol. LII, No. 7 (March, 1971), p. 407.

to note that the contractors approach the job of teaching skills with considerable enthusiasm and positive expectation.

Mecklenburger and Wilson list a number of generalities in contracted projects. The fundamental policy is similar: ". . . contractors anchor their practice in the belief that every child can learn. If children fall short, the companies regard themselves as inaffective." There also exists a similarity of approach in most of the projects: ". . . a student's needs are diagnosed, a series of instructional activities are outlined for him, and he takes a pre-test and later a post-test monitored by an adult." Teaching materials in these projects are abundant and available to students. There is heavy reliance upon programmed materials, para-professionals, and in many instances, extrinsic reward systems. The value of extrinsic rewards has been argued vehemently in the past few years, but Mecklenburger and Wilson point out that for children who have lost their motivation may be the most effective way back to intrinsic motivation."[4]

There are a number of terms that schools and private corporations have used to describe educational accountability, particularly related to performance contracts. Leon Lessinger, one of the most signficant promoters of accountability, defined such concepts as independent audit, educational engineering, risk capital, management support groups, request for proposal, and a number of other ideas as components of accountability. The primary consideration, however, is that educational accountability aims to provide the community with an effective instructional program in which learning is the collective responsibility of the community and the school, and children themselves are not held accountable for their failures to learn. All of this is to be accomplished through efficient management of all available resources.

SHARED RESPONSIBILITY

The question then comes down to who is responsible for what? In what areas should educators assume the mantle of accountability? For what should the home be held accountable? What is the community's area of accountability? Who decides these questions?

Educators cannot assume total responsibility for the educational program. Parents and citizens, in addition to assuming responsibility for financing the program, must agree to become involved in assisting with program development. Only through this cooperative arrangement will communities begin to approach the development of adequate educational opportunities for their children. Once roles are identified, costs are determined, and priori-

[4]James A. Mecklenburger and John A. Wilson, "The Performance Contract in Grand Rapids." *Phi Delta Kappan,* Vol. LII, No. 10 (June, 1971), pp. 590–93.

ties are set, then accountability becomes a total school-community responsibility.

The Georgia Association of Educators has published a report, prepared by the Commission on Teacher Education and Professional Standards, entitled *Educational Effectiveness: Accountability.* The Commission outlined six steps for achieving the process of accountability:

1. The professional staff restudies its basic beliefs about education today.
2. Students, educators, parents, and other community leaders cooperatively establish the school's goals as related to community needs.
3. The professional staff determines, in terms of desired student and/or teacher performance, the objectives, content, process, and materials for attaining the goals.
4. The professional staff determines the competencies needed for implementing the established goals and objectives.
5. The professional staff implements the goals and objectives.
6. Evaluation in terms of student accomplishments is made continuously at all points, and information is disseminated to all individuals concerned with decision making.

Division of responsibility is defined by how the professionals and the public will share in accounting for the effectiveness of the educational program. More specifically, "when the public grants to the profession autonomy in determining means to be employed in achieving goals, the public may, and indeed should be concerned with whether or not its policies and goals are being implemented effectively." This leads to establishing objectives in areas of attitudes and values as well as in subject matter areas.[5]

Evaluation is essential to the total process of accountability. Through the process of a comprehensive plan of evaluation, certain guarantees are established, one of which is to provide the feedback necessary to evaluate continuous improvement. As the needs change, so will the programs. In making assessments, the Commission suggests that accomplishments be measured in terms of stated behaviors. When objectives are not met, a recycling process should be initiated until the stated objectives are met. The teacher's responsibility is to determine why a student has not achieved the stated "level of attainment" so that the situation can be remedied. This does not imply that the teacher is remiss, but rather that some component of the process is lacking. For example, a teacher may point out that for a certain child to accomplish a specific task, an entirely different set of materials are required. This may in turn mean that the principal or central office personnel is responsible for providing this support.

[5]James A. Mecklenburger and John A. Wilson. *Educational Effectiveness, Accountability.* Georgia Association of Educators (March 1971).

Trend Toward Accountability

The trend toward accountability should direct our attention toward instruction based on objectives and not the instructional process as an end in itself. This implies clearly defined statements of who is responsible and for what. Don Davies states the problems well in his comments:

> How do we move from a mass approach to teaching and learning to a highly individualized approach? How do we go about the 'simple' task of treating each child as an individual human being? How do we succeed with those youngsters who have never experienced success?
>
> How do we substitute a vigorous, enjoyable classroom atmosphere for one that has too often been marked by competition, pain, fear, and failure?
>
> And last, how do we build into ourselves the capacity for continuing self-renewal, for meeting increasing demands, for adapting to new roles?[6]

The question is, what kind of accountability is most workable? Two approaches have emerged. One is the analysis of invested resources in relation to achieved results. The other emphasizes consumer choice: this approach is best described through the voucher system, which is designed to provide parents the choice among schools.

In a brilliant article, Kliebard in a discussion of curriculum theory, traces the development of the "growing acceptance of a powerful and restrictive bureaucratic model for education which looked toward the management techniques of industry as its ideal of excellence and source of inspiration." Although Kliebard does not use the term accountability it is clear that his fears concerning the mechanization of education are encompassed in the concept of accountability if conceived in its most limited application.

According to Kliebard, the efficiency movement although generally applied to the administration of schools has had a profound influence upon curriculum theory itself. In expressing this point of view he writes:

> Modern curriculum theory currently being influenced by systems analysis, tends to regard the child simply as input inserted into one end of a great machine from which he eventually emerges at the other end as output replete with all the behaviors, the "competencies," and the skills for which he has been programmed. Even when the output is differentiated, such a mechanistic concept of education contributes only to man's regimentation and dehumanization rather than to his autonomy.[7]

Again, let it be said that a very few people advocate the overthrow of the institution of public schools. However, the warning is clear: if the school systems do not produce acceptable criteria and procedures for accountability,

---

[6]Don Davies, "The Relevance of Accountability." *Journal of Teacher Education*, Vol. XXI, No. 1 (Spring 1971), p. 129.

[7]Herbert M. Kliebard, "Bureaucracy and Curriculum Theory." *Freedom, Bureaucracy and Education*, ASCD Yearbook (1971), p. 93.

educators will have to face the fact that the public may very well seek out alternatives that are more effective.

A public education system based on accountability will require change on the part of all the people involved with the schools. Parents, teachers, administrators, school board members, state departments of education, colleges, universities, and federal agencies will all be involved and will all be responsible.

The answers to the questions posed by Don Davies are not solely the task of the teachers or the school. The solutions must come from the community and the schools together in a cooperative effort. If educators can lead the way toward making the community a partner in educational accountability, then and only then will ways be found to prepare our children for successful lives in an uncertain future.

CONTRIBUTORS TO SECTION I

Accountability is not new to education. Perhaps the intensity of present day demands gives a sense of urgency that was not apparent in the past. The accountability theme of the seventies is a useful way of calling attention to the fact that the needs of students today are much different than they were ten or fifteen years ago. As these needs have changed, so has the direction of the schools and the allocation of responsibility. Ralph Tyler's contribution to this section of the book clearly makes this point. His treatment of the preparation of students for the "world of work" provides the kind of insight that is necessary for educating children by placing emphasis "upon the development of generally useful abilities and skills, rather than confining the training to skills limited to specific jobs." In defining the responsibility of the school, Tyler suggests that ". . . an important educational aim today is to teach students to learn and to develop in them a strong interest in continued study together with the skills required to keep on with their learning after graduation." Tyler's guidelines for determining the process of accountability offer a positive approach to the challenges that must be met by educators.

The charge of restructuring the goal system of public schools as set forth by Ralph Tyler is further amplified by Romeo Eldridge Phillips and Edward Frierson. They reaffirm that schools are responsible for the education of *all* children. They admit that schools cannot meet all the needs of all the children, but rather that schools must identify the needs that can be met and set about accomplishing the task.

Friedrich Edding reacts to the economic principles that apply in education. He sets forth 26 points that should assist educators and laymen toward accomplishing the principle of achieving ". . . optimal relation between cost and quality."

W. James Popham reemphasizes the outcomes-oriented approach to education. He states:

> Because the criterion by which the success of an instructional process will be judged must be measurable learned behavior, the outcomes-oriented educator cleaves exclusively to objectives amenable to measurement. Whether they are called 'performance objectives', 'behavioral goals', 'operational objectives', or some equivalent phrase, they must be capable of post-instructional assessment.[8]

Organization of curriculum by subject and grade level, according to Popham, is not the most functional or effective way of "categorizing instructional outcomes."

Section I is concluded by Felix M. Lopez, who summarized the reasons why certain accountability programs have failed, and the requirements that must be met before accountability programs will succeed. Lopez describes the criteria for a "Teacher Accountability Program," "Instruments of Accountability," and the "Accountability Review," which in his words are means by which educators will be freed, ". . . for the real responsibilities of managing one of the most vital enterprises in society—the school system."

[8]W. James Popham, "Focus on Outcomes: A Guiding Theme of ES '70 Schools." *Phi Delta Kappan.* Vol. 50 (December, 1969), p. 208.

Ralph W. Tyler

Purposes for Our Schools[*]

From their beginning the schools of our country have been sensitive to the needs and opportunities of our changing society. In the debates that took place in the early days of our nation over the establishment of free public education, two primary purposes were emphasized. For the individual child, education was to provide the opportunity to realize his potential and to become a constructive and happy person in the station of life which he would occupy because of his birth and ability. For the nation, the education of each child was essential to provide a literate citizenry. Since the new nation was ruled by its people, ignorance among the people would threaten the survival of the country.

INDIVIDUAL SELF-REALIZATION

Today, these remain two of the educational functions of our schools, recognized by the public generally and firmly imbedded in our thinking in the light of changed social conditions, new knowledge, and prevailing attitudes of the times. The goal of individual self-realization is even more necessary for the schools to stress in our mass society where economic, political, and social demands are frequently heard more distinctly than demands of the individual for education that will enable him to use the rich resources of an industrial society for his own fuller life. Kenneth Boulding, speaking in June, 1966, at the Eight-State Conference on "Prospective Changes in Society by 1980," eloquently expressed the contemporary problem in achieving this purpose.

The final problem is subtle and hard to put one's finger on; nevertheless, it

*Reprinted from *The Bulletin* of *The National Association of Secondary School Principals*, 52 (December, 1968), pp. 1–12, by permission of the author and The National Association of Secondary School Principals.

may be the most important problem of all. This is the problem of the role of the educational system in creating what might be called a moral identity. The obsolescence of older moral identities in the face of enormous technological changes is a problem which underlies almost all others in the social system. . . . In its solution, the educational system would play an absolutely crucial role. It would be precisely indeed in the things which our conservatives despise as "frills" that the development of satisfying human identities may have to be found. It must never be forgotten that the ultimate thing which any society is producing is people. . . . If this principle is stamped firmly in the minds of those who guide and operate our educational system, we can afford to make a great many mistakes, we can afford to be surprised by the future, we can afford to make some bad educational investments, because we will be protected against the ultimate mistake, which would be to make the educational system a means, not an end, serving purposes other than man himself.

One test of our success in educating the individual for self-realization is whether at the end of each year of education he has a wider range of realistic choices in life available to him. If he is being narrowly specialized to fit into a niche in life with a real possibility of very limited choices, he has been miseducated. Each year should open new doors for him and develop new abilities to enable him to go through these doors as he chooses.

LITERATE CITIZENS

The reinterpretation of the development of literate citizens is profoundly important today when both the political problems and the functioning of the political system have increased enormously in scope and complexity. When the activities of government were largely restricted to maintaining law and order, providing shcools, roads, and postal services, and protecting property from fire, the issues were easily grasped, and the agents and officers of government were generally known to a majority of the community. Now, the preservation of the nation, the health of the economy, the welfare of those in need, as well as education, have become mammoth operations with national and international implications. The agents and officers of government are known personally to only a small fraction of the people. Moreover, effective citizenship requires participation in a much more complex social system. A few years of schooling are not sufficient to prepare an intelligent citizen, nor are the simple myths, which pass for American history in many places, adequate background for reasoned understanding. Educating a literate citizenry is in itself a major educational task.

SOCIAL MOBILITY

A third purpose of our schools has been recognized ever since the immigrating tide from Europe reached massive proportions in the latter part of the last century. As the children of recent immigrants became a considerable proportion of the school population in several of the states, many of the new citizens began to perceive the American schools as a means by which their children could have a chance through education to get better jobs and to enjoy the benefits of American life which they had been unable to do. Hence, in addition to providing opportunities for individual self-realization and educating for intelligent citizenship, the American schools have become a major avenue for social mobility—the means by which the American dream has been made a reality by many thousands of families and by which new streams of vigorous leadership have been injected into our maturing society.

But educating for social mobility has also required new interpretations with each generation. In the 90's, the prevailing notion among educators was that there were a few children among the many immigrant families whose moral character and native intelligence were equal to those of pupils from the middle class, old-American stock. They could make superior records in school if certain handicaps were eliminated. The handicaps recognized then were: limited knowledge of English, little time for study because of the need for their wages or help at home, and lack of supporting encouragement. Equality of educational opportunity meant, in that day, furnishing special help in acquiring the English language, raising money to reduce the time the child had to work, and for teacher and principal to give him friendly encouragement.

Now, we have learned that most children have capabilities in one or more areas and that, in place of estimating educational potential by a single scale of scholastic aptitude, we need to use various means of finding the strengths of each child on which further educational development can be based. Not only do we now expect to find many more children with potential social mobility than did our predecessors, but we have also learned about a broader range of handicaps that we need to eliminate in order that children and youth may move ahead. These include limited experience with standard English, limited access to the influence of educated people, nutritional and other health problems, lack of experience in successful learning, lack of disciplined work experience, and lack of confidence in ability to learn. The particular learning objectives and the kinds of educational programs that can enhance social mobility, we now know, must be designed in terms of the particular strengths and limitations of the pupils concerned.

PREPARATION FOR THE WORLD OF WORK

The expectation that the public elementary and secondary schools would prepare the workers needed in our expanding economy was not commonly held until the close of World War I. Farm laborers, construction workers for railroads and highways, domestic servants, and unskilled "helpers" comprised the majority of the labor force. Skilled tradesmen came from Europe or were trained through apprenticeship in this country. But the rapid rate of industrialization and business development after 1910 required many workers with higher levels of skills and understanding such as mechanics, stenographers, clerks, and sales people. The level of education required came to be expressed increasingly in terms of a high school diploma. Furthermore, specific vocational education was introduced in many high schools with grants-in-aid provided by the federal government. By 1925, the public generally, and the schools as well, were including as one of the purposes of American education the preparation of young people for the world of work.

Since 1925, and particularly since World War II, the rapid rate of technological development in agriculture, industry, commerce, defense, and the health services has so changed the occupational distribution of the total labor force that the chance for a youth or young adult without high school education to obtain employment is less and less. Farmers and farm laborers, who made up 38 percent of the labor force at the turn of the century, now comprise only 7 percent. Similarly, opportunities for employment in unskilled occupations have almost disappeared. Last year, only 5 percent of the labor force was unskilled. The proportion employed in skilled trades is not likely to increase. But there are large increases in the percentage of people employed in engineering, science, the recreational fields, accounting, and administration. Now, not only is high school education essential for most employment, but the percentage of jobs requiring college education is increasing at a rapid rate. Education as preparation for employment is more important than ever before.

But this function also requires continuing reinterpretation. Recent reports, such as the one by President Kennedy's Commission of Vocational Education, chaired by Benjamin Willis, and that of the National Association of Secondary School Principals, have documented the failures of our schools to maintain continuing contact with the needs, problems, and opportunities in educating youth for the world of work.

Mention was made earlier of the sharp shifts taking place in the composition of the labor force. In 1960, only 45 percent of the United States labor force was engaged in the production and distribution of material goods, while 55 percent was employed in providing non-material services in areas like the health services, education, recreation, social services, science and engineering, accounting, and administration. In 1967, it was estimated that only 40 percent of our labor force was required to produce and distribute material goods, and this is predicted to shrink to 25 percent by 1980. In spite of these great changes, high school vocational programs are still predominantly focused on production jobs, including farming, although only 7 percent of the labor force is engaged in agriculture.

The shift in demand to persons who provide nonmaterial services poses a particular problem for males. A majority of boys from working-class homes have a self-image of being strong and manually dexterous. This is their notion of a "real man." But the opportunities where physical strength and manual dexterity are important are becoming more and more limited. Instead, the new jobs that are increasingly available require primarily intellectual competence and social skills. Education that helps boys to prepare for employment really begins in the early grades, aiding them to develop a more realistic picture of the world of work and to perceive more clearly what characteristics are required for employment. In these early years, children can develop habits of responsibility, of thoroughness in work, of punctuality, as well as intellectual and social skills. In the junior high school period, career exploration and planning are important phases of the program. One of the most significant changes in occupational education is based on the recognition that every child needs to learn things that will prepare him for the world of work, that what is to be learned is much more than certain specific vocational skills, and that appropriate educational experiences will need to extend throughout the schools years. Furthermore, the continuing transformation taking place in the nature and distribution of jobs requires not only the use of current projections of employment demands but also emphasis upon the development of generally useful abilities and skills, rather than confining the training to skills limited to specific jobs. This shift of emphasis will insure that reeducation and training, when needed, will be more easily accomplished.

WISE CHOICES OF NONMATERIAL SERVICES

To maintain and to increase the productivity of the American economy requires not only an ample supply of workers at higher levels of competence but also consumers who want and are willing to pay for the wide range of consumer goods and services which the economy can produce. If the American people wanted only food, clothing, and shelter, a major fraction would be unemployed because these goods can be produced by a small part of our labor force. The desire and the willingness to pay for health, education, recreation, including art, music, literature, sports, and the like create the demand which enables the economy to shift its patterns of production to take advantage of the greater efficiency of technology, without stagnation. This sets a fifth major function of American education, namely, to develop in students understanding and appreciation of the wide range of experiences, services, and goods which can contribute much to their health and satisfaction. Only through education can people learn to make wise economic choices as well as wise choices in the personal, social, and political fields.

The consumer education courses which were constructed in the '20's and

'30's emphasized the development of the abilities required to make choices among material products, using information about the serviceable qualities and relative costs of these goods. The chief consumer problem of that period was believed to be to obtain useful products at lowest prices commensurate with necessary quality. Few of these courses dealt with the problems involved in making wise choices of goods and services that furnish nonmaterial values, like the aesthetic values in music, art, and drama; the recreational values of sports; the personal and social values in various educational opportunities; the health values in different forms of health and medical programs. Frequently, English courses sought to develop an appreciation for literature that could afford continuing meaning and satisfaction to the reader, and a small number of courses were devoted to motion picture appreciation aimed to help students make wise choices of the movies they viewed.

Now that a majority of the labor force is engaged in the production of nonmaterial services, the range of possible choices for the consumer is increasing greatly. Hence, the reinterpretation of this purpose in our age opens up a whole new area of consumer education and requires the development of relevant objectives and learning experiences. The wise choice of these services is profoundly important, in the development both of individuals and of our culture. Choices of literature, art, music, recreation, leisure time, educational opportunities, health services, and contributing social services have more to do with the quality of life than most of our material choices.

However, the relatively simple calculations involved in comparing the value of steak at one price with that of chicken at another is not the kind of decision process involved in choosing among nonmaterial alternatives. The educational program will need to extend the opportunities for students seriously to explore experiences and services in ways that help them to perceive values, to find meaning in them and to discover how far they afford satisfaction. Furthermore, to help in making rational decisions, students will need opportunities to review their experiences, to reflect on their impact, to assess the probable future consequences, and to develop the habit of appraising the values of nonmaterial experiences. This is a new area for many schools.

LEARNING TO LEARN

Teaching students how to learn has, in the last ten years, been accepted as another function of our schools. With the rapid acquisition of new knowledge, it is no longer possible to give the student in school an adequate command of the facts in each major subject which will serve him throughout the balance of his life. The school can only start him on a life-long career of continued learning. Hence, an important educational aim today is to teach students to learn and to develop in them a strong interest in continued study

together with the skills required to keep on with their learning after graduation.

At educational gatherings, the comment can be heard that this has always
been a major purpose of our schools. It has certainly been stated as a desirable
aim by educational leaders for centuries; but not only have the particular
sources of learning and procedures for study changed with the times but for
generations the pattern of school performance has been in sharp contrast to
what is involved in learning outside of the formal school situation. In life
outside the school, one encounters problems that are not clearly formulated,
and he must analyze the situation sufficiently to identify particular problems
or to see what questions are involved. He needs to know where he can get
relevant information; he needs to be able to attack the particular problems
appropriately in terms of fields in which they can be placed—that is, science,
literature, economics, politics, and the like. He needs to be able to verify or
validate the procedures he follows and/or the answers or solutions he pro-
poses.

These abilities can be acquired through experience which requires their
use. But most schools do not provide much opportunity for this. Typically,
the teacher poses the problems of questions rather than the student finding
them as we works. The textbook or the teacher is most likely to furnish the
answers rather than to require the student to work them out or to find
dependable sources. If this new purpose is to be attained, the contrast between traditional study in school and the procedures of life-long learning
must be eliminated through making the school experiences examples of
continued learning. This requires teachers and students to take on new roles.

The increase in the number of functions which the American schools are
expected to serve is the natural result of the changes in our whole society.
In the nearly 200 years since this country was founded, society has increased
enormously in complexity. Yet, today, the human individual at birth does not
differ appreciably from the babies born at the time of the American Revolution. All of the knowledge, skills, and attitudes required to live in modern
society must be acquired by each individual after birth. Since society is
continuing to increase in complexity and scope, the development of youth
for effective modern life increases in difficulty and in magnitude with each
generation.

CRITICAL NEW TASKS

The aforementioned six still remain the major functions of American
schools, but from time to time special tasks take on immediate urgency. Two
of them are stressed today.

We have seen that with the increasing use of technology the demand for unskilled labor has diminished to about 5 percent of the labor force. Yet, in the United States and in other advanced nations, between 15 percent and 20 percent of the population have not acquired significant skill and general literary ability to qualify for skilled or higher levels of employment. The fact that more than 80 percent of our children have achieved an educational level above the minimum requirements for modern literacy and employment is a tribute to the determination of our people and the efforts of our schools. But this is not enough. Today, 19 out of every 20 of our children can and must be effectively reached by education. We know how to stimulate and guide the learning of children who come from homes where education is valued and where the basis for it has been laid in the home experiences. However, we do not have widely accepted means for reaching children whose backgrounds have given them little or no basis for school work. To reach all or nearly all of these children is a critical task of the present period.

A second urgent task of today is also partly a result of modern technology. As automation has sharply reduced the demand for unskilled labor, the occupations in which there are increasing demands, as noted earlier, are those requiring a fairly high level of education. However, to provide employment opportunities for all our people and to keep our economy fully productive requires a much larger proportion of our youth to complete high school —many more than in the past—to gain professional, semiprofessional, or technical competence. To provide these educational opportunities and to insure effective learning for youth from varied backgrounds of training, experience, and outlook is another new and important educational task which we now face. Neither the United States nor any other country has previously attempted it.

Mention is made of these two new tasks that the schools are being urgently asked to undertake, not because they involve additions to the basic functions or purposes of the schools but because they should be viewed as important tasks with purposes of their own.

Both of them—reaching the disadvantaged and making the high school effective for a large proportion of the population—must be undertaken with the six basic purposes in mind: to help each individual achieve his highest potential, to develop a broader base of intelligent and active citizens, to make possible social mobility, to prepare each person for the world of work, to help him choose nonmaterial services that will furnish the greatest meaning and satisfaction, and to become a life-long learner.

In making education effective for a larger number of students, consideration must be given to the criticism made by students themselves of the high school program.

The most common complaint they make is its "irrelevance." In many cases, what is being taught could be highly relevant to the activities, interests, and problems of the students, and they fail to perceive the connection. Much of this is due to the separation of the school from the rest of life. For example, the separation of the school from the world of work and the world of community service results in several unfortunate consequences. Many students see the school as something apart from the adult world into which they will be going. This is one of the factors in dropping out of school: and for many students who do not drop out, the apparent lack of connection between the school work and their future lives results in low interest and effort in their studies. From the standpoint of the society, the separation of the school makes more difficult the transition from school to work and from school to constructive community membership.

What is needed is the development of bridges to the rest of the community and greater openness in the school to outside persons and activities. We need to be providing cooperative education (work-study programs), community service programs, and other means by which school youth can be actively involved in work experiences, in community services, in joint civic participation with adults, and the like. Students are not likely to use what they learn unless they have practice in identifying problems and difficulties. Dealing with these requires learning—and practice in using what is learned—in situations outside of school.

RESPONSE OF THE SCHOOLS TO CHANGE

Although the American schools, when compared to those of Western Europe, have not rigidly adhered to obsolete programs but have been responsive to changing needs and opportunities of the times, these educational changes have lagged some years behind the initiating forces, and the adaptation or transformations required in the schools have not always been largely effective. The lag appears to have been due both to the lack of continuing attention within the school to developments in the society and to the common failure of school leaders to translate needed changes into educational purposes and operations that guide the actual conduct of school work.

It has become modern business practice for the corporation to make continuing projections of environmental factors, such as population shifts, new technologies becoming available, and changing patterns of consumer preferences, that importantly affect its work. From these assessments and reassessments of changing conditions, the corporation commonly plans its production and distribution programs, adjusting the future plans each year in the light of facts of the past year. In this way, the company is able to respond quickly to changing conditions and frequently anticipates the changes before they actually take place. Educational systems and organizations could benefit from similar practices. A rationale for such planning procedures exists, and modifications to fit a particular system can be worked

out. With such studies and with the attitude that change is the natural characteristic of our society and its institutions, our schools in the future can anticipate new educational needs as well as respond to present conditions more
promptly.

Our failure to translate changing needs into guiding purposes and operational plans seems to be largely due to our following the pattern of leadership
characteristic of a slowly changing society. Under conditions of very gradual
shift, the operational modifications in the system are commonly made by the
operators before they are recognized by the leaders. Then, the role of leadership is to explain these changes in terms of accepted principles so that the new
practices now in operation are legitimized. Many statements of educational
policy have been justifications of changes already under way rather than
pointing the direction for new efforts.

Because our society is changing more rapidly with each decade, we must
develop educational procedures that can reduce the lag between changing
needs and educational programs that meet the needs. The American schools
have shown their flexibility in responding to needs in the past. By developing
procedures to scan the social horizon, we can anticipate impending changes
and understand their probable impact. By employing task forces of scholars,
scientists, curriculum makers, and teachers to translate needs into educational
objectives and operational plans, we can expect to respond more promptly
and more effectively in the future than we have in the past. Over the years,
the purposes for our schools have been expanding, and in each generation
older purposes require reinterpretation. This is necessary for schools to serve
adequately the individual and the society of the times.

Romeo Eldridge Phillips

Whose Children Shall We Teach?*

The writer recently served on a panel with a political scientist and a sociologist. The topic for the evening was given the ambiguous title, "The Polarization in Our Society." Our assignment was to ad lib as to our perceptions of this phenomenon.

The sociologist gave an analogy of the social stratification within the American society and delivered an excellent dissertation on acculturation and enculturation.

The political scientist, who has a degree in divinity, outlined the whys and wherefores of the American political system and how the church fits into it.

The writer supported the pontifications of the two speakers. However, I stated that the public schools are the only places where the sons and daughters of college professors, maids, janitors, pimps, prostitutes, and preachers are found. In a typical college town where there is only one senior high school, they are found in the same building.

TEACHING ALL THE CHILDREN

It would appear plausible that the sons and daughters of employers and employees meet on a continuum of sociality daily. To look at this conglomerate of upper, middle and lower income youths, one realized that the public school is truly an arena. The writer submitted then and submits now that the home and church have abdicated their individual responsibility to the young people of this nation. Therefore, the public schools by inheritance and default now must really and completely "teach" *all* the children of *all* the public! Let us cite some observations to support this hypothesis.

*Reprinted from *Educational Leadership,* 27 (February, 1970), pp. 471–474, by permission of the author and the editor.

Many white Americans have contended that they did not leave the large cities to "get away" from black Americans, but because they desired a better quality of education for their children. On the other hand, many chose to live in a particular neighborhood because they, too, desired a better quality of education for their children. If a person's income permitted him, the movement became a living reality. One must remember, however, that an exodus from a given area does not render it a ghost town. To the contrary, living bodies remain—and in large numbers.

Let us follow the public school sojourn of a child whose parents have moved to a certain neighborhood in a typical college town. It is amazing how shortsighted we can be.

When one moves into a "certain" neighborhood, it is his intention to be with those of his kind, that is, at his level within the bourgeoisie. It is reasonable to assume that the schools will be populated with these types of children. This assumption is one-third accurate: the middle-junior high school will have children from several neighborhoods; the senior high school will have children from *all* neighborhoods!

It appears that the runner ran in a circle. If one had wanted to expose a son or daughter to the "best" families, it would appear that this should be during the period of early pubescence when discriminate taste develops. During this period, it is not what Mom or Dad desires, it is what "I" want. We call this the period of adolescent rebellion. It is logical to conclude, then, that only the elementary school can supply the "quality education" sought by the mover-runner. Let us look into the high school where all three "types" are housed.

The teachings, mores, fears, prejudices, etc., of parents are placed on public display in the senior high school. It is in the senior high school that the 14-or-so years of neighborhood values training bears fruit. It is in the senior high school that the realities of heterogeneous living are tried. Truly, the senior high school is an educational arena. The public schools have been given the task either of curing all the social ills or of serving as a deterrent. For some 180-odd days each year the public schools face these problems head on.

Often potential teachers are heard repeating statements of veteran teachers about certain schools in certain school districts. They may express a desire not to work in certain schools in certain school districts. When reminded that they are seeking a certificate to teach in the *public* schools and not in certain types of public schools, expressions of ambivalence about teaching pour from their lips. The shock of being expected to teach *all* the children of *all* the public—including poor whites, blacks, American Indians, and Spanish speaking—creates a form of academic amitosis. One would guess that when they are reminded of this, the potential teachers may experience a form of ametropia. Sometimes it appears that such beginners no longer see public school teaching as before. Yet and still, a horrible disservice would be created if they were not made to acknowledge such a commitment as being realistic.

The writer has often been asked these questions: What types of teachers are in the public schools? and, What sub-roles must we play, since the church and home no longer appear to really care?

TYPES OF TEACHERS

There are five types of teachers currently drawing wages in the public schools. Each is easily recognized.

1. The Rebel—is against the entire system, but has no suggested plan of change.

2. The Retreatist—wants out of teaching, is constantly seeking other employment, and leaves, usually, with his or her leave bank empty.

3. The Ritualist—has retired on the job, and continues to repeat the same lessons year in and year out. The teacher can quote page, paragraph, and sentence of the text.

4. The Conformist—goes along with what is current without making an effort to contribute. In many cases this person and the ritualist are related.

5. The Innovator—sees the need for change and seeks to bring it about without antagonism. This effort ranges from his/her classroom to the district.

One who teaches must be conditioned to accept the following sub-roles:

1. —a mediator of learning;

2. —a judge;

3. —a disciplinarian;

4. —a confidant;

5. —a parent substitute;

6. —a surrogate of middle-class values.

If, in fact, we have five types of teachers currently in the public schools and if teaching should subscribe to these six sub-roles, we must look at the teacher-preparing institutions.

Since the orbiting of Sputnik I, men with names such as Bestor, Rickover, Conant, Clark, Malcolm X, and McKissick have charged that the teacher education institutions are not doing their job. Of these various charges, the one heard most often is that potential teachers are being prepared to work with just one segment of our society—the middle!

The truth of the matter, they are saying, is that one does not really teach, per se, the middle segment. This highly motivated segment needs only guidance. Teaching must be at the extremes of the continuum. Because of this fact many veteran "teachers" obtain and seek assignments in such schools. Knowing this, potential teachers seek such non-available assignments. Teacher education institutions contribute to this dastardly deed by holding back two-thirds of the information needed—the fact that we have three types of communities within the public school arena. It is inexplicable why neophyte teachers must develop this awareness by empirical design.

Too many teacher education institutions have developed what the writer calls "slogan shibboleths." Many of these are really polite euphemisms, for they appear to be evasive in nature. One does not talk about "teaching the whole child" only to point out negatives, for example, low IQ scores, a product of an illegitimate affair, and too much freedom and money. Children may be dumb, but they are not stupid. They need not be told which type of teacher so-and-so is. They know that actions speak louder than words. For potential teachers not to be prepared to teach *all* the children of *all* the public is malfeasance. Potential teachers must be told what is expected of them and the professor is professionally obligated to "tell it like it is!"

PROBLEM OF ACCOUNTABILITY

The problem on hand now is what must be done to teach students currently enrolled. The problem is compounded by the fact that many teachers are aware of these differences but choose not to adapt their presentations to fit the experiences of their charges. What can be done to rectify this situation?

Teachers unions appear not to be concerned about making teachers accountable, it is a personal desire. Accountability in labor unions known to the writer revolves around wages. As a worker produces so is he paid. When he works up to expectations he is, naturally, praised; when he works under basic standards he is moved.

A teacher is protected by state law plus a master contract. However, unlike the members of labor unions, a teacher has no demands made on him to produce. He is not accountable and accepts all pay raises with no scruples of conscience. Knowing this to be true, citizens have resorted to extralegal means to gain teacher accountability.

In the suburbs, parents often check the content of their children's assignments. The same is true in "choice" neighborhoods in large cities and college communities. It is not unusual for Bobby's father, who is a professor of math at the local college, to challenge the teacher's math competency. Knowing the level of academic sophistication of his students' parents, the teacher usually shapes up or ships out. The ghetto poor lack academic sophistication; they measure results. They know that they send their children to school for an education. The children may remain for some 13 inclusive years only to emerge lacking the ability to read. Parents are not stupid. They are now seeking methods of community control via the purse strings of school employees. They measure step-by-step what their children learn. If it is adjudicated that the learning did not take place, they want the teachers' wages affected, union master contract to the contrary notwithstanding.

When the ghetto poor rise up, it is unusual. A case in point is the Ocean Hill-Brownsville fiasco in New York in the fall of 1968. The public schools can expect more of the same as parents, ghetto poor parents, demand education of a quality comparable to that found outside their community. In the process the teacher education institutions will not come out unscathed. After all, it is they who trained the present cadre so inadequately. Pedagogics must expand to include the three socioeconomic levels. Teachers must be, so to speak, educational chameleons.

The business of teaching in this country is now, more than before, very serious business. Politicians no longer can afford to use the public schools as vehicles for reelection. Adequate funds are needed, and all three groups are united in this effort. Politicians react favorably to pressure. The ghetto poor know that a person without a marketable skill is a drain on society. They expect the public schools to provide the training. Our country has been made aware of the reality of the waste of brain power by not tapping the resources of the poor.

THE ANSWER IS EASY

Whose children shall we teach? It appears that the answer is quite easy. We teach *all* the children of *all* the public, regardless of circumstance of birth, status of parents, and innate ability. If we do *not* believe in public education, we had better say so and commence to provide for those who will be eliminated. If we believe that the public *should* have the opportunity to be educated, then we had better act that way.

This means that the power structure, commencing with the teacher education institutions, must make the present and future cadre accountable. Ivan Pavlov used food with his dogs; perhaps money would be a viable control stimulus for humans, that is, pay would be determined by the quality of the work. No work—no pay! After all, we must stop the brain drain. If we can put men on the moon, surely we should be able to work with the known. Our greatest investments are our children. *All* of them must be taught!

Since the ghetto poor, like the members of the middle and upper class, desire and are now demanding results from their children's education, the public school arena has become a battleground. The "haves" have the resources to supplement via the tutoring route that which the public schools fail to accomplish. The "have-nots" do not have the resources, but they are demanding the same results within the same period of time. Since both sets of children are to compete in the same society, it is fair that both be given equal opportunities. The only "resource" available to the "have-nots" is the ability to destroy. We need not go into the psychological reasoning why this "resource" is used, for we know that it is used. We must concentrate our efforts so that the ghetto poor will feel that there is no need to use this "resource." Although they have nothing to lose, likewise they will not gain by using this "resource." It is better for the "have-nots" to gain a fair shake than for the "haves" to be reduced to the status of "have-nots."

The acculturation and enculturation outlined by the sociologist, as well as the role of the church and the politics of our society outlined by the political scientist, highlight the responsibility of the public schools. No matter how lucid the oratory about the need for a high quality of public education for every child, it boils down to what was said by the late Dr. Martin Luther King, Jr.: "Either we're going to live together as brothers and sisters or we're going to die together like fools." It appears that the only light in the lighthouse to guide our society is the public school. The light must not go out.

Edward C. Frierson

Determining Needs*

Cultural deprivation, a source of exceptionality among children, creates a handicapping condition in most school settings. Until recently, curriculum planners and textbook writers apparently ignored the fact that culturally homogeneous groups are not established as a function of age-grade groupings. Indeed, an investigation of several primary classes within any large school district will reveal differences in children's experiences comparable to the differences in intellect, emotional stability, social maturity, and physical traits which they possess.

It is a distinct advantage to determine the extent of any physical, emotional, or intellectual disability early in the school career of the exceptional child. Early identification leads to early inclusion in educational programs specifically designed to minimize the negative influence of disabilities. Parents and community resources further reduce the effects of disabilities when the specific needs of the exceptional child are identified. The disadvantaged child whose preschool experience has resulted in intellectual malnutrition will need to be identified at a similarly early point in his school career lest his retarded educational development be mistakenly attributed to mental retardation.

DEFINING EDUCATIONAL OBJECTIVES

Determining the needs of the disadvantaged child poses some difficult problems which are related to values, norms, and educational objectives as well as to rudimentary problems of measurement. Much has been written about the middle class value structure which prevails in the public school.

*Reprinted from *Education*, April, 1965, pp. 461–466, by permission of the author and the editor.

28

The use of age-grade norms is being critically examined as ungraded administrative patterns emerge in elementary schools. However, the basic problem which faces the educator is that of defining his objectives in unambiguous terms. For it is only within such a framework of objectives that the educational needs of any child should be determined.

Once the needs of the child are identified with respect to the objectives toward which he is advancing, the means for meeting these needs can be ascertained. Thus we have the primary question clearly before us: What are the specific goals of educational programs? The secondary question is then placed in perspective: How should the specific needs of any child be determined? It is upon these questions that the present discussion focuses.

In order to emphasize the importance of educational goal definition, let us consider the following example. Let us suppose that a healthy twelve-year-old boy enrolls for his first extended summer camping experience. He has been reared by a widowed mother in an environment devoid of physical aggressiveness, stern commands, keen competition, and athletic involvement. This camper is, on the other hand, widely read, highly articulate, good with numbers, and accomplished in musical performance. His needs (from the observer's point of view) can be understood only in light of camp life and the objectives established by the camp administration.

If our camper's past experience has not included swimming lessons and the camp administration is determined to display every camper in a synchronized swim show on the last day of camp, certain problems are immediately apparent.

First, our camper is retarded. Not only is he retarded but he has hidden attitudes, feelings, and motives which may or may not cause him to commit himself to the task of swimming. If he is conscious of his atypical experience as he observes "normal" campers, he may adopt behaviors in keeping with his past experience but certainly out of tune with the camp staff's definition of good adjustment. In short, his "disadvantaged" rearing becomes a handicap to the degree that the objectives of the camp are not extensions of his family's goals but are, indeed, alien to the life patterns created in his home.

It would be appropriate to analyze the wisdom or value of the goal that everyone should execute synchronized swim strokes. Likewise, it would be appropriate to question the practice of grouping all twelve-year-olds regardless of experience and letting them "sink or swim" day after day. Yet the former takes us into philosophy and the latter into administrative practice; consequently, while both issues are crucial with respect to disadvantaged children, the issue before us is how to determine the specific needs of the child who is caught up in a program which did not consider his needs in its inception. Clearly, the first step is to identify the specific goals of the program within which he is expected to function.

SYMPTOMS OF DEPRIVATION

The next step toward identifying needs of the disadvantaged child is to review the general effects of cultural deprivation upon children. Many fine studies are now available to help us in this effort.

Riessman characterizes the deprived child in school as a slower student.

> There is little doubt that the deprived child typically works on academic problems in a slower manner. This is shown in many ways: he requires more examples before seeing a point, arriving at a conclusion or forming a concept. He is unwilling to jump to conclusions or to generalize quickly. He is a slower reader, slower problem solver, slower at getting down to work, slower in taking tests (1).[1]

Middle and lower class children "differ with respect to norms and values in the area of personal achievement (2)." In fact, higher correlations have been found between socioeconomic status and achievement than between intelligence and achievement (3).

The absence of long-range educational aspiration among deprived is translated into reduced motivation, with the result that school drop-out rates are five times greater for children from families whose income is $3,000 than for children whose family income is $5,000. The dropout rate for those from $3,000 income families is 22 times greater than for those from $9,000 income families (4).

The language development of lower class children is poorer than that of other social classes. Poor models, lack of stimulation and limited experience are among the causes cited (5). The possibility of poor verbal skills depressing I.Q. scores of low-income children is now acknowledged.

Contrasting the lower-class child with normative behavior and behavior of other socioeconomic class groups, Reissman holds that the following characteristics are fairly typical of the deprived child's style:

1. Physical and visual rather than aural.
2. Content-centered rather than form-centered.
3. Externally oriented rather than introspective.
4. Problem-centered rather than abstract-centered.
5. Inductive rather than deductive.
6. Spatial rather than temporal.
7. Slow, careful, patient, persevering, rather than quick, clever, facile and flexible.

Much potential ability goes unidentified among lower class children. A factor contributing to the obscurity of ability among lower class children is poor verbal facility. Davidson and Balducci found that among high IQ children "the high social class children are always superior to the low social class

[1]Numbers in parentheses refer to reference list at end of article.

children (6)." Findings similar to this have led many to support Schreiber's claim that present tests do not measure the full potential of lower class children (7).

Oppel has reported that changes in IQ reflect social class. The upper class background is associated with rising IQ's; the lower class background with declining IQ's (8). In order not to discriminate against the lower class gifted child, Levinson suggests that the IQ rating necessary for selection as "gifted" be put at the ninety-eighth percentile for each socioeconomic level (9).

The problem of identifying the needs of the educationally retarded and disadvantaged child is now considered within a frame of reference which requires the school to define its objectives and which recognizes the deleterious effects of cultural deprivation.

RETARDATION AND CULTURAL FACTORS

Gray has reviewed the findings of many researchers in an attempt to account for the progressive retardation which characterizes the educational performance of culturally deprived children (10). The findings are fairly consistent and may be grouped into two broad categories, those relating to attitudes toward achievement and those relating to aptitude for achievement.

Attitudes toward achievement are strikingly different in the lower class culture and in the middle class cluture. Winterbottom (11) and Rosen (12) have related achievement motivation to differences in child rearing.

Delay of gratification is a necessary condition for school achievement (the adolescent must delay immediate gratification for future gains). Mischel (13, 14) has shown that delay of gratification is related specifically to social class and to parental attitudes.

Persistence toward a goal is a variable which is an essential condition for academic achievement, but Gray (10) found that this variable was related to a given task rather than a general trait, at least at early ages.

Another variable is a family environment which places high or low value upon achievement, and specifically upon academic performance. Strodbeck's studies suggest that values and subsequent achievement may be related to social class patterns. Attitudes toward school type activities have been shown to differentiate a group of culturally deprived six-year-olds from a group of (upper middle class) kindergarten youngsters.

Language development, perceptual development, and concept formation are related to a culturally deprived environment. Studies such as Milner's (15) have documented the relationship between reading readiness and the language interactions of parents and children. Major differences were found between middle and lower classes. In addition to marked deficiency on language tests, the deprived show up as even more handicapped on nonlanguage tests that demand discriminations, comparisons, and use of symbols (10).

An important aspect of the conceptual performance of the culturally deprived child contrasts with the greater efficiency of the middle class child who uses more abstract language categories. Since school experience places major emphasis upon ability to order the world in terms of formal categories, a learning approach that is chiefly concrete may lead the child into increasing difficulties as he progresses through the elementary grades.

Social interaction patterns which are established in the preschool years provide another factor influencing educational retardation. Lower class children have been found to be more aggressive in relationships with peers than middle class children. The attitudes toward authority figures may not follow the same pattern. There is some indication that the lower class child may be more passive in the face of authority than the middle class child. This may be another reason for less adequate school development or learning among the culturally deprived (10).

THREE TYPES OF NEEDS

The needs of the educationally retarded and the disadvantaged child are of three kinds: first, the experiential needs that are demanded by the educational objectives which exist at each grade level and in each subject area; second, the needs which are associated with the symptoms of cultural deprivation; lastly, the fundamental needs which may only be met by dealing with the culture or environment which has "created" the disadvantaged child.

The first type of need may be explored by using standard aptitude and achievement tests. Because such tests are standardized on "normal" populations and are used to compare a particular child with an age-grade norm, they usually produce a label for the child rather than a description of his educational needs. It is suggested, therefore, that clinical education diagnostic procedures be used to determine which skills, experiences, and prerequisite knowledges are lacking in the educationally retarded child. Merely labeling him slow learner, under achiever, or poor reader cannot substitute for a documented statement of learning needs.

The second type of need has been described in clinical terms and has served as the basis for adjustment counseling and psychotherapy. It is suggested that a thorough diagnosis such as that used in remedial education be employed as the basis for classroom and tutorial planning. In this way, needs associated with cultural deprivation may be met in educational settings in ways comparable to those used by special educators in other areas of exceptionality.

Identifying needs of this type requires an interdisciplinary effort. The social psychologist, anthropologist, educational specialist, sociologist and clinical psychologist and others have developed instruments which the specialist could interpret and translate into classroom teacher terminology. Without this translation, identification of needs may be meaningless.

Clearly, the fundamental needs of the disadvantaged child cannot be divorced from the needs of families and communities. The problems of employment, income, desertion, illegitimacy, mobility, adult education, aesthetic stimulation, and community life combine to produce a living status which the child does not choose and usually cannot escape.

The identification of family related needs is generally a by-product of the case study approach. The value of environmental data in determining the fundamental needs of the educationally retarded child cannot be overestimated. Environmental data can sometimes explain behavior which is mistakenly associated with mental retardation, emotional disturbance and delayed neurological development.

SUMMARY

The need of the educationally retarded and disadvantaged children is related to the educational objectives of our schools. Therefore, these objectives must be carefully identified. Cultural deprivation produces behavior which is best described as symptomatic. Needs related to desired changes in behavior must be identified from the remedial education perspective. Some needs must be understood as needs of families and communities.

Identification of the needs of educationally retarded and disadvantaged children is clearly an interdisciplinary task. Translation of identified needs into terms meaningful to the classroom teacher is essential for meeting the needs of all exceptional children.

REFERENCES

1. Frank Riessman, *The Culturally Deprived Child* (New York: Harper and Row, 1961).
2. Elizabeth Douvan, "Social Status and Success Striving." *Journal of Abnormal Psychology*, Vol. 52 (March, 1956), pp. 219–223.
3. Walter H. Friedhoff, "Relationships among Various Measures of Socioeconomic Status, Social Class Identification, Intelligence, and School Achievement." Unpublished doctoral dissertation, State University of Iowa, 1955. *Dissertation Abstracts*, Vol. 15 (1955), p. 2098.
4. Patricia C. Sexton, *Education and Income* (New York: Viking Press, 1961).
5. Leonard Carmichael (ed.), *Manual of Child Psychology* (New York: John Wiley and Sons, 1946).

6. Helen H. Davidson and Dom Balducci, "Class and Sex Differences in Verbal Facility of Very Bright Children." *Journal of Educational Psychology,* Vol. 47 (December, 1956), pp. 476–480.
7. Daniel Schreiber, "Identifying and Developing Able Students from Less Privileged Groups." *High Points,* Vol. 40 (December, 1958), pp. 5–23.
8. W. Oppel, Boland U. Rider, and Gerald Weiner, "Some Correlates of IQ Changes in Children." *Child Development,* Vol. 34 (March, 1961), pp. 61–67.
9. Boris Levinson, "Rethinking the Selection of Intellectually Gifted Children." *Psychological Reports,* II (1956), p. 127.
10. Susan W. Gray, "The Performance of the Culturally Deprived Child: Contributing Variables." *Proceedings of Section II, Seventh Annual Professional Institute of the Division of School Psychologists,* American Psychological Association, (1962).
11. M. Winterbottom, "The Relation of Need for Achievement to Learning Experiences in Independence and Mastery." In J. W. Atkinson (ed), *Motives in Fantasy, Action, and Society* (Princeton, N. J.: Van Nostrand, 1958).
12. B. C. Rosen and R. B. Andrade, "The Psychosocial Origins of Achievement Motivation." *Sociometry,* 22 (1959), pp. 185–218.
13. W. Mischel, "Preference for Delayed Reinforcement: An Experimental Study of a Cultural Observation." *Journal of Abnormal and Social Psychology,* Vol. 56 (1958), pp. 57–61.
14. W. Mischel, "Preference for Delayed Reinforcement and Social Responsibility." *Journal of Abnormal and Social Psychology,* Vol. 62 (1961), pp. 1–70.
15. E. Milner, "A Study of the Relationship between Reading Readiness in Grade One School Children and Patterns of Parent-Child Interactions." *Child Development,* Vol. 22 (1951), pp. 95–112.

Friedrich Edding, Berlin

Efficiency in Education *

1. The title of this article will cause librarians some difficulty. They may have in their classification scheme the heading "economics of education," and they may have subheadings like "educational finance," "education and manpower needs" and "education and economic growth." They probably have these headings because there is quite a body of literature on these subjects. If they have difficulty in classifying an article on "efficiency in education," it is because there are relatively few publications which fall or seem to fall under such a heading. [1]

2. Reflecting on the possible reasons for this neglect, I formed the hypothesis that this subject is nearest to the core of economics, and is consequently most difficult to approach. It is concerned with one fundamental principle, namely, to achieve given ends with a minimum of resources and energy, or put another way, to achieve an optimal relation between cost and quality. Since the beginning of this century education has been following industry in expansion of plant and manpower employed. We know, however, that these were not the most significant features of industrial development. The increase in productivity of these inputs was the greatest single achievement. In this regard education has failed to advance, and efforts to improve cost/quality relationship are still in the initial stages. Efficiency in education is comparatively underdeveloped, even in the most advanced countries. At a time when a new and enormous expansion of education is planned in the less industrialized countries, this lagging behind in a most essential field of research and practice needs to be rectified.

3. Research in this area is handicapped by a certain unwillingness on the

*Reprinted from *International Review of Education,* 10, No. 4 (1964), pp. 393–403, by permission of the author and the editor.
[1]See the bibliographies in: R. Callahan, *Education and the Cult of Efficiency* (University of Chicago Press, 1962), and F. Edding, *Okonomie des Bildungswesens* (Freiburg: Rombach, 1963).

part of educators to have the economic principle applied in their province. They sometimes tend to confuse economics with economies[2] and often claim that in contrast to industry, education cannot be subjected to rational principles. Education, it is argued, has to do mainly with an incalculable growth process of body and mind and with imponderable spiritual values. Allowances must certainly be made for such values.[3] But they should not be allowed to hinder research. The purpose of research is to clarify issues. Responsibility for action rests with the politicians. They should see to it that both the rational and irrational are given a fair chance of expression in all their consequences. Economic research in this field is also strongly opposed on grounds of tradition, prejudice and vested interest. If not supported firmly by farseeing politicians, research into efficiency in education will always remain underdeveloped. Hardly any major research on this subject can be done without the co-operation of public agencies.

4. Some much-debated educational issues spring to mind such as: small schools distributed widely over the countryside *versus* large schools situated only in central places; conventional teaching by fully trained teachers *versus* teaching by teachers with different lengths of training using modern techniques. The comparison of costs is usually the first type of assistance offered by economic research towards the clarification of such issues. It is always worthwhile to ask how a change in the organization, staffing, equipment or methods of education affects costs. Costs can be expressed in terms of student and staff manhours. But it is practically impossible to compare facilities, equipment, transport and other services in kind. Desirable as such calculations in real terms would be particularly for international comparison, I see no way of obtaining them. It is, therefore, indispensable to use the money expression for comparisons.

5. In order to make costs comparable, total expenditure for an educational institution is divided by the number of students in enrollment or attendance. This is the method used so far in most countries. It is a very crude measurement. Since students attend school for varying lengths of time, either a standard full-time equivalent should be taken as a unit or a standard hour. In most countries so far, this simple refinement in the method of calculation cannot be made because of inadequate basic statistics. The insufficiency of educational statistics has been criticized so often,[4] that I can abstain here from going further into this matter. Any larger investigation in this field presup-

[2]This is understandable if one looks through the volume on economies published during the crisis of the thirties, where governments recommended and practised the reduction of salaries and the prolongation of teaching duties. *Les economies dans le domaine de l'instruction publique* (Bureau International d'Education, Genéve, 1934).

[3]See F. Edding, "Bildung und Wirtschaft." *International Review of Education,* Vol. VI (1960), p. 129 ff.

[4]See for instance, *Policy Conference on Economic Growth and Investment in Education,* Vol. II, (OECD, Paris, 1962), p. 60 ff.

poses a strong effort to improve accounting statistics.

6. Assuming proper unit cost calculations, what could we learn from them for the present purpose? We could probably learn that unit costs in small schools are, as a rule, higher than in big schools. We would also probably find that beyond certain limits of school size, unit costs tend to increase. The cost curve would show us the optimum size as far as unit costs are concerned, assuming that the product remains the same.

7. Investigations in various countries confirm, as a rule, what has been said in the foregoing paragraph, but they show also considerable deviations from the general rule. This situation necessitates further analysis of the factors influencing unit costs. Anybody who is, for noneconomic reasons, in favor of small schools, can point to some example where these schools entail the lowest unit costs. The expenditure related to the unit can comprise, in very different proportions, outlays on staff, maintenance, equipment, learning materials, auxiliary services, debt service, etc. If the cost of teaching per student hour in small rural schools is very low, the cause can be a high student teacher ratio, extremely long hours and poor quality and pay of the teacher (or perhaps nuns receiving no pay). It may happen that in larger schools, supporting the same unit costs as the smaller schools, all these circumstances are completely reversed. Here we have highly qualified well paid teachers teaching small classes using all modern equipment. In this case, advantages of scale are not reflected in unit cost which simply relates the total expenditure on teachers of an educational institution to its number of students.

8. More refined methods of calculation are needed for many reasons, one of which is to find out how the size factor influences unit costs under various conditions. Whenever we want to discover how a certain change in school organisation or teaching will influence costs, we require a method of calculation which enables all the relevant factors to be brought into a formula as variables. Such a more refined method of costing gives the opportunity to play around with a great number of factors in various combinations. In this way and using a computer, any educational program can be expressed quickly in unit and total costs. If a certain size of school seems for noneconomic reasons desirable, this size can be put into the formula as a fixed factor. If, nevertheless, a certain level of costs should not be exceeded, all other factors named above have to be chosen so as to suit this purpose.

9. This approach permits the calculation of the numerous alternative combinations of educational goods and services which can be acquired for a given outlay and alternatively, enables plans and estimates of future needs to be translated into monetary terms. This method is also ideal for comparisons, because only in this way can one find out the real comparative merits of complex different systems of education in terms of costs. The computers are available, but we are far behind in the provision of statistics and the development of methodology. To date, only the first steps

have been taken to translate the ideas outlined above into reality. The main point to be borne in mind is that the work can be done, and this with increasing precision.

10. The number of factors can be increased so as to include new techniques of teaching, new methods of building and new ways of overcoming the handicaps of distance. To begin with the last, I refer to the study of W. P. McLure on the effect of population sparsity on schools costs.[5] We can find there most of the relevant factors quantified and brought into mathematical relation. A population sparsely distributed over a wide area, means that consideration must be given to the cost-increasing effect of small schools serving sometimes not more than ten children and, on the other hand, to the costs of a transport system as part of the cost of big central schools. In recent years we think also of direct assistance to pupils scaled according to the distance between their homes and the school. Those who have to commute long distances or pay for room and board away from home receive assistance in cash or kind; this is then another cost factor which should be included in an attempt to calculate the comparative unit costs of centralized or decentralized systems of school organization.

11. School size also affects building costs and other facilities not coming under the heading supplies, but rather under capital. To date, it is uncommon to find costs expressed as annual costs and added to the recurring expenditure. But it seems necessary to do this in order to improve investigation into efficiency. At present, capital costs are accredited, as a rule, to the year when the bills for the construction of a school were paid. This expenditure cannot be considered as an input serving the production of knowledge in this year. It has to serve this purpose for at least 50 years. And it cannot be assumed that there is a steady flow of new construction which permits the adding of the actual building costs of one year to other educational outlays of this year. On the contrary, the proportion of actual capital costs in total educational expenditure differs considerably from one year to another. For proper unit cost calculations it is, therefore, necessary to find out which amount of capital is used up per student per year or per hour in school. This can be done and has been done by studying life-time expectancies of replacement periods[6] of buildings and equipment.

12. It is important to differentiate properly in the accounts of durable equipment, because replacement periods of tables or blackboards differ considerably from those of teaching machines or television sets and because it is particularly interesting to see the effect of modern equipment on unit costs.

[5]Teachers College Columbia University, *Contribution to Education*, No. 929 (New York, 1947).

[6]See, W. Wasserman, *Education Price and Quantity Indexes* (Syracuse University Press, 1963), p. 59 ff.

So far, I have rarely seen any data on the life-expectancy of the various new audiovisual teaching devices. Neither can I remember, with few exceptions, such data for buildings and calculations of total capital consumed per student and per year. These very calculations may reveal important differences in unit costs. They may or may not be justified, but as long as they are unknown, all talk about efficiency is mere tongue wagging.

13. The analysis of building costs must be pursued in depth if unit-cost comparisons are to be established which really give an insight into the causes of differences and into the great variety of possible combinations of cost factors in the same total unit cost. The unit in these calculations can be the student-place, the square meter or the cubic meter. Total costs of a building, for instance, are related to the number of students for which it has been designed. But such a total unit cost may deviate between 40 and 60 percent from the average in twenty out of a hundred schools of the same size and type. The normal checks on government expenditures are unlikely to uncover the cause of such disparities. Indeed, it is singificant that those appointed to act as watchdogs on the public purse are usually preoccupied with checking the integrity of civil servants, spotlighting outlandish or extravagant expenditures and examining the profit margins of government contractors. While such investigations are certainly justified, they may be regarded as being superficial in so far as attention is not concentrated on probing basic causes.

14. Thus, in the case of differences in school building costs, the causes may only be found by relating each major cost-element in a structure to the unit. Such elements are, for instance, the area or cubic meter per student in the classrooms, in the circulation areas, common rooms, workshops, laboratories etc. The height, number and quality of windows and doors may be another important element. One school has plenty of outdoor space with swimming pool, gymnasium, cafeteria. Another school has none of these facilities, considered by some as unessentials, by others as strictly necessary. The same can be said of all these elements, as has been mentioned above about cost factors, like the student/teacher ratio or the size of school in the recurrent account. With the help of a computer, it is possible to make a choice between various combinations inside the same total unit cost. If one element, for instance, a swimming pool, is considered in space and quality as being strictly necessary, then other elements may have to be reduced in cost or left out. Vice versa this method enables us to translate any specific building program quickly into money terms and enables us, at the same time, to pinpoint the detailed causes of differences we want to compare in total costs of school buildings. We can also learn the effect of size on building costs by keeping all other factors constant and by changing only the number of student places.

15. The methods outlined here have been developed and carried farthest by a special department in the Ministry of Education in London.[7] It can claim to have lowered unit costs in British schools considerably, mainly with the help of cost limits and cost analysis. I have reason to believe that in many countries, average unit costs of buildings could be lowered by 30 and more percent, just by applying and adapting the British methods. In order to do this, special research is needed in individual countries or regions, because conditions and requirements vary so much that mere copying methods which have proved successful in other countries are insufficient.

16. Harold Clark[8] has pointed to the fact that during this century the ratio of investment in buildings to investment in equipment has changed radically in industry but not in education. In the case of the latter, outlays on equipment remain, on average, around 10 percent of total capital outlay, whereas in American industry in recent years the proportion of equipment was around 75 percent of total capital investment. Mainly because of expansion in upper secondary and higher education, facilities requiring costly equipment have multiplied during the last decades. But this has had only small effect on the average proportion cited above. The mass of educational institutions are still rather "labor intensive." The probability is that this will be altered drastically before this century ends. Programmed and televised instruction, language laboratories and other modern devices will increase the capital intensity of all types and levels of education and change the proportion, inside total capital investment, in favor of the outlay for equipment.

17. As far as these new inputs are concerned, no particular difficulties of costing will arise. It will merely mean that unit cost calculations will have to take into account some new factors, whose prices and depreciation rates will have to be studied. Comparative cost analysis will reveal the break-even points, where for instance unit costs of conventional instruction are about the same as in televised instruction, but each student beyond a certain number in the closed-circuit televised course means decrease in unit costs.[9] There seems no doubt that airborne television, reaching far greater numbers of students, can lower unit costs or at least marginal unit costs drastically. The same is true of programs, tapes, records, and other massproduced teaching devices. They can, in principle, provide instruction of the highest quality at a very low price, and attainment tests combined with cost analysis can help to find out how far, and under which conditions, they do this in practice.

18. In addition to new technical teaching devices, new ways of organiz-

---

[7]See particularly *Building Bulletin*, No. 4, published by this Ministry in March, 1957. See also, F. Edding, *Problems of Expanding Investment in Education*, Regional technical assistance seminar (Bangkok, April, 1964), UNESCO/AD/AS/29, Paris 13 (March, 1964).

[8]*Cost and Quality in Public Education*, (Syracuse University Press, 1963), p. 8 ff.

[9]*Instructional Television Research. An Invewtigation of Closed-Circuit Television for Teaching University Courses* (The Pennsylvania State University, 1958), p. 101 ff.

ing instruction are under investigation. Flexible class-size, team teaching and payment of teachers according to performance may change the educational landscape in the future no less than is to be expected from new technical means. Proper job descriptions and investigations into the possible division of labor between trained teachers and auxiliary personnel will probably lead to a liberation of the master teacher from many nonprofessional chores. Here again, the costing of the change in inputs presents no serious difficulties. One can say without calculation that a flexibility in class size can result in an increase in the average student/teacher ratio thus tending to lower unit costs. This may be offset by lower average teaching duties or higher pay to teachers. The possible combinations can be worked out in the way indicated above without encountering any serious methodoligical problems.

19. The difficulties really begin when one questions the effects which the various input combinations have had, or will have, on the output, product or results of education. A lot of circumstantial evidence has led most experts in the field to the belief that educational investment is, on the whole, bringing comparatively good returns. Marginal returns also seem to be, in general, defensible in comparison with other possible investments. We have furthermore a great number of experiments intending to prove that one method of teaching gives better results than another. But these experiments are rarely linked with costing. The question as to whether the better results are obtained with higher or lower unit costs has, as a rule, been left open. In consequence, we are fairly sure that it is economically justified to continue with the expansion of educational investment. But we know amazingly little about the economic merits or demerits of the various possible ways to operate education.

20. Most educational reformers assume that increased expenditures which may arise from changes they propose will bring proportionate returns in terms of a higher quality of achievement. There is a widespread belief in educational circles that any increase in expenditure will have this result and is, therefore, perfectly justified. Non-educators are less sure about this. The more education expands the more important it will be to have reliable cost/quality analysis in this field.

21. This necessitates experimental research and development as is to be found in industry and the natural sciences. It calls for controlled experiments with sufficiently large numbers of groups under various conditions. It requires a strict isolation of factors and, more specifically, the efficient exclusion of that particular factor known as experimental enthusiasm. A strong effort to improve the means of testing is also called for. All this can be achieved. It is already in reach of the research institutes farthest advanced in this field. It can really be done there, and can become common practice if sufficient support is made available. The costs of such research are rather high and the degree of cooperation required from schools and administrations is unusual.

But so much depends on such work being undertaken that an unusual effort is certainly justified.

22. The principle of doing this type of research seems simple. In a sufficient number of student classes or groups, education has to be organized so that either only one fact is changed during a period of observation, or a specific factor combination is changed. The first may be appropriate if, for instance, the effect of class-size is to be investigated. The second seems indicated, if the effect of operating with teachers' aids in combination with certain new technical devices, is to be studied. All other factors, then, have to be fairly constant in all groups under observation, that is, in the groups where the change is operated and in the control groups where instruction is continued in the conventional way. The effects of change on unit costs can be easily assessed. The effect on quality has to be measured by tests. As far as tests can measure quality, it can then be established how much unit costs and achievement have been increased or decreased.

23. Changes in class-size exert a considerable influence on unit cost. Many experiments have been carried out to discover whether a corresponding lowering or improvement of achievement can be assumed to be the normal consequence of such changes. However, the results obtained so far are rather confusing and provide little help in the solution of practical problems. My impression is that none of the experiments has been either large enough or sufficiently well prepared to exclude all possible sources of error. Experts state that it could be done in such a way as to ensure that the results are universally acceptable. They assure us that practically any new combination of inputs could be tested for output if only research were given all the opportunities of experimenting it needs.

24. In this connection and in other respects, the teacher performance factor merits the closest examination. The development of methods to evaluate this performance has made slow progress considering the vital importance of what teachers can do and whether they give of their best. Experiments as outlined above, make little sense if it is assumed that each input of a teaching hour is equal. The quality of teachers is usually measured by the years and type of training they have had and sometimes by the salary they receive. But the measurement of actual performance is rarely undertaken. Somehow it is assumed that length of training is a sufficient yardstick by which to gauge quality.

25. More research activity directed towards the evaluation of teachers' performance seems necessary to improve the reliability of cost quality analysis. The fact that it constitutes one of the bases on which merit systems of teachers' compensation are erected, makes such research all the more essential. In many countries, teachers receive salaries according to the status achieved by graduating from training institutions with the addition of some allowances for age, number of children and local conditions. Few systems

grant premiums to teachers for educational performance during their careers, the reason being the difficulty of measuring performance. If this could be changed, it would revolutionize the efficiency in education. Without proper incentives most people fall back to a kind of routine work.[10] But teaching is an art as well as a gift and requires an active interest, dedication and continuous learning throughout the working life.

26. This leads to the last point made in this paper which seems to the writer to be essential for the improvement of efficiency in education. It is that ways and means must be provided to make sandwich courses the rule for both teachers and those engaged in many other professions and vocations.[11] Knowledge has been growing and continues to expand at so fast a rate, that it seems absurd to cling to the old notion that most of the knowledge that has to be acquired by systematic learning must be taught in institutions of education between the ages of 5 and 25. Inefficiency resulting in wastage of valuable teacher and student man hours is a consequence of the continued implementation of this traditional concept. Too much is frequently pressed into poor brains in too short a time. During the years of compulsory school, pupils are often neither really interested nor willing to learn. Even in higher education, many students are enrolled mainly because it is the conventional thing to do. But we know that a real transfer of knowledge can be brought about only if the recipient is willing and interested to learn. It is part of the art of teaching to evoke such willingness and to keep it alive. The chances of attaining success in this great art are enhanced if the student is strongly motivated towards learning. Such keenness is characteristic of persons returning to systematic learning during, or at intervals in, gainful employment. This category of student is able to bring to the classroom a fresh interest based on his experience of the problems of everyday working life. Normal eagerness to make the best use of the interval of study is increased if, as is frequently the case, he has to consider income or scarce leisure time forgone. There is a strong probability that the returns accruing to educational expenditure are highest in these circumstances. The verification of this hypothesis by research, and the study of the consequences of any findings arising from such an investigation, would appear to be crucial to the future organization of education.

.

[10]See Economic Aspects of the Teachers' Role. In C.S. Benson, *Perspectives on the Economics of Education. Readings in School Finance and Business Management* (Boston, 1963), p. 399 ff.

[11]See Selma J. Mushkin, *Resource Requirements and Educational Obsolescence.* Paper prepared for the Conference of the International Economic Association at Menthon St. Bernard, 1963 (to be published by MacMillan).

W. James Popham

Focus on Outcomes: A Guiding Theme of ES '70 Schools*

The single most important deficiency in the American education is its preoccupation with instructional process. This overriding concern with procedures rather than the results produced by those procedures manifests itself in myriad ways. We see teachers judged according to the methods they use ("She has excellent chalkboard techniques and fine bulletin boards.") Innovation is lauded for its own sake ("Now there's a *really* new instructional approach!"). Teachers design classroom instructional sequences by asking themselves "What shall I do?" rather than the appropriate question, which is "What do I wish my learners to become?" Schools in the ES '70 network, fortunately, do not suffer from this debilitating affliction. Perhaps their example will stimulate other American educators to attend to more fruitful instructional concerns. Perhaps by their example they can promote a focus on outcomes. Only such a focus can remedy the educational ills fostered by process preoccupation.

A MEANS ORIENTATION

Before turning to the schemes used by ES '70 schools in counteracting the devotees of process, a closer look at the culprits is in order. Essentially, the distinction is between educators who possess a means orientation and those who possess an outcomes orientation. Those who are captivated by questions of instructional process may well be descendants of the educational methods enthusiasts so prevalent during the early half of this century. More

*Reprinted from *Phi Delta Kappan,* 50 (December, 1969), p. 208, by permission of the author and the editor.

likely, they bear no such lineage—it's just a great deal easier to be concerned with instructional methods rather than with whether those methods are effective. For when you commit yourself to assessing whether a given instructional process is worthwhile, there are two frightfully aversive concomitants. First, you have to go to the very considerable trouble of devising adequate criterion measures. Second, you run the risk that you may be held accountable for producing satisfactory results.

Anyone who has seriously tried to develop criterion measures with which to assess a major instructional program will readily attest to the difficulty of such an enterprise. Simple, low-level objectives, of course, are easily assessed. All educators, or so it seems, are skilled in testing a student's ability to memorize. But assessing high-level cognitive outcomes or attitudinal attainments—this is a taxing task. The really worthwhile goals of education are invariably the most difficult to measure. Preparing adequate devices to assess such goals is onerous indeed.

Further, the accountability for instructional growth that is absent in means-oriented education is awesome, particularly for the incompetent. If one's responsibility ceases with the generation of instructional procedures, then there is no fear. The merits of the procedures will not be measured. One simply conjures up new ways of teaching people, then forgets it—or at most collects some impressionistic data from biased participants. Did the "experimental" teachers really like the new instructional method (with which they are clearly identified)? How did the "experimental" pupils respond to the new approach? Having summarized such reactions, the means-oriented educator moves off to explore new instructional galaxies. The just-completed project has been a success.

But despite these two aversive elements, an outcomes-oriented approach to education is the only defensible stance open to the responsible educator. ES '70 educators have committed themselves to such an orientation. Let's examine the ingredients of such a commitment.

AN OUTCOMES ORIENTATION

An educator who focuses on outcomes, not process, is usually committed to the belief that teachers exist primarily to modify learners. More generally, formal education is viewed as an enterprise which is designed to *change* human beings so that they are better, wiser, more efficient, etc. If this basic assumption is correct (alternative assumptions appearing eminently untenable), then the educator's principal tasks are to (1) identify the kinds of modifications he wishes to promote, (2) design instructional procedures which he hopes will promote them, and (3) find out whether the procedures were successful. Judgments about the success of an instructional procedure are made exclusively on the basis of results, that is, the changes in learner behavior which emerge as a consequence of instruction. Only if the hoped-for changes in learner behavior have been attained is the instructional process considered effective. Only when such changes have not been attained is the process judged ineffective.

This concern with results, as reflected in the modified performance of learners, leads the outcomes-oriented educator to focus the bulk of his attention on the formulation of instructional objectives and, subsequently, on measuring the degree to which they have been achieved. Because the criterion by which the success of an instructional process will be judged must be measurable learner behavior, the outcomes-oriented educator cleaves exclusively to objectives amenable to measurement. Whether they are called performance objectives, behavioral goals, operational objectives, or some equivalent phrase, they must be capable of post-instructional assessment.

But is the outcomes-oriented educator oblivious of instructional process? Clearly not. However, only *after* an appraisal of outcomes are modifications in procedures recommended. In other words, means are judged according to the ends achieved. Modifications of instructional means are often made, but only as dictated by the learner's post-instruction behavior.

ES '70 SCHOOLS

As pointed out earlier, the 19 ES '70 schools have committed themselves, in diverse ways, to an outcomes orientation. An examination of the several schemes by which these schools are employing measurably stated instructional objectives will illustrate the nature of this commitment.

Several of the schools are really just getting under way with respect to the employment of performance objectives. But at the very least, all network schools have provided specific training experiences, e.g., institutes, workshops, short courses, etc., to make their professional staffs more conversant with the manner in which instructional objectives can be most profitably formulated.

A few of the schools have engaged in what might be characterized as a generalized task analysis of the levels of specificity at which objectives should be stated. Two of the schools, for example, report attempts to explicate different levels of instructional objectives. The Breathitt County, Kentucky, ES '70 school has attempted to organize its instructional objectives at five levels of generality ranging from what are called "ultimate behavioral objectives" through the increasingly specific goals statements that follow, i.e., terminal behavioral objective, terminal intermediate behavioral objective, intermediate behavioral objective, and subbehavioral objective. The Bloomfield Hills, Michigan, school district organized instructional objectives into the following categories: "system objectives, discipline objectives, terminal performance objectives, interim performance objectives, and course objectives." While these attempts to classify instructional objectives have not yet been validated by experimental investigations, they illustrate considerable concern about the nature of instructional outcomes in these schools.

Several of the ES '70 schools have shown remarkable progress in developing instructional materials and evaluation measures based upon performance objectives. The accomplishments of Nova High School in Broward County, Florida, have been reported frequently during the past few years. This ES '70 school has developed small instructional units designated as Learning Activity Packages (LAPs) in science, mathematics, social studies, and technical science. These materials are used extensively in the school and, because of a liberal distribution policy, by a number of other secondary schools which have secured copies of the Nova LAPs. Development of additional learning activity packages in the areas of music, English, physical education, and language arts are now under way at Nova. The Monroe, Michigan, ES '70 school has also developed learning activity packages in metal shop, physics, and applied science. Monroe High School staff members have been willing to prepare these materials in addition to their regular instructional responsibilities. Some of the ES '70 schools have been able to provide more released time for these kinds of developmental activities than other network schools. The Philadelphia, Pennsylvania, school district has had a writing team working on the development of interdisciplinary instructional materials based on performance objectives for a number of months, even though their ES '70 school will not open until September, 1970.

In Duluth, Minnesota, the ES '70 high school has been using performance objectives in a highly individualized instructional program which, like the innovations at Nova, has been reported widely in recent years. One of the principal techniques for using measurable instructional objectives in Duluth is the development of student learning contracts. The key to the student learning contract is the performance objective. Students are provided with contracts in a variety of fields, each contract specifying the general purpose as well as the specific, measurable objective of the instructional activity. Sample test situations for the instructional objectives are provided along with resource materials which the student is to use in an attempt to achieve the instructional objective. The student then takes a test which measures attainment of the objective. If the student achieves the stated level of proficiency on the test, he is permitted to go on to another contract. If he fails to achieve the desired level, other instructional procedures (frequently a teacher-led presentation) help him to achieve the objective. A second test of equal difficulty is given to the student before he moves on to the next contract.

The ES '70 school in Mineola, New York, reports an unexpected dividend from focusing on measurable objectives. Eliot G. Spack, ES '70 coordinator in Mineola, described this incident as follows:

> Quite recently one of our elementary schools began to undertake a revision of its curriculum through the development of behavioral objectives in certain subject areas. At the time there was great concern registered by the teachers as to whether or not the central office would financially underwrite all the equipment and materials which they felt would be necessary for any individualized program. This group worked for several months under the guidance of the school principal. After almost a year of writing objectives, and performance criteria the teachers were ready to review the array of resources which would be incorporated into the learning activities. The principal invited eight representatives of leading software producers to display their wares at a conference day session. The materials available reflected a potential expenditure in the thousands of dollars. Using their predefined objectives as their guide, the teachers surveyed the "market." When their review was completed the principal dismissed the salesmen and, mopping his brow in expectation of the worst, queried his staff on their desires. The sum total of their requests for purchase came to $12.60. The teachers had learned to become sophisticated consumers by applying their own objectives. It was quite a lesson for all!

As these varied uses of measurable objectives illustrate, there are certainly many procedures for employing specific outcomes in instructional planning and evaluation. But although the procedures were different, the central focus persisted, namely, that high quality instructional planning requires the explication of instructional intents in terms of measurable learner behaviors.

RECLASSIFYING OUTCOMES

As the number of outcomes-oriented educators increases, the possibility of restructuring the basic curriculum patterns of American education also increases. Whereas the organization of curriculum according to classical subject and grade level boundaries is a time-honored tradition, there may be more functional ways to categorize instructional outcomes. Two research projects are currently under way at Rutgers University and at the University of California at Los Angeles to test the adequacy of alternative methods of classifying instructional outcomes. It is apparent that if we can find a large enough number of school personnel who are willing to consider outcomes rather than standard discipline and grade level classifications, there may be some merit in rethinking the basic organizational pattern of the curriculum. To illustrate, a child may acquire certain analytic skills in one course which are precisely the same as the analytic skills acquired in another course. It may be more efficient to organize the curriculum around that particular outcome, namely, that particular kind of analytic skill, than around the customary subject boundaries. The Rutgers and UCLA project staffs will be working closely with ES '70 schools to test both the adequacy of alternative methods of classifying instructional outcomes as well as the practical utility of such classification schemes in the public school classroom.

The major advantage of an outcomes-oriented approach to education is that our instructional outcomes have an increased probability of being realized. The major danger of such an approach is that we may be pursuing the wrong outcomes. Efforts to scrutinize methods of categorizing objectives, coupled with the highly visible outcomes orientation of the ES '70 network, offer the promise of both identifying and accomplishing truly worthwhile educational achievements.

Felix M. Lopez

Accountability in Education[*]

Accountability refers to the process of expecting each member of an organization to answer to someone for doing specific things according to specific plans and against certain timetables to accomplish tangible performance results. It assumes that everyone who joins an organization does so presumably to help in the achievement of its purposes; it assumes that individual behavior which contributes to these purposes is functional and that which does not is dysfunctional. Accountability is intended, therefore, to insure that the behavior of every member of an organization is largely functional.

Accountability is to be distinguished from responsibility by the fact that the latter is an essential component of authority which cannot be delegated. It is the responsibility of a board of education to insure the effective education of the children in its community. Board members cannot pass this responsibility on to principals and to teachers. But they can hold teachers and principals accountable for the achievement of tangible educational effects *provided* they define clearly what effects they expect and furnish the resources needed to achieve them.

REASONS FOR FAILURE

A review of accountability programs underlines its uneven, trial-and-error progress and its current inadequacies. Initiated when psychometric theory was largely underdeveloped, embedded early in unrealistic management and legislative mandates, imposed usually from above on an unwilling and uncomprehending supervisor, the program has struggled with the common conception that it is an end rather than a means and with an administra-

[*]Reprinted from *Phi Delta Kappan,* 52 (December, 1970), pp. 231–235, by permission of the author and the editor.

tive naivetè that treats it as a student's report card. Personnel textbooks have stressed the idea that an accountability plan must be characterized by simplicity, flexibility, and economy. Ignoring the fact that these qualities are not wholly compatible, administrators have attempted to develop programs along these lines. Their inevitable failures have led to the current disillusionment and distrust and, in some quarters, to the belief that the establishment of an effective program is impossible. Nevertheless, a careful examination of efforts to establish accountability programs suggests some underlying misconceptions that explain the many failures.

1. Most accountability programs have been installed in organizational settings that lack the necessary background and organizational traditions to assimilate them. Insufficient emphasis has been placed on the development of an organizational philosophy and on the determination of accountability policies before the implementations of the program.

2. The administrative procedures governing the program have not been attuned to its purposes. There has been a tendency to make the program accomplish a great deal with an oversimplified procedure. The evidence strongly suggests that despite the ardent wish for economy and simplicity, only a program designed for a specific purpose or involving a multimethod approach is likely to succeed.

3. Accountability systems have not been designed to gain acceptance by those who are covered by them nor by those who have to implement them. For the most part, they have been designed by specialists, approved at the highest levels, and imposed without explanation on those who have to implement them. This occurs because the problem is approached from an organizational rather than an individual perspective.

4. The measures of accountability so far developed have not met even minimum standards of reliability and relevancy. This failure is known as the "criterion problem" and can be summarized briefly as follows:

   (a)   Criteria of effectiveness in a position generally lack clear specifications.

   (b)   Objective measures, when examined closely, are usually found to be either nonobjective or irrelevant.

   (c)   Subjective measures, when examined closely, are usually found to be biased or unreliable.

   (d)   Seemingly adequate criteria can vary over time.

   (e)   Position effectiveness is really multidimensional. Effectiveness in one aspect of a position does not necessarily mean effectiveness in others.

   (f)   When effectiveness in different aspects of a position is measured, there is no sure way to combine these measures into a single index of effectiveness.

(g)   Different performance patterns achieve the same degree of effectiveness in the same job.

To be successful, therefore, the accountability program must meet the following requirements:

1. It must be an important communications medium in a responsive environment through which members are informed of what is to be accomplished, by whom, and how; wide participation in the obtainment of organization goals must be invited; and the attention of top management must be focused on the accomplishment of individual employees' personal goals.

2. It must reflect an organizational philosophy that inspires confidence and trust in all the members.

3. It must be based on ethical principles and sound policies that can be implemented by a set of dynamic, flexible, and realistic standards, procedures, and practices.

4. It must clearly specify its purposes so that standards, procedures, and practices can be conformed to them.

5. It must be designed primarily to improve the performance of each member in his current job duties. Other effects, such as the acquisition of information on which to base salary and promotion decisions and the personal development of the employees' capacities, may accompany the main effect of improved job performance, but these must be considered merely by-products of the main process.

6. The manner in which the supervisor discusses his evaluation with the subordinate constitutes the core of the process. If this is handled poorly, the program, no matter how well designed and implemented, will fail.

7. To be effective and accepted, both those who use it and those who will be judged by it must participate in the design, installation, administration, and review of the total accountability system.

These principles, then, outline the dimensions of an approach to the establishment of accountability in education. The approach encompasses three broad interventions into the current system, each aimed initially at a distinct level of the organization structure: the top, the middle, and the base, the last named being the teachers themselves. Ultimately, however, all three levels will be involved in all three phases of the accountability program.

INTERVENTION AT THE TOP

Basically, intervention at the top consists of the establishment of organizational goals by the use of a technique referred to in private industry as "Management by Objectives" (MBO) and in government as the "Planning, Programming, and Budgeting System" (PPBS). Since there are many excellent books describing these techniques in detail, we shall confine ourselves here to a brief summary of the method.[1]

Goal Setting

The underlying concept of the goal-setting approach is simple: The clearer the idea you have of what you want to accomplish, the greater your chance of accomplishing it. Goal setting, therefore, represents an effort on the part of the management to inhibit the natural tendency of organizational procedures to obscure organizational purposes in the utilization of resources. The central idea is to establish a set of goals for the organization, to integrate individual performance with them, and to relate the rewards system to their accomplishment.

While there is general agreement that this method represents the surest approach to effective management, there is no primrose path to its practical implementation.

In its most commonly accepted form, MBO constitutes an orderly way of goal setting at the top, communication of these goals to lower-unit managers, the development of lower-unit goals that are phased into those set by the higher levels, and comparison of results in terms of goals. The program operates within a network of consultative interviews between supervisor and subordinate in which the subordinate receives ample opportunity to participate in the establishment of his own performance objectives. Thus, the whole concept is oriented to a value system based upon the results achieved; and the results must be concrete and measurable.

When properly administered, Management by Objectives has much to recommend it:

1. It involves the whole organization in the common purpose.

2. It forces top management to think through its purposes, to review them constantly, to relate the responsibilities of individual units to pre-set goals, and to determine their relative importance.

3. It sets practical work tasks for each individual, holds him accountable for their attainment, and demonstrates clearly how his performance fits into the overall effort.

4. It provides a means of assuring that organization goals are eventually translated into specific work tasks for the individual employee.

It is, therefore, virtually impossible to conceive of an effective accountability program that does not operate within the umbrella of the goal-setting process. When properly designed and implemented, goal setting becomes an ideal basis for other forms of performance evaluation. It insures that subordi-

[1]For example, G. S. Odiorne, *Management by Objectives* (New York: Pitman Publishing Co., 1965) and C. L. Hughes, *Goal Setting: Key to Individual and Organizational Performance* (New York: American Management Association, 1965).

nate goals and role performances are in support of the goals of the higher levels of the organization and that ultimately the institutional purposes will be achieved.

The Charter of Accountability

One way of implementing the goal-setting process that has been found useful in education is through the development of a charter of accountability. This approach was originally developed by the Ground Systems Group of the Hughes Aircraft Company.[2] The charter is agreed to by two individuals or groups—one in a superordinate and the other in a subordinate capacity—after consultation, discussion, and negotiation. Ultimately, the entire organization is covered by the series of charters beginning at the top with a major organization unit, say, the English department in a local high school. Each teacher's goals are shaped by his unit's charter of accountability. Each unit head is held accountable for the results specified in his charter, which he draws up and which he and his superiors sign. Ultimately, all charters are combined into a system-wide charter that provides the basis of accountability for the board of education and the superintendent of schools.

A charter contains a statement of purposes, goals, and objectives. *Purpose* constitutes the organization's reason for existence and gives meaning and direction to all its activities. Purposes, therefore, are usually stated in broad inspirational terms.

Goals and *objectives* are the tangible expressions of the organization's purposes. Goals are long-range, concrete, end results specified in measurable terms. Objectives are short-range, specific targets to be reached in a period of one year, also specified in measurable terms.

Specifically, a charter of accountability contains the following features:

1. A statement of system-wide purposes or areas of concern and the purposes of the next level above the unit completing the charter of accountability.
2. A statement of the specific purposes of the unit completing the charter.
3. A description of the functional, administrative, and financial accountability necessary to accomplish the unit's purposes.
4. A set of basic assumptions about the future economic, socio-political, professional, and technological developments likely to affect the attainment of goals but which are beyond the control of the accountability unit.

---

[2]P. N. Scheid, "Charter of Accountability for Executives." *Harvard Business Review* (July-August, 1965), pp. 88–98.

5. A listing of the major goals of the unit to be aimed at for the immediate five-year period.

6. A subseries of performance tasks that provide unit supervisors with definitive targets toward which to orient their specialized efforts and with which to define the resources necessary to accomplish them.

7. Statements of the authority and responsibility necessary to complete these tasks.

Space does not permit the full exposition of the process of establishing a charter of accountability. Very broadly, and quite superficially, it would follow this pattern:

1. A central committee or council composed of representatives of key members of the system—school board, local school boards, union, teachers, parent and community groups—would convene to define the broad purposes of the school system. Putting it simply, their job would be to answer these questions: What is the business of the school system? What are we trying to accomplish? While the answers to these questions may seem obvious, in practice they are difficult to articulate. Answering them serves the larger purpose of clarifying thinking about the realistic aims of a schools system. In business, the definition of purpose has led to dramatic changes in organization structure, business policies, product mix, and, ultimately, in return on investment.

The purposes delineated by this council are then discussed widely in the community. In particular, they serve to determine the major areas of concern of the school system that have been assigned to it by the community. Both the purposes and the areas of concern, however, must be considered at this point to be tentative and subject to modification by lower levels of the system. They will provide, however the necessary guidelines for the goal-setting process and the development of charters of accountability by the school districts and other lower level units.

2. Each major subunit—school district, division, or department—meets to define its goals and objectives and to prepare its charter of accountability. Since these goals and objectives can differ substantially according to the needs of specific localities, the criteria of accountability will also differ. This is the important, even crucial point that constitutes the major ad vantage of the goal-setting process. It provides for multiplicity of measures of accountability that are tailored to the needs and hence the goals of specific operating units. The objectives of a principal of an inner city-school will differ from those of a principal of a surburban school, and so must the measures of accountability. Reading grade equivalents may be an appropriate measure of teacher effectiveness in one school and not in the other.

3. The charters of all units are collated and reviewed by the central council or school board with the advice and assistance of the planning and budgeting unit of the office of the superintendent of schools. Appropriate approvals are granted in accordance with existing policy and legislation. Thus, the combined charters constitute *the* charter of accountability for the board of education and the entire school system. While there will be some uniformity to this charter, it is apparent that it will resemble more a patchwork quilt than a seamless cloak and will, therefore, adhere more closely to the reality it attempts to reflect.

4. As each charter is approved, subcharters are developed in the same way for individual units in each district. Obviously, the heads of these units will have had a voice in the formulation of the district charter so that this will not be a new task for them. But in developing the subunit charters in the schools themselves, all the members of the system will ultimately have a voice.

5. Once the charters have been adopted, they are implemented. In some cases, new inputs will eliminate or change previously stated objectives. In others, objectives will be found to be quite unrealistic. Provisions must be made, therefore, to amend the charters of accountability as experience dictates. In most cases, however, it is advisable to stick with the original charter until the year-end review and appraisal of results.

6. The evaluation of the achievement of the period's objectives is made as plans for the next charter are formulated. This is the essence of accountability: results compared to objectives. It is important to note, however, that this evaluation is made not in a punitive, policing climate to check up on people, but rather in a supportive, constructive atmosphere to find out how objectives were achieved and, if they were not, why not. Both parties to this process assure the responsibility for the results and approach the task with the idea of exploring what happened for purposes of problem solving and resetting goals and objectives.

INTERVENTION IN THE MIDDLE

The implementation of an accountability program depends, to a large extent, on the attitudes and the skills of the supervisory force. If it is skeptical, anxious, or hostile to the plan, it will fail no matter how well it is conceived. This has been the bitter experience of many firms that have attempted to install goal-setting and performance-evaluation programs without first preparing their managers and supervisors to implement them.

Thus, a second essential step in introducing accountability into a school system is the establishment of a massive supervisory development program. Such a program must be practical, intensive, and primarily participative in nature. Its purpose is not merely to disseminate information but rather to change attitudes and to impart specific skills, particularly the skill of conducting accountability interviews with subordinates.

This will not be easy. Most supervisors, principals, and teachers have had no experience with such a program to prepare them for the tasks involved. A development program must be tailor-made to meet their needs.

The development program must also begin at the top with the superintendents. There is a practical reason for this. When presenting this subject matter to middle managers in other organizations, an almost universal response from them is, "Why can't our bosses take this course? They need it more than we do." Since the program content is likely to be quite strange, even revolutionary, to many of the lower middle-management participants, its credibility can be insured only by its being accepted at the highest levels and applied there first.

The program must enable the top-level people to examine the basic assumptions on which they operate and give them as much time as possible to get these assumptions out in the open. The specific objectives of the program would be:

1. To emphasize the influence process in handling subordinates, managers, and supervisors, as well as teachers, and to de-emphasize the formal authority-power-coercion approach to supervision and administration.[3]

2. To provide a deeper understanding of the communications process itself. Such a program must heighten the awareness of the supervisor as to how he comes across best to others and develop his flexibility in dealing with the broad spectrum of personalities encountered in the fulfillment of his responsibilities. Each supervisor should be given an opportunity to prepare a plan for his self-growth and development.[4]

3. To consider ways of dealing with the more routine aspects of teaching by considering job enrichment techniques.

4. To emphasize the sociopyschological realities that education faces today. The program should make supervisors aware that they simply cannot rely on authoritarianism alone to get results with people.

The format of the program should be primarily participative in nature —that is, it should consist of learning experiences and exercises which require the supervisors to participate actively in the training sessions. Frequent use should be made of audio-visual displays, role playing, conference discussions, and case study techniques. Theoretical ideas and concepts that help

---

[3]Felix M. Lopez, *Evaluating Employee Performance* (Chicago: Public Personnel Association, 1968).
[4]For an expansion of this principle, see Lopez, *op. cit.,* pp. 68–69.

develop new ways of thinking and approaching problems can be introduced and amplified through specifically designed case studies. The solutions which result from the systematic examination of these case studies should be applied directly to specific school system problems. And, finally, attention must be given to problem areas that may be unique to an individual supervisor.

INTERVENTION AT THE BASE

The third phase of the accountability system, and the most pertinent, is the development of specific instruments and techniques to evaluate how individual members of the school system are performing their assigned roles. Since this phase touches the teachers directly, it is the most difficult and also the most delicate. If it is handled properly, it can accelerate the educational development of the community's children. If it is handled poorly, or indifferently, or as just another routine task (as it so often has been in other public agencies), problems of academic retardation will persist.

Description and discussion of the design, development, and installation of individual performance standards and measures for teachers is beyond the scope of this paper. There are a number of approaches to this effort utilizing both objective and subjective measures. But regardless of the measures and procedures employed, there are some general principles that warrant mention here.

REQUIREMENTS OF A TEACHER

Accountability Program

First, an individual teacher accountability program can function effectively only within the context of a goal-setting program, such as the charter of accountability previously described, and a program of continuous supervisory development in coaching and evaluation interviewing.

Second, it must be quite clear from the outset that the purpose of the accountability program is improvement of present role performance. If the measurements and standards developed are used for other purposes—such as discipline, promotion, and salary increases—the program will fail, positively and absolutely. Of course there must be a relationship between the measures of accountability and these other personnel actions, but the relationship must be indirect and antecedent rather than direct and causal.

Third, the immediate intentions of the instruments developed as part of the accountability program should be to provide the teacher (or other professional worker) with feedback on his efforts and to provide him and his supervisor with material for discussions of ways to strengthen his professional performance.

Instruments of Accountability

The instruments or standards of measurement of performance must be designed to fulfill two purposes:

1. They must be meaningful and acceptable to the person who is evaluated by them.
2. They must permit quantitative consolidation in the form of means, standard scores, and percentiles to serve as criteria with which to evaluate the department, school, and district achievement of objectives.

Such instruments can be of two basic types:

1. *Results oriented data.* These are hard data geared to the effects of the teacher's performance—attendance, standardized achievement test scores, grade point averages, etc.
2. *Person-oriented data.* These consist of ratings completed by peers, superiors, and subordinates describing the *style* of the teacher's performance—that is, his initiative, technical competence, interpersonal competence, etc. It is possible to design the instrument so that the person completing it cannot consciously control the outcome.

None of the information obtained at this level should go beyond the school principal except in a consolidated and hence anonymous form.

To insure the acceptance of these instruments, it is necessary that the teachers themselves and their supervisors actively participate in this research, design, and implementation. This is done in two ways. First, in the initial development of the program, teachers and supervisors should actively assist the professional researchers at every stage. Second, and even more important, in the accountability interview, the teacher takes an active role in what is essentially a problem-solving process.

The Accountability Interview

The entire program described in this paper pivots around the accountability interview between supervisor and teacher. If it is conducted well throughout the school system, then the educational process in that community will thrive. If it is done poorly, the whole accountability program will fail and the school system will be in trouble. Therefore, this encounter is crucial.

To make the interview effective, a number of conditions must exist before, during, and afterward. First, the supervisor must have discussed his own performance with his superior—the principal or the superintendent. He must also have participated in the development of his charter of accountability and that of his school or district. Both the teacher and the supervisor must be familiar with these documents.

They must also be aware of the department's and the school's goals and objectives. The supervisor must have adequate preparation in coaching and interviewing skills. Both the supervisor and the teacher must have met earlier to agree on the dimension of the teacher's role and on acceptable standards of performance. The teacher must be given adequate time for self-evaluation, and both must have reviewed the data resulting from the accountability instruments referred to previously.

During the interview, both discuss the material collected on the teacher's performance. They analyze the teacher's strengths and explore ways of capitalizing on them. They identify areas for improvement, develop an improvement plan, and choose the resources to implement it. The teacher also discusses his professional problems with his supervisor and ways in which the latter can be of greater assistance to him. They establish follow-up schedules with milestones to determine progress. And they put all of this—the plan, the schedule, and the milestones—in writing for subsequent review and follow-up.

This accountability program, sincerely pursued at all these levels, is guaranteed to achieve positive results. There will remain, however, one major obstacle—time. It is obvious that the program will make major demands on a supervisor's time. Consequently, most supervisors will assert that they do not have the time for such a meticulous and detailed approach. In part they will be wrong, and in part they will be right.

They will be wrong, first, because they are not really using the time they now have to maximum advantage. If they are like most managers, they waste a good deal of time in superfluous activities. Secondly, they will be wrong because they are mistaken in their notions of the proper functions of their job. They tend to overemphasize the professional and functional aspects of their responsibilities and to underemphasize the managerial and supervisory concerns that are of paramount importance in the organizational system.

But they will be right because their present school system, like nearly every other organizational system in the United States, requires them to perform many functions that interfere with their basic duties of manager and supervisor.[5]

The answer to this problem, which is one of the chief stumbling blocks to the implementation of an accountability program, seems to lie in a searching examination of the functions performed at each level of supervision. Many of these, upon closer examination, will be found to be delegatable, thus enriching the jobs of their subordinates and freeing them for their real responsibilities of managing one of the most vital enterprises in society—the school system.

[5]See, for example, F. M. Lopez, *The Making of a Manager: Guidelines to His Selection and Promotion* (New York: American Management Association, 1970), Chapter 4 ("What Does a Manager Do?")

Application to the Curriculum

section **II**

Introduction

Since the time of the Greek philosophers and assuredly before, the question of what is worth knowing has periodically been raised by man. At certain periods in the development of educational thought the question was thought to be answered only to be asked again and again at later dates as society became more complex. In our time the question is still unresolved.

Within the last decade the disputes surrounding the curriculum have reached the proportions of a verbal war. The conflicts have revolved around not only the relative merits of some fields, but the amount of time which should be spent on specific areas of knowledge. Heated arguments have also been heard regarding whether or not some areas are worthy of being taught within the confines of the school educational experience. What subject matter, experiences and attitudes are most apt to contribute to the development of a secure, self-activating individual who is prepared to live in a changing world? This question must be answered if some semblance of order in our educational system is to evolve, at least a partial answer must be found—and quickly.

Accountability and all that it implies, is not an answer to the question raised but it does help us to focus on that which is basic for survival in our society. Accountability should not, however, be confused with the stated philosophy of the Council for Basic Education (CBE). The CBE completely rejects any school concern for the mental health of the child, training for citizenship, or the need for solving social problems. The CBE philosophy is not necessarily encompassed in the philosophy of accountability as conceived by the authors. Accountability in our philosophy of the curriculum means that the teacher should be held responsible for teaching the student the basic skills in order that he can learn. We do not believe in the concept that if it cannot be tested it does not exist. But it would be foolish for educators to disregard those skills and abilities which can be evaluated just because we do not have the technical know-how to test concepts, attitudes, beliefs and behavior as accurately.

63

Our concept of the accountable curriculum would teach and test those skill elements which we know to be of value and to use the best measurement technology to evaluate results. But, we would also teach and evaluate growth in concept development related to social problems, citizenship and all of the other affective areas of the curriculum using the best measurement technology available to aid us in judging our effectiveness in these areas as well.

EITHER-OR THINKING

The pendulum type swing which is characteristic of the school curriculum is an example of the either-or thinking. In their zeal for reform, proponents of the CBE philosophy and those of the free floating child-centered philosophy often discount the school program that would basically provide for a school setting where the strengths of both extremes could be employed to advantage. Many zealist reformers of the contemporary curriculum are academicians whose first commitment and interest is in the subject matter with little or no regard for the mental health of the individual student. Others, proponents of the child-centered curriculum, would have us develop a program that would eliminate any structured teaching of subject matter content. Neither approach is balanced and both can do great harm to the students attending our schools.

Sudden shifts in educational thinking can have unfortunate outcomes upon the achievement of our educational product—the children. Abrupt shifts in the program of the schools that have resulted in harm are not unknown within the last decade. Not all changes are harmful, nor are they unconstructive, but mindless changes made on the basis of "bandwagon" thinking have done damage. Some of the changes which have resulted in irritating the educational balance are:

1. Team teaching.
2. Cross grade grouping.
3. Content area grouping.
4. Ungraded units.
5. Modern mathematics.
6. Phonics in reading.
7. Programmed materials.

Team Teaching

Within many schools in our nation the team teaching approach was enforced upon all of the teachers regardless of the abilities of the teachers involved, the characteristics of the student population to be served or the philosophical makeup of the school. The results of the enforced organization have done some damage. Let us look at just an example.

Point

—In school A, in a primary grade unit, the teachers (4) divided the content areas with each taking the area they liked to teach best. The newest member of the team and a first year teacher was given the responsibility for teaching mathematics. The new teacher did an extremely poor job in teaching the mathematics and her contract was not renewed. It seems that no one checked to find out that mathematics was the weakest area in her college preparation and that she was aware of her weakness. She was unfortunate enough to be placed on a team where she was the newest member and was being assigned on the basis of what no one else wanted to teach.

Grouping

Cross grade and content area grouping share a common weakness. Both grouping practices are organized for ease of instruction by reducing the ability range to be taught, but no claim has ever been made that the practice improves the learning environment. There is also no evidence in the research that cross grade or content area grouping procedures improve achievement.

Point

—At the sixth grade level in a local school the children were assigned to a homeroom and then sent to different "sixth" grade teachers for instruction in science, math, etc. In reading, the students were cross graded in order to lessen the range of reading ability to be accommodated by any one teacher. The grouping for reading did provide for instruction at the level of the children's achievement but when they went to spelling class, mathematics, social studies and other they were all given a "sixth" grade book.

Ungraded Unit

The ungraded primary unit is (in our opinion) a philosophically and educationally sound plan. If operated in the way in which it is conceived it would allow the child to progress along the educational continuum in the manner most suited to his individual growth and developmental patterns. In order to succeed however, the philosophy of the plan must be completely understood by the teachers and the philosophy must be translated into classroom practice. In many school situations the "plan" is in operation but the philosophy is not.

Point

—In X school the early elementary grades are organized on a primary unit plan. All of the grade level indicators have been removed from the doors and it is considered in bad taste to mention what grade you teach. In Miss Y's room however, all of the basal reading books are at the second grade level and every child is in one of the books, on different pages certainly. At the end of the school year Miss Y hurries in her instruction to get all of the children through the second grade material so they will be ready for Mrs. Z's room next year.

—Such practices leave one to wonder what would happen to Miss Y if we promoted children in March and taught all summer.

Mathematics

The majority of mathematics educators agree that mathematics is being taught more effectively today than prior to the "Modern Mathematics" revolution of the 1950's. In general, today's students are more interested in the subject. Current instruction in mathematics is characterized by a multiplicity of teaching materials and instruction strategies. However, in spite of this improvement of teaching in this field, many of the problems related to what students are actually learning that existed prior to the "revolution" continue to exist today. Specifically there are large numbers of students who proceed through our elementary grades who use the "new language" of sets, number theory and non-metric geometry, but do not have command of fundamental computational skills in the basic operations of addition, subtraction, multiplication and division.

Another important dimension of current mathematics instruction is the utilization of the discovery method. However, we are finding that unless children possess knowledge of the basic hierarchy of skills, very little discovery takes place.

Point

—A third grade teacher prided herself in the fact that "nearly all my children knew the addition facts in base five even though it took five weeks to teach them."

—This is perhaps an exaggerated example of a misguided teacher. It would seem that this was not a sound use of student and teacher time. Utilization of different numeration systems can be an effective technique for learning the base ten system, but there is very little utility in knowing the addition facts in base five.

Reading

The pendulum has swung to such extremes in reading instruction that it is a wonder that anyone learns to read. The cycle appears to be that approximately every eight to ten years an exposé of reading instruction appears in print and the "obvious" answer to solve all of our problems is phonics. Phonics instruction does have a place in the reading instructional program but it is not THE program. We often complain about the low interest appeal of reading material to students and yet the following example is not unfamiliar.

Point 1

The child has been taught the sound for the combination -*an* and the sound of the letters *n, c, f* and *d*. Now he reads:

Nan can fan Dan.
Dan can fan Nan.
Can Dan fan Nan?
Nan can fan Dan.

Point 2

The child is taught the sounds of *c* (k), *a* and *t*. He is then expected to put the sounds together *c-a-t* to pronounce the word cat. The problem appears to be that not all children can combine isolated sounds into a known word.

Programmed Materials

Programmed materials of the workbook type are in many instances being used as total programs and all inclusive for teaching skill areas; i. e., reading and mathematics. An advertized advantage of the materials is that they teach the child the required skills in a sequential manner with constant reenforcement and feedback. In actual use of the material it has been observed by the authors that the material is being used extensively with children from low socio-economic backgrounds who have low motivation and poor attention spans. The following example is taken from an observation made in the school system of a metropolitan area.

Point

The children were working in different workbooks depending upon their level of ability in learning to read. The children were enthusiastic about the program in the beginning as were the teachers because they were able to see progress in moving from one level book to another. When I asked several children to read from the workbook one level below the one they were currently working on however, I found that they could not read. The children had learned the technique in order to put down the correct response in the blank, but they were not learning.

Postcript

At the end of the school year when the children were being administered an achievement test one of the children ran out of the room during the middle of the test. When the teacher went after him and asked why he ran out, he responded, "You bastard, you told me I could read and I can't."

The examples cited are unfortunately not unrare in our schools. One cannot help but wonder if the practices would have occurred if someone had indicated that those responsible for the practice would have been held accountable for the results attained.

ACCOUNTABLE—WHAT FOR?

School administrators and teachers are professionally trained and certified to guide the educational development of children. They have only one commodity to sell and that is their ability to create a learning environment in which the child can acquire the skills and abilities necessary to make him an independent and productive learner. If the educational system is not organized and administered in a manner which provides for this function there is no reason for it to exist.

All of the elements for the successful operations are available to us if we will only use them wisely and truly make our school accountable for their function. The assets which we have are many.

1. Within limits, we know what is a good teaching practice and what is a poor practice.
2. We have much information available on how children learn and principles of learning are available as guidelines.
3. Within the skill areas we have a good idea of a logical learning sequence and we can place the skills in a hierarchical order.
4. Much research is available to enable us to evaluate organizational structures and use them wisely.
5. The teacher has more teaching materials available to her to meet all levels of ability then ever before.
6. Teachers are well trained and are encouraged to improve their professional qualifications.
7. Professional journals and textbooks are readily available to all teachers.

Although there are many good things about our educational system there are also some liabilities which, unless corrected, could accelerate the criticism directed toward us.

1. Many school administrators know little or nothing about the school curriculum and how it functions.
2. Programs and materials are placed in the school without any consideration of the research related to their value.
3. Teachers do not put into practice the techniques and information they possess about how children learn.

4. Our educational philosophy is not broad enough to enable us to provide meaningful programs for all our children.
5. We rigidly impose a standard of performance which we equate with grade level.
6. Our administration is not flexible enough to allow for several organizational instructional programs to exist within the same school.
7. We do not adjust to the instructional needs of minority groups that exist within our society.

The possibility for improvement is not beyond the capabilities of educators. The abilities reside within our own professional group to put the schools on a truly accountable basis, but some changes need to be made by both the administrators and the teacher if we are to succeed.

Teachers

The key to any change in education resides with the teacher in the classroom. Edicts can be sent down through the administrative ladder, but if the teacher does not change the practice in the individual classroom or as a group within the school, all is to no avail. Teachers have the charge to meet what might be called achievement accountability. Achievement accountability simply means that the classroom teacher has the responsibility to find out where the student is in his skill development and to teach him in a manner and at a rate that will assure continuous progress.

The concept of achievement accountability is not an unusual charge for teachers but what is amazing is that the charge although supposedly implicit in the concept of teaching is not commonly practiced. Accountability should not be considered by teachers as a threat but as a reaffirmation of purpose.

Millman (see Section III) in his discussion of how to judge student progress takes a common sense approach which can be understood by all teachers. He states quite clearly that standardized tests for evaluation of teaching performance have distinct limitations but that evaluation of students on skill performance in relation to what they have been taught is not unreasonable. Teachers are indeed accountable for the progress or lack of progress which students make during a year.

Administrators

School administrators, since they are operating in a supervisory and administrative capacity, are in final analysis those who are ultimately accountable for student progress. They must work with the teacher in creating an environment where the teacher and student perform at a maximum.

A factor which is often overlooked by administrators in translating the concept of accountability to the classroom teacher is that in most private contracts made with industry, the industry has the option to eliminate a portion of the school population from the contract. Naturally, the students frequently eliminated are those who pose the greatest risk in teaching—the low ability and emotionally disturbed child. Another group frequently excluded are those children who are having remedial problems. It is important for the school however to make a distinction between those who have never been taught and are thus manifesting learning difficulties and those who have learned skill fragments and are confused. It is a serious mistake in judgment for administrators to apply achievement accountability to situations that private industry will not touch and at the same time expect miracles from the teacher.

It is also amazing that Boards of Education are willing to give large sums of money to industry to purchase materials for instruction and to organize for instruction in the most educationally advantageous way possible while denying the same opportunity to teachers. It would seem that if there is a question concerning who can do some educational jobs more efficiently than others that a judgment can be rendered only after each has been given equal opportunity to perform.

From the administrators point of view perhaps one of the best ideas that has developed out of the accountability concept is the idea of developmental capital as advocated by Leon Lessinger. Lessinger suggests that Boards of Education should authorize a percentage of the total school budget to be used for the exploration, implementation and evaluation of new ideas into the school program. It is impossible for the schools to engage in a process of self-renewal if positive directions are not taken. Lessinger (1970, p. 43) expresses the rationale for the developmental capital extremely well in the following statement.

> . . . . In its recent distinguished report on the schools, the Committee for Economic Development revealed that *much less than one percent* of our total national education investment goes into research and development. On the local level, of course, the percentage is even smaller. "No major industry," the report observes, "would expect to progress satisfactorily unless it invested many times that amount in research and development." Our failure to provide development capital for schools is a very costly saving, the same kind of false economy that might send a firm into bankruptcy. In contrast, if we allow the schools a chance at meaningful development, it is possible that the cost of producing a given unit of educational accomplishment, as independently assessed, might actually *decline* relative to other prices within our economy. In that case, we might still wish to devote the same or even a somewhat higher percentage of our national income to education, but we could expect to receive a substantial increase in effective services from the system. This would be very big news after a period such as the present, in which some parts of the educational system are collapsing even as they absorb a greater share of public resources.

Evaluation of Achievement

The inadequacy of our testing instruments is perhaps the greatest technical difficulty in expanding accountability, particularly in relation to performance contracting. It is interesting to note that school administrators who were often reluctant to have standardized tests used in evaluating their efforts are very willing to pay industry to use the same measures.

The inconsistencies in using standardized tests for measuring individual or class growth are many.

1. Students should not be measured against an artificial norm (national norm) which is constantly changing and which by definition necessitates that half of the test takers score above it, and half below.
2. Test norms are revised every ten years on an average. With the known improvement in achievement of children, it is possible for large numbers of children and certainly intact classes to have raw scores that place them above the national norm.
3. If the class mean on pre- and post-tests are used as a measure of performance, high performance by a few can outweigh the poor performance of many.
4. Different forms of the same test are not necessarily equivalent.
5. The statistical regression to the mean is operating in every testing situation. The odds are, that regardless of the instructional program, children who score very low on a pre-test will get a higher score on the post-test.
6. Standardized tests are probably not valid for children with severe deficiencies.

The problem of evaluation in relation to accountability has raised some interesting questions of which most professional educators are aware but which place us in a most uncomfortable position. Standarized test scores have been used to produce intense pressure to do something about achievement; i.e., reading, math. Yet, regardless of their shortcomings, school administrators and private industry insist upon objective, quantitative measures of performance to indicate growth.

Educators' Responsibilities

Accountability implies that the educator has the responsibility of the total school performance. But, an analysis of the performance contracts in operation indicate heavy concentration in the areas of reading and mathematics. The reason for the emphasis is these two areas are not difficult to evaluate. Reading and mathematics are areas in which standardized tests exist, there is reasonably good agreement among educators on the skills to be taught and the sequencing of the skills is fairly well established. The two areas also have the added advantage of being agreed upon as having high priority by parents, teachers and administrators.

The emphasis upon "the fundamentals" is hardly original with the concept of accountability. It is certain that with our present educational technology, that if we set our goals to teach certain skills, we can succeed. It is also perfectly clear however that the school must teach more than the 3 R's.

CONTRIBUTORS TO SECTION II

Accountability and its application to curriculum reform is the focal point of the movement. Leon Lessinger in the introductory article to this section speaks to the point of reform in his statements related to the promises we have made the public concerning our intent as educators to teach all children to our maximum ability as teachers. Barro follows Lessinger with suggestions of how schools can be made accountable and suggests a model for the development of accountability measures. Wildavsky, in the third article, follows the theme by suggesting that we may need to create differing normative data for different groups of students. He also suggests that if the school accountability movement is to work that the school principal should probably be held accountable for what goes on in his school in relation to curriculum development.

The article by Henry S. Dyer provides the valuable contribution of bringing us back to the question of what are the goals of education. He develops the theme that we can not effectively release ourselves from the "word game" concerning the curriculum until we first find out where we are. Until this is done he sees no chance for us to determine where we ought to be. Smith and Walberg further develop the importance of goals in relation to curriculum development by the Smith's discussion of how we identify the criterion structure of goals and Walberg's insistence upon the necessity for the reassessment of educational evaluative theory, practice and their interdependency.

Since instructional technology is so important to the accountability movement as it is currently practiced, the article by Engler is included to present the viewpoint of an official of a large publishing house concerning the contributions that educational technology can make to the curriculum.

The final article in this section (Leon M. Lessinger) is a fitting summary to the discussion of applications to the curriculum. Dr. Lessinger presents four key ideas which he feels will strengthen public education.

REFERENCE

Leon M. Lessinger. *Accountability: Every Kid a Winner* (New York: Simon and Schuster, 1970).

Leon M. Lessinger

Accountability and Curriculum Reform [†]

A growing number of people are becoming convinced that we can hold the schools—as we hold other agencies of government—to account for the results of their activity.

In his education message of March 3, 1970, President Nixon stated "From these considerations we derive another new concept: accountability. School administrators and school teachers alike are responsible for their performance, and it is in their interest as well as in the interest of their pupils that they be held accountable."

The preamble to the agreement between the Board of Education of the City of New York and the United Federation of Teachers for the period September 1969 to September 1972, under the title *Accountability,* says "The Board of Education and the Union recognize that the major problem of our school system is the failure to educate all of our students and the massive academic retardation which exists especially among minority group students. The Board and the Union therefore agree to join in an effort, in cooperation with universities, community school boards and parent organizations, to seek solutions to this major problem and to develop objective criteria of professional accountability."

Many more pronouncements and program activities of a similar sort to these quoted above from key groups and important decision makers could be added. Clearly, a new educational movement is under way. We are entering the age of accountability in education.

The call for accountability in education is a summons to review and

*Leon M. Lessinger is Calloway Professor of Urban Education at Georgia State University.
†Reprinted from Educational Technology, 10 (May, 1970), pp. 56–57, by permission of the author.

reform the educational system. The concept rests on two foundations: demonstrated student learning and independent review. These legs of accountability can have substantive effects upon the school curriculum and operation. This paper attempts to describe some of the more important of these potential impacts.

If schools are to be accountable for results, a new approach to their basic mission becomes mandatory and a new educational tradition will begin to emerge. Let us see why.

In the first place, emphasis will shift from teaching to learning. A growing research literature shows that, with respect to learning, teaching can be independent or influential, and that learning can take place without teaching. So independent is this relationship that some have termed it a teaching/learning paradox. This suggests that the present and traditional methods of requesting resources for education as the principal bases for accrediting schools will undergo basic change. Instead of equating quality in terms of resources allocated, such as kinds and numbers of teachers, space available, materials for use and books in the library, the independent variable will become *student accomplishment*. This will lead to a revised educational commitment for the nation.

In principle, the American educational commitment has been that every child should have access to adequate education—this is the principle of equal educational opportunity. This commitment has been translated into dollar allocations for the people and the "things" of education. When a child has failed to learn, school personnel have assigned him a label—slow, unmotivated, or retarded. Accountability triggers a revised commitment—that every child shall learn. Such a revision implies the willingness to change a system which does not work, and find one which does; to seek causes of failure in the system, its personnel, its organization, its technology or its knowledge base, instead of focusing solely on students. This revised commitment can be properly called the principle of equity of results.

The second major effect of accountability on school curriculum reform centers on a technology of instruction and the notion of better standard practice. Without accountability for results, educational practice is unverified, and good educational practice is not identified. Technology is more than equipment, although equipment may be a part of technology. Technology refers to validated practice—the use of tested means to produce desired ends. When the author was a child, his father, a medical doctor, treated sore throats by swabbing them with a black substance called Argyrol. This caused gagging and was most unpleasant. Medical technology of that day suggested the medical practice of throat "painting" as good practice. It was the standard practice for treating sore throats. Today, given a better technology, the improved practice is the use of antibiotics. The use of Argyrol, a standard practice once, would today be malpractice. If cure and results were not the criterion, there would be little impetus for improved technology and better medical practice. The same logic applies to education. The generation of an improved technology of instruction is allied to another benefit of accountability. Since World War II, several fields have been developed to enable leaders of very complex enterprises to operate effectively and efficiently. These emerging fields include: systems design and analysis, management by objectives, contract engineering (including warranties, performance contracts, incentives), logistics, quality assurance, value engineering, and the like. The coordination of these fields around educational concerns for an improved technology of instruction may be conveniently called *educational engineering.* Engineering has traditionally been a problem-solving activity, a profession dedicated to harnessing and creating technology to the accomplishment of desired ends, the resolution of difficulties and the promotion of opportunities. The American education system is experiencing continuing and growing criticism and even overt challenge. Virtually everyone agrees that something has gone wrong and that something dramatic ought to be done about it. Engineering accountability into public education can be that dramatic "something."

The process of change in education starts with the design or location of good practice and ends with the installation of that good practice in the classroom and learning centers of the nation, where it becomes standard practice. We know that the change process involves adaptation of good practice and adoption. Education engineering is the field designed to produce personnel with competence in this change process. Accountability for results in education is mere rhetoric without an engineering process to sustain it.

The "eye" of accountability lies in the phrase "modes of proof." Recognition of an expanded notion of assessment of results is the third major effect of accountability on school reform. For too long we have confused measurement of results in education with standardized achievement testing of the paper and pencil, normal curve based variety. Limited to this useful but restricted means of assessment, the pursuit of accountability would be frightening and even potentially destructive, for not everything in education can be (or ought to be) quantified in such a manner. But accountability in education, like accountability in other governmental enterprise, can make use of "evidence" from a variety of modes of attaining evidence. One thinks immediately of hearing, of juries, or expert witnesses, of certified auditors, of petitions and the like. Education can make use of all these modes, and can use such means of acquiring evidence as videotape and pupil performance in simulated real-life situations, to mention a few. To argue that scientific measurement is limited to narrow so-called objective tests is to display both ignorance of the rich field of assessments, limited experience with science, and an inability to foresee the rapid development of creative output instruments and strategies which money and attention can promote.

The outside review component of accountability, another spur to school curriculum reform, can bring education more closely in line with the main-stream of science. Science relies for its very existence on qualified, independent review and replication. Thus, literally nothing is established in science unless and until it can be demonstrated by someone other than he who claims discovery or invention. The scientist defines a problem clearly, separates complex problems into their individual components, and clarifies their relationships to each other. He records data in a communicative and standard form and ultimately accepts an audit from objective peers by seeking publication in a journal. Scientists are neither better people nor better scholars than educators; they do not pursue more "scientific" or intrinsically "better" problems than teachers. They are simply subject to better monitoring by a system that both encourages and mobilizes the criticism of competent peers throughout their lives. Education, on the other hand, substitutes the gaining of a credential or license at a single point in a career for a continuing process of independent review and mandated accomplishment replication. Accountability addresses this lack by insisting upon techniques and strategies which promote objectivity, feedback of knowledge of results and outside replication of demonstrated good practice.

Outside review tied to public reporting probably explains the popularity of the emerging concept of accountability to the public at large. Schools in America serve and are accountable to the citizenry, not the professionals. Since the public served is in reality many "publics," each of whom have legitimate needs for information, accountability can lead to an opening up of the system to bring in new energy and support.

All of us in the business of formal education need to be reminded that we have promised each family sending its children to school and each community employing our services that we will do all within our power and competence to have each student succeed. In a very real sense, failure to deliver on promises is a test of our professional integrity. Failure may be a measure of our commitment, of our technology, of our resources, or of factors inherent in the human condition of our client. Varying processes to achieve results in each student can generate that "Can Do" spirit so refreshing in a professional, be he a doctor, an engineer, or a teacher. So much in the current drama of student unrest and boredom stems from irrelevant processes and outmoded expectancies.

Stephen M. Barro

An Approach to Developing Accountability Measures for the Public Schools*

THE CONCEPT OF ACCOUNTABILITY

Although the term "accountability" is too new in the educational vocabulary to have acquired a standard usage, there is little doubt about its general meaning and import for the schools. The basic idea it conveys is that school systems and schools, or, more precisely, the professional educators who operate them, should be held responsible for educational outcomes—for what children learn. If this can be done, it is maintained, favorable changes in professional performance will occur and these will be reflected in higher academic achievement, improvement in pupil attitudes, and generally better educational results. This proposition—that higher quality education can be obtained by making the professionals responsible for their product—is what makes accountability an attractive idea and provides the starting point for all discussion of specific accountability systems and their uses in the schools.

The unusual rapidity with which the accountability concept has been assimilated in educational circles and by critics of the schools seems less attributable to its novelty than to its serviceability as a unifying theme. Among its antecedents, one can identify at least four major strands of current thought and action in education: (1) the new, federally stimulated emphasis on evaluation of school systems and their programs; (2) the growing ten-

---

*Reprinted from *Phi Delta Kappan,* 52 (December, 1970), pp. 196–205, by permission of the author and the editor.

dency to look at educational enterprises in terms of cost effectiveness; (3) increasing concentration on education for the disadvantaged as a priority area of responsibility for the schools; and (4) the movement to make school systems more directly responsive to their clientele and communities, either by establishing decentralized community control or by introducing consumer choice through a voucher scheme. Under the accountability banner, these diverse programs for educational reform coalesce and reinforce one another, each gaining strength and all, in turn, strengthening already powerful pressures for educational change.

HOW THE SCHOOLS CAN BE MADE ACCOUNTABLE

Accountability in the abstract is a concept to which few would take exception. The doctrine that those employed by the public to provide a service—especially those vested with decision-making power—should be answerable for their product is one that is accepted readily in other spheres and that many would be willing to extend, in principle, to public education. The problems arise in making the concept operational. Then it becomes necessary to deal with a number of sticky questions:

To what extent should each participant in the educational process—teacher, principal, and administrator—be held responsible for results?

To whom should they be responsible?

How are "results" to be defined and measured?

How will each participant's contribution be determined?

What will be the consequences for professional educators of being held responsible?

These are the substantive issues that need to be treated in a discussion of approaches to implementing the accountability concept.

Various proposals for making the schools accountable differ greatly in the degree to which they would require existing structures and practices to be modified. In fact, it is fair to say they range from moderate reform to revolution of the educational system. The following paragraphs summarize the major current ideas that, singly or in combination, have been put forth as approaches to higher quality education through accountability.

Use of Improved, Output-Oriented Management Methods

What is rapidly becoming a new "establishment" position—though it would have been considered quite revolutionary only a few years ago—is that school district management needs to be transformed if the schools are to become accountable and produce a better product. The focus here is on accountability for effective use of resources. Specific proposals include articulation of goals, introduction of output-oriented management methods (planning-programing-budgeting, systems analysis, etc.) and—most important— regular, comprehensive evaluation of new and on-going programs. Mainly internal workings of the school system rather than relations between school and community would be affected, except that better information on resource use and educational outcomes would presumably be produced and disseminated.

Institutionalization of External Evaluations or Educational Audits

Proposals along this line aim at assuring that assessments of educational quality will be objective and comparable among schools and school districts and that appropriate information will be compiled and disseminated to concerned parties. They embody the element of comparative evaluation of school performance and the "carrot" or "stick" associated with public disclosure of relative effectiveness. A prototype for this function may be found in the "external educational audit" now to be required for certain federal programs. However, the need for consistency in examining and comparing school districts suggests that a state or even a federal agency would have to be the evaluator. This would constitute a significant change in the structure of American public education in that it would impose a centralized quality-control or "inspectorate" function upon the existing structure of autonomous local school systems.

Performance Incentives for School Personnel

Perhaps the most direct way to use an accountability system to stimulate improved performance is to relate rewards for educators to measures of effectiveness in advancing learning. One way to do this is to develop pay schedules based on measured performance to replace the customary schedules based on teaching experience and academic training. An alternative approach would be to use differentiated staffing as the framework for determining both pay and promotion. The latter is a more fundamental reform in that it involves changes in school district management and organization as well as changes in the method of rewarding teachers. Professional organizations have tended to oppose such schemes, partly out of fear that performance criteria might be applied subjectively, arbitrarily, or inequitably. Although this may not be the only objection, if a measurement system could be developed that would be widely recognized as "objective" and "fair," the obstacles to acceptance of a system of performance incentives might be substantially reduced.

Performance or Incentive Contracting

Performance contracting rests on the same philosophy as the proposals for incentives, but applies to organization outside the school system rather than individual professionals within it. A school district contracts with an outside agency—a private firm, or conceivably, a nonprofit organization—to conduct specified instructional activities leading to specified, measurable educational results. The amount paid to the contractor varies according to how well the agreed-upon objectives are accomplished, thereby providing a very direct incentive for effective instruction. At present, there is too little experience with performance contracting to support conclusions about its potential. However, a large number of experiments and several evaluation efforts are under way.[1] Should they prove successful, and should this very direct method of making the purveyor of educational services responsible for his product become widely used, there would undoubtedly be substantial and lasting effects on both the technology and organization of American public education.

Decentralization and Community Control

These are two conceptually distinct approaches to accountability that we lump together under one heading only because they have been so closely linked in recent events. Administrative decentralization, in which decision-making authority is shifted from central administrators to local area administrators or individual school principals, can itself contribute to accountability. The shift of authority should, for example, favor greater professional responsiveness to local conditions and facilitate the exercise of local initiative. Also, it allows responsibility for results to be decentralized and, in so doing, provides the framework within which various performance incentives can be introduced.

The movement for community control of the highly bureaucratized, big-city school systems aims at accountability in the sense of making the system more representative of and responsive to its clientele and community. In the context of community control, accountability can be defined very broadly to include not only responsibility for performance in achieving goals, but also for selecting appropriate or "relevant" goals in the first place. Most important, community control provides the means of enforcing accountability by placing decision-making and sanctioning powers over the schools in the hands of those whose lives they affect.

Alternative Educational Systems

Probably the most radical proposal for achieving better education through improved accountability is this one, which would allow competing

[1]An experiment involving 18 districts and testing several different forms of performance contracting is being carried out in 1970–71 under sponsorship of the Office of Economic Opportunity. Also, the Department of Health, Education, and Welfare has contracted with the Rand Corporation to carry out an evaluation of other efforts to plan and implement performance contracts.

publicly financed school systems to coexist and would permit parents to choose schools for their children. Usually this is coupled with a proposal for financing by means of "educational vouchers,"[2] although this is not the only possible mechanism. The rationale for this "consumer-choice" solution is that there would be direct accountability by the school to the parent. Furthermore, there would be an automatic enforcement mechanism: A dissatisfied parent would move his child—and funds—to another school. Of course, the burden of becoming informed and evaluating the school would be on the individual parent. At present, there is very little experience with a system of this kind and little basis for judging how well it would operate or what effect it would have on the quality of education.

THE NEED FOR ACCOUNTABILITY MEASURES

These proposals, though not mutually exclusive, are quite diverse both with respect to the kinds of restructuring they would imply and the prospective educational consequences. However, they are alike in one important respect: Each can be carried out only with adequate information on the individual and the collective effectiveness of participants in the educational process. At present, such information does not exist in school systems. Therefore, a major consideration in moving toward accountability must be development of information systems, including the data-gathering and analytical activities needed to support them. This aspect of accountability—the nature of the required effectiveness indicators and the means of obtaining them—will be the principal subject of the remainder of this paper.

Progress in establishing accountability for results within school systems is likely to depend directly on success in developing two specific kinds of effectiveness information: (1) improved, more comprehensive pupil performance measurements; and (2) estimates of contributions to measured pupil performance by individual teachers, administrators, schools, and districts. As will be seen, the two have very different implications. The first calls primarily for expansion and refinement of what is now done in the measurement area. The second requires a kind of analysis that is both highly technical and new to school systems and poses a much greater.challenge.

The need for more extensive pupil performance measurement is evident. If teachers, for example, are to be held responsible for what is learned by their pupils, then pupil performance must be measured at least yearly so that gains associated with each teacher can be identified. Also, if the overall effectiveness of educators and schools is to be assessed, measurement will

---

[2]See *Education Vouchers: A Preliminary Report on Financing Education by Payments to Parents*, Center for the Study of Public Policy, Cambridge, Mass., (March, 1970).

have to be extended to many more dimensions of pupil performance than are covered by instruments in common use. This implies more comprehensive, more frequent testing than is standard practice in most school systems. In the longer run, it will probably require substantial efforts to develop and validate more powerful measurement instruments.

But no program of performance measurement alone, no matter how comprehensive or sophisticated, is sufficient to establish accountability. To do that, we must also be able to attribute results (performance gains) to sources. Only by knowing the contributions of individual professionals or schools would it be possible, for example, for a district to operate an incentive pay or promotion system; for community boards in a decentralized system to evaluate local schools and their staffs; or for parents, under a voucher system, to make informed decisions about schools for their children. To emphasize this point, from now on the term "accountability measures" will be used specifically to refer to estimates of contributions to pupil performance by individual agents in the educational process. There are described as "estimates" advisedly, because, unlike performance, which can be measured directly, *contributions* to performance cannot be measured directly but must be *inferred* from comparative analysis of different classrooms, schools, and districts. Ths analytical methods for determining individual contributions to pupil performance are the heart of the proposed accountability measurement system.

A PROPOSED APPROACH

In the following pages we describe a specific approach that could be followed by a school system interested in deriving accountability measures, as they have just been defined. First, a general rationale for the proposed approach is presented. Then the analytical methodology to be used is discussed in more detail.

For What Results Should Educators be Held Responsible?

Ideally, a school system and its constituent parts, as appropriate, should be held responsible for performance in three areas: (1) selecting "correct" objectives and assigning them appropriate priorities, (2) achieving all the stated (or implicit) objectives, and (3) avoiding unintentional adverse effects on pupils. Realistically, much less can be attempted. The first of the three areas falls entirely outside the realm of objective measurement and analysis, assessment of objectives being an intrinsically subjective, value-laden, and often highly political process. The other two areas can be dealt with in part, subject to the sometimes severe limitations to the current state of the art of educational measurement. The answer to the question posed above must inevitably be a compromise, and not necessarily a favorable one, between what is desirable and what can actually be done.

Any school system aims at affecting many dimensions of pupil performance. In principle, we would like to consider all of them—appropriately weighted—when we assess teacher, school, or district effectiveness. In practice, it is feasible to work with only a subset of educational outcomes, namely, those for which (a) objectives are well defined and (b) we have some ability to measure output. The dimensions of performance that meet these qualifications tend to fall into two groups; first, certain categories of cognitive skills, including reading and mathematics, for which standardized, validated tests are available; second, certain affective dimensions—socialization, attitudes toward the community, self-concept, and the like—for which we have such indicators or proxies as rates of absenteeism, dropout rates, and incidence of vandalism and delinquency. For practical purposes, these are the kinds of educational outcome measures that would be immediately available to a school system setting out today to develop an accountabiliy system.

Because of the limited development of educational measurement, it seems more feasible to pursue this approach to accountability in the elementary grades than at higher levels, at least in the short run. Adequate instruments are available for the basic skill areas—especially reading—which are targets of most efforts to improve educational quality at the elementary level. They are not generally available—and certainly not as widely used or accepted—for the subject areas taught in the secondary schools. Presumably, this is partly because measurement in those areas is inherently more difficult; it is partly, also because there is much less agreement about the objectives of secondary education. Whatever the reason, establishing accountability for results at the secondary level is likely to be more difficult. Pending further progress in specifying objectives and measuring output, experiments with accountability measurement systems would probably be more fruitfully carried on in the elementary schools.

Fortunately, existing shortcomings in the measurement area can be overcome in time. Serious efforts to make accountability a reality should, themselves, spur progress in the measurement field. However, for the benefits of progress to be realized, the system must be "open"—not restricted to certain dimensions of performance. For this reason, the methodology described here has been designed to be in no way limiting with respect to the kinds of outcome measures that can be handled or the number of dimensions that can ultimately be included.

Who Should be Accountable for What?

Once we have determined what kinds of pupil progress to measure, we can turn to the more difficult problem of determining how much teachers, principals, administrators, and others have contributed to the measured results. This is the key element in a methodology for accountability measurement.

The method proposed here rests on the following general principle:

Each participant in the educational process should be held responsible only for those educational outcomes that he can affect by his actions or decisions and only to the extent that he can affect them.

Teachers, for example, should not be deemed "ineffective" because of shortcomings in the curriculum or the way in which instruction is organized, assuming that those matters are determined at the school and district level and not by the individual teacher. The appropriate question is, "How well does the teacher perform, given the environment (possibly adverse) in which she must work and the constraints (possibly overly restrictive) imposed upon her?" Similarly, school principals and other administrators at the school level should be evaluated according to how well they perform within constraints established by the central adminsitration.

The question then arises of how we know the extent to which teachers or administrators can affect outcomes by actions within their own spheres of responsibility. The answer is that we do not know *a priori*; we must find out from the performance data. This leads to a second principle:

The range over which a teacher, a school principal, or an administrator may be expected to affect outcomes is to be determined empirically from analysis of results obtained by all personnel working in comparable circumstances.

Several implications follow from this statement. First, it clearly establishes that the accountability measures will be relative, involving comparisons among educators at each level of the system. Second, it restricts the applicability of the methodology to systems large enough to have a wide range of professional competence at each level and enough observations to permit reliable estimation of the range of potential teacher and school effects.[3] Third, it foreshadows several characteristics of the statistical models needed to infer contributions to results, To bring out the meaning of these principles in more detail, we will explore them from the points of view of teachers, schools administrators, and district administrators, respectively.

---

[3]This does not mean that accountability cannot be established in small school districts. It does mean that the analysis must take place in a broader context, such as a regional or statewide evaluation of performance, which may encompass many districts.

Classroom Teachers

We know that the educational results obtained in a particular classroom (e.g., pupils' scores on a standard reading test) are determined by many other things besides the skill and effort of the teacher. The analyses in the Coleman Report,[4] other analyses of the Coleman survey data,[5] and other statistical studies of the determinants of pupil achievement[6] show that a large fraction of variation in performance levels is accounted for by out-of-school variables, such as the pupils' socioeconomic status and home environment. Another large fraction is attributable to a so-called "peer group" effect; that is, it depends on characteristics of a pupil's classmates rather than on what takes place in the school. Of the fraction of the variation that *is* explained by school variables, only part can be attributed to teachers. Some portion must also be assigned to differences in resource availability at the classroom and school level and differences among schools in the quality of their management and support. Thus, the problem is to separate out the teacher effect from all the others.

To illustrate the implications for the design of an accountability system, consider the problem of comparing teachers who teach very different groups of children. For simplicity, suppose that there are two groups of pupils in a school system, each internally homogeneous, which we may call "middle-class white" and "poor minority." Assume that all nonteacher inputs associated with the schools are identical for the two groups. Then, based on general experience, we would probably expect the whole distribution of results to be higher for the former group than for the latter. In measuring gain in reading performance, we might well find, for example, that even the poorest teacher of middle-class white children obtains higher average gains in her class than the majority of teachers of poor minority children. Moreover, the ranges over which results vary in the two groups might be unequal.

If we have reason to believe that the teachers associated with the poor minority children are about as good, on the average, as those associated with the middle-class white children—that is, if they are drawn from the same manpower pool and assigned to schools and classrooms without bias—then it is apparent that both the difference in average performance of the two groups of pupils and the difference in the range of performance must be taken into account in assessing each teacher's contribution. A teacher whose

[4]James S. Coleman et al., *Equality of Educational Opportunity* (Washington, D.C.: Office of Education, 1966).

[5]George W. Mayeske et al., "A Study of our Nation's Schools" (a working paper, Office of Education, 1970).

[6]E.g., Eric A. Hanushek, "The Education of Negroes and Whites," unpublished Ph.D. dissertation, M.I.T. (1968); and Herbert J. Kiesling, "The Relationship of School Inputs to Public School Performance in New York State," The Rand Corporation (October, 1969), P-4211.

class registers gains, say, in the upper 10 percent of all poor minority classes should be considered as effective as one whose middle-class white group scores in the upper 10 percent for that category, even though the absolute performance gain in the latter case will probably be much greater.

This illustrates that accountability measures are relative in two senses. First, they are relative in that each teacher's contribution is evaluated by comparing it with the contributions made by other teachers in similar circumstances. In a large city or state school system, it can safely be assumed that the range of teacher capabilities covers the spectrum from poor to excellent. Therefore, the range of observed outcomes, after differences in circumstances have been allowed for, is likely to be representative of the range over which teacher quality can be expected to influence results, given the existing institutional framework. It may be objected that the range of outcomes presently observed understates the potential range of accomplishment because present classroom methods, curricula, teacher training programs, etc., are not optimal. This may be true and important, but it is not relevant in establishing teacher accountability because the authority to change those aspects of the system does not rest with the teacher.

Second, accountability measures are relative in that pupil characteristics and other nonteacher influences on pupil performance must be taken fully into account in measuring each teacher's contribution. Operationally, this means that statistical analyses will have to be conducted on the effects of such variables as ethnicity, socioeconomic status, and prior educational experience on a pupil's progress in a given classroom. Also, the effects of classroom or school variables other than teacher capabilities will have to be taken into account. Performance levels of the pupils assigned to different teachers can be compared only after measured performance has been adjusted for all of these variables. The statistical model for computing these adjustments is, therefore, the most important element in the accountability measurement system.

School Administrators

Parallel reasoning suggests that school administrators can be held accountable for relative levels of pupil performance in their schools to the extent that the outcomes are not attributable to pupil, teacher, or classroom characteristics or to school variables that they cannot control. The question is, having adjusted differences in pupil and teacher inputs and having taken account of other characteristics of the schools, are there unexplained differences among schools that can be attributed to differences in the quality of school leadership and administration? Just as for teachers, accountability measures for school administrators are measures of relative pupil performance in a school after adjusting the data for differences in variables outside the administrators' control.

Consideration of the accountability problem at the school level draws attention to one difficulty with the concept of accountability measurement that may also, in some cases, be present at the classroom level. The difficulty is that although we would like to establish accountability for individual professionals, when two or more persons work together to perform an educational task there is no statistical way of separating their effects. This is easy to see at the school level. If a principal and two assistant principals administer a school, we may be able to evaluate their relative proficiency as a team, but since it is not likely that their respective administrative tasks would relate to different pupil performance measures there is no way of judging their individual contributions by analyzing educational outcomes. Similarly, if a classroom teacher works with a teaching assistant, there is no way, strictly speaking, to separate the contributions of the two. It is conventional in these situations to say that the senior person, who has supervisory authority, bears the responsibility for results. However, while this is administratively and perhaps even legally valid, it provides no solution to the problem of assessing the effort and skills of individuals. Therefore, there are definite limits, which must be kept in mind, to the capacity of a statistically based accountability system to aid in assessing individual proficiency.

District Administrators

Although the same approach applies, in principle, to comparisons among districts (or decentralized components of larger districts), there are problems that may limit its usefulness in establishing accountability at the district level. One, of course, is the problem that has just been alluded to. Even if it were possible to establish the existence of overall district effects, it would be impossible to isolate the contributions of the local district board, the district superintendent, and other members of the district staff. A second problem is that comparisons among districts can easily fail to take account of intangible community characteristics that may affect school performance. For example, such factors as community cohesion, political attitudes, and the existence of racial or other intergroup tensions could strongly influence the whole tone of education. It would be very difficult to separate effects of these factors from effects of direct, district-related variables in trying to assess overall district performance. Third, the concept of responsibility at the district level needs clarifying. In comparing schools, for example, it seems reasonable to adjust for differences in teacher characteristics on the grounds that school administrators should be evaluated according to how well they do, given the personnel assigned to them. However, at the district level, personnel selection itself is one of the functions for which administrators must be held accountable, as are resource allocation, program design, choice of curriculum, and other factors that appear as "givens" to the schools. In other words, in assessing comparative district performance, very little about districts can properly be considered as externally determined except, perhaps, the total level of available resources.[7] The appropriate policy, then, seems to be to include district identity as a variable in comparing schools and teachers so that net district effects, if any, will be taken into account. Districts themselves should be compared on a different basis, allowing only for differences in pupil characteristics, community variables, and overall constraints that are truly outside district control.

A PROPOSED METHODOLOGY

The basic analytical problem in accountability measurement is to develop a technique for estimating the contributions to pupil performance of individual agents in the educational process. A statistical method that may be suitable for that purpose is described here. The basic technique is multiple regression analysis of the relationship between pupil performance and an array of pupil, teacher, and school characteristics. However, the proposed method calls for two or three separate stages of analysis. The strategy is first to estimate the amount of performance variation that exists among classrooms after pupil characteristics have been taken into account, then, in subsequent stages, to attempt to attribute the interclassroom differences to teachers, other classroom variables, and school characteristics.[8] This methodology applies both to large school districts, within which it is suitable for estimating the relative effectiveness of individual teachers and schools in advancing pupil performance, and to state school systems, where it can be used, in addition, to obtain estimates of the relative effectiveness of districts. However, as noted above, there are problems that may limit its utility at the interdistrict level.

Pupil Performance Data

Since we are interested in estimating the contributions of individual teachers and schools, it is appropriate to use a "value-added" concept of output. That is, the appropriate pupil performance magnitudes to associate with a particular teacher are the *gains* in performance made by pupils in her class. Ideally, the output data would be generated by a program of annual (or more frequent) performance measurement, which would automatically

---

[7]In addition, of course, there are constraints imposed by state or federal authorities, but these are likely to be the same across districts.

[8]The statistical method described here is essentially the same as that used by Eric A. Hanushek in a study, *The Value of Teachers in Teaching*, to be published in late 1970 by the Rand Corporation.

provide before and after measures for pupils at each grade level. It is assumed that a number of dimensions of pupil performance will be measured, some by standarized tests and some by other indicators or proxy variables. Specific measurement instruments to be used and dimensions of performance to be measured would have to be determined by individual school systems in accordance with their educational objectives. No attempt will be made here to specify what items should be included.[9] The methodology is intended to apply to any dimension of performance that can be quantified at least on an ordinal scale. Therefore, within a very broad range, it is not affected by the choice of output measures by a potential user.

Data on Pupils, Teachers, Classroom, and Schools

To conform with the model to be described below, the variables entering into the analysis are classified according to the following taxonomy:

1. Individual pupil characteristics (ethnicity, socioeconomic status, home, family, and neighborhood characteristics, age, prior performance, etc.).

2. Teacher and classroom characteristics.

(a)   Group characteristics of the pupils (ethnic and socioeconomic composition, distribution of prior performance levels, etc., within the classroom).

(b)   Teacher characteristics (age, training, experience, ability and personality measures if available, ethnic and socieconomic background, etc.).

(c)   Other classroom characteristics (measures of resource availability: class size, amount of instructional support, amount of materials, condition of physical facilities, etc.).

3. School characteristics.

(a)   Group characteristics of the pupils (same as 2a, but based on the pupil population of the whole school).

(b)   Staff characteristics (averages of characteristics in 2b for the school as a whole, turnover and transfer rates, characteristics of admistrators same as 2b).

(c)   Other school characteristics (measures of resource availability: age and condition of building, availability of facilities, amount of administrative and support staff, etc.).

[9]Realistically, however, almost every school system will be likely to include reading achievement scores and other scores on standardized tests of cognitive skills among its output variables. Also, it will generally be desireable to include attendance or absenteeism as a variable, both because it may be a proxy for various attitudinal output variables and because it may be an important variable to use in explaining performance. Otherwise, there are innumerable possibilities for dealing with additional dimensions of cognitive and affective performance.

No attempt will be made to specify precisely what items should be collected under each of the above headings. Determiniation of the actual set of variables to be used in a school system would have to follow preliminary experimentation, examination of existing data, and an investigation of the feasibility, difficulty, and cost of obtaining various kinds of information.

Steps in the Analysis

The first step is to determine how different pupil performance in each classroom at a given grade level is from mean performance in all classrooms, *after* differences in individual pupil characteristics have been allowed for. The procedure consists of performing a multiple regression analysis with gain in pupil performance as the dependent variable. The independent variables would include (a) the individual pupil characteristics (category 1 of the taxonomy), and (b) a set of "dummy" variables, for identifiers, one for each classroom in the sample. The latter would permit direct estimation of the degree to which pupil performance in each classroom differs from pupil performance in the average classroom. Thus, the product of the first stage of the analysis would be a set of estimates of individual classroom effects, each of which represents the combined effect on pupil performance in a classroom of all the classroom and school variables included in categories 2 and 3 of the taxonomy. At the same time, the procedure would automatically provide measures of the accuracy with which each classroom effect has been estimated. Therefore, it would be possible to say whether average performance gains in a particular classroom are significantly higher or lower than would be expected in a "typical" classroom or not significantly different from the mean.

Heuristically, this procedure compares performance gains by pupils in a classroom with gains that comparable pupils would be likely to achieve in a hypothetical "average" classroom of the system. This can be thought of as comparison of class performance gains against a norm, except that there is, in effect, a particular norm for each classroom based on its unique set of pupil characteristics. It may also be feasible to carry out the same analysis for specific subgroups of pupils in each class so as to determine, for example, whether there are different classroom effects for children from different ethnic or socioeconomic groups.

Estimation of Teacher Contributions

The second stage of the analysis has two purposes: (1) to separate the effects of the teacher from effects of nonteacher factors that vary among classrooms; and (2) to determine the extent to which pupil performance can be related to specific, measurable teacher attributes. Again, the method to be used is regression analysis, but in this case with a sample of classroom observations rather than individual pupil observations. The dependent variable is now that classroom effect estimated in stage one. The independent variables are the teacher-classroom characteristics and "dummy" variables distinguishing the individual schools.

Two kinds of information can be obtained from the resulting equations. First, it is possible to find out what fraction of the variation in performance gains among classrooms is accounted for by nonteacher characteristics, including group characteristics of the pupils and measures of resource availability in the classroom. The remaining interclassroom differences provide upper-bound estimates of the effects that can be attributed to teachers. If there is sufficient confidence that the important nonteacher variables have been taken into account, then these estimates provide the best teacher accountability measures. They encompass the effects of both measured and unmeasured teacher characteristics on teacher performance. However, there is some danger that such measures also include effects of group and classroom characteristics that were inadvertently neglected in the analysis and that are not properly attributable to teachers. This problem is referred to again below.

Second, we can find out the extent to which differences among classrooms are explained by measured teacher characteristics. Ideally, of course, we would like to be able to attribute the whole "teacher portion" of performance variation to specific teacher attributes and, having done so, we would be much more confident about our overall estimates of teacher effectiveness. But experience to date with achievement determinant studies has shown that the more readily available teacher characteristics—age, training, experience, and the like—account for only a small fraction of the observed variance. It has been shown that more of the variation can be accounted for when a measure of teacher verbal ability is included.[10] Still more, presumably, could be accounted for if a greater variety of teacher ability and personality measurements were available. At present, however, knowledge of what teacher characteristics influence pupil performance is incomplete and satisfactory instruments exist for measuring only a limited range of teacher-related variables. This means that with an accountability information system based on current knowledge, the excluded teacher characteristics could be at least as important as those included in determining teacher effectiveness. For the time being, then, the interclassroom variation in results that remains after nonteacher effects have been allowed for probably provides the most useful accountability measures, though the danger of bias due to failure to include all relevant nonteacher characteristics must be recognized.

The principal use of these estimates would be in assessing the relative effectiveness of individual teachers in contributing to gains in pupil performance. More precisely, it would be possible to determine whether each

[10]Hanushek, *The Value of Teachers in Teaching, op. cit.*

teacher's estimated contribution is significantly greater or significantly smaller than that of the average teacher. At least initially, until there is strong confirmation of the validity of the procedure, a rather stringent significance criterion should be used in making these judgments and no attempt should be made to use the results to develop finer gradations of teacher proficiency.

The analysis will also make it possible to determine the extent to which measured teacher characteristics are significantly correlated with teacher effectiveness. Potentially, such information could have important policy implications and impacts on school management, resource allocation, and personnel practices. A number of these potential applications are noted at the end of the paper.

Estimation of Contributions by School Administrators

The same analytical techniques can be used in estimating the relative effectiveness of different schools in promoting pupil performance. Conceptually, a school accountability index should measure the difference between pupil performance in an individual school and average pupil performance in all schools after all pupil, teacher, and classroom variables have been accounted for. Such measures can be obtained directly if school dummy variables are included in the regression equation, as described earlier. Of course, the results measure *total* school effects, without distinguishing among effects due to school administration, effects of physical attributes of the school, and effects of characteristics of the pupil population. It may be feasible to perform a third-stage analysis in which the results are systematically adjusted for differences in the latter two categories of variables, leaving residual effects that can be attributed to the school administrators. These would constitute the accountability measures to be used in assessing the effectiveness of the principal and his staff. The results may have policy implications with respect to differential allocation of funds or resources among the different schools and, of course, implications with respect to personnel. Also, as would be done for teachers, an attempt could be made to relate measured characteristics of the school administrators to the estimated school effects. By so doing, it might be possible to learn whether administrator training and experience and other attributes are reflected in measured school output. Even negative results could provide important guidance to research on administrator selection and assignment.

Comparisons Among Districts

For reasons that have already been stated, it would probably be desirable to treat comparisons among districts separately from comparisons among classrooms and schools. This could be done by means of yet another regression analysis, with individual pupil performance gain as the dependent variable and with independent variables consisting of pupil and community characteristics, measures of resource availability, and a dummy variable or identifier for each district being compared. The purpose would be to determine whether there are significant differences in results among districts once the other factors have been allowed for. If there are, the findings could be interpreted as reflections of differences in the quality of district policy making and management. But as pointed out earlier, there would be uncertainty as to the causes of either shortcomings or superior performance. Nevertheless, the results could have some important, policy-related uses, as will be noted shortly.

THE NEED FOR EXPERIMENTAL VERIFICATION OF THE APPROACH

The methodology described here carries no guarantee. Its success in relating outcomes to sources may depend both on features of the school systems to which it is applied and on the adequacy of the statistical models in mirroring the underlying (and unknown) input-output relationships in education. The validity and usefulness of the results must be determined empirically from field testing in actual school systems. Experimental verification, possibly requiring several cycles of refinement and testing, must precede implementation of a "working" accountability system.

Potential Problems

Three kinds of technical problems can threaten the validity of the system: intercorrelation, omission of variables, and structural limitations of the models. None of these can be discussed in detail without mathematics. However, a brief explanation of each is offered so that the outlook for the proposed approach can be realistically assessed.

Intercorrelation

This is a problem that may arise where there are processes in a school system that create associations (correlations) between supposedly independent variables in the model. An important example is the process—said to exist in many systems—whereby more experienced, better trained, or simply "better" teachers tend to be assigned or transferred to schools with higher socioeconomic status (SES) pupils. Where this occurs, pupil SES will be positively correlated with those teacher characteristics. On the average, high SES children would be taught by one kind of teacher, low SES children by another. This would make it difficult to say whether the higher performance gains likely to be observed for high SES pupils are due to their more advantaged backgrounds or to the superior characteristics of their instructors. There would be ambiguity as to the magnitude of the teacher contribution and a corresponding reduction in the reliability of estimates of individual teacher effectiveness. Thus, the quality of accountability information would be impaired.

This problem can take many forms. There may be strong correlations between characteristics of pupils and characteristics of school staffs, between teacher characteristics and nonteacher attributes of the schools, between classroom-level and district-level variables, and so on. The general effect is the same in each instance: ambiguity resulting in diminished ability to attribute results to sources.[11]

There are several things that can be done to mitigate the effects of intercorrelation. One is to stratify the data. For example, if teacher characteristics were linked to pupil SES, it would be possible to stratify the classrooms by pupil SES and to perform separate analyses for each stratum. This would eliminate some of the ambiguity *within* strata. On the other hand, comparisons of teachers *across* strata would be precluded. Another possible solution would be to take account of interdependence explicitly in the statistical models. Some attempts along this line have been made in studies of determinants of school performance. However, this solution is likely to raise a whole new array of technical problems as well as questions about the feasibility of routine use of the methodology within school systems.

The Problem of Omitted Variables

The validity and fairness of the proposed approach would depend very strongly on inclusion of all major relevant variables that could plausibly be cited by teachers or administrators to "explain" lower-than-average estimated contributions. This means that all variables would have to be included that (a) have significant, independent effects on performance and (b) are likely to be nonuniformly distributed among classrooms and schools.

It will never be possible to demonstrate in a positive sense that all relevant variables have been included. Many intangible, difficult-to-measure variables, such as pupil attitudes, morale, "classroom climate," etc., can always be suggested. What can be done is to determine as well as possible that none of the additional suggested variables is systematically related to the estimated teacher and school contributions. In an experimental setting, administrators could be interviewed for the purpose of identifying alleged special circumstances, and tests could be carried out to see whether they are systematically related to performance differences.

---

[11]The existence of this type of ambiguity in analyses of the Coleman survey data is one of the principal findings reported in Mayeske, *op. cit.*

Structural Limitations of the Models

The models described here may be too simple to take account of some of the important relationships among school inputs and outputs. One such shortcoming has already been noted: The models do not allow for possible interdependencies among the various pupil and school characteristics. Another, which may prove to be more troubling, is that interactions among the various output or performance variables have also not been taken into account.

Researchers have pointed to two distinct kinds of relationships. First, there may be trade-offs between performance areas.[11] A teacher or school may do well in one area partly at the expense of another by allocating resources or time disproportionately between the two. Second, there may be complementary relationships. Increased performance in one area (reading, for example) may contribute directly to increased performance in others (social studies or mathematics). Therefore, treatment of one dimension of output at a time, without taking the interactions into account, could produce misleading results.

Econometricians have developed "simultaneous" models consisting of whole sets of equations, specifically to take account of complex, multiple relationships among variables. Some attempts have been made to apply these models to studies of determinants of educational outcomes.[12] It may prove necessary or desirable to use them in an accountability measurement system, despite the complexity they would add, to eliminate biases inherent in simpler models.

Validity

Another important reason for thoroughly testing the accountability measurement system is that its validity needs to be assessed. Some of the procedures mentioned above contribute to this end, but more general demonstration would also be desirable. Two procedures that may be feasible in an experimental situation are as follows.

Replication

A strong test of whether the method really gets at differences in effectiveness instead of differences in circumstances would be to apply it to the same teachers and schools during two or more years. Consistency in results from year to year would strongly support the methodology. Lack of consistency

---

[11]See Henry M. Levin, "A New Model of School Effectiveness." *Do Teachers Make A Difference?* (Washington, D.C.: Office of Education, 1970), pp. 56-57.
[12]*Ibid.*, pp. 61ff.

would show that major influences on performances remained unmeasured or neglected. Certainly, if the results were to be used in any way in connection with personnel assignment, reward, or promotion, the use of several years' estimate would be an important guarantee of both consistency and fairness.

An External Test of Validity

The most direct way to test the validity of the statisical approach is to compare the results with alternative measures of teacher and school effectiveness. The only measures that are likely to be obtainable are subjective assessments by informed and interested parties. Though such evaluations have many shortcomings, it could be valuable in an experimental situation to see how well they agreed with the statistical results. Two important questions that would have to be answered in making such a comparison are: 1) Who are the appropriate raters—peers, administrators, parents, or even pupils? and 2) What evaluation instruments could be used to assure that subjective assessments apply to the same dimensions of performance as were taken into account in the statistical analysis? It may not be possible to provide satisfactory answers. Nevertheless, the feasibility of a comparison with direct assessments should be considered in connection with any effort to test the proposed accountability measurement system.

POTENTIAL USES OF ACCOUNTABILITY MEASURES

Space does not permit a full review of the potential uses of an accountability measurement system. However, an idea of the range of applications and their utility can be conveyed by listing some of the main possibilities.

Identification of Effective Schools

The most rudimentary use of the proposed accountability measures is as an identification device. Once relative school effectiveness is known, a variety of actions can follow, even if there is ambiguity about causes. As examples, less formal evaluation efforts can be more precisely targeted once school effectiveness with different kinds of children is known and campaigns can be initiated to discover, disseminate, and emulate good practices of high-performing schools.

Personnel Assignment and Selection

Accountability measures may help to improve both staff utilization and selection of new personnel. Personnel utilization could be improved by using information on teacher effectiveness in different spheres and with different types of students for guidance in staff assignment. Selection and recruitment could be aided by using information from the models as a guide to performance-related characteristics of applicants and as a basis for revising selection procedures and criteria.

Personnel Incentives and Compensation

An accountability measurement system can be used to establish a connection between personnel compensation and performance. One use would be in providing evidence to support inclusion of more relevant variables in pay scales than the universally used and widely criticized training and experience factors. Another possibility would be to use accountability measures as inputs in operating incentive pay or promotion systems. The latter, of course, is a controversial proposal, long resisted by professional organizations. Nevertheless, putting aside other arguments pro and con, the availablity of objective measures of individual contributions would eliminate a major objection to economic incentives and help to make the idea more acceptable to all concerned.

Improved Resource Allocation

An accountability measurement system could also contribute to other aspects or resource allocation in school systems. Analytical results from the models could be of value, for example, in setting policies on class size, supporting services, and similar resource variables. More directly, school accountability measures could provide guidance to district administrators in allocating resources differentially among schools according to educational need. Similarly, state-level results could be used in determining appropriate allocations of state aid funds to districts.

Program Evaluation and Research

Models developed for accountability could prove to be valuable tools for program evaluation and research. They could be readily adapted for comparing alternative ongoing programs simply by including "programs" as one of the classroom variables. Also, "norms" provided by the models for specific types of pupils could be used as reference standards in evaluating experimental programs. This would be preferable, in some cases, to using experimental control groups. Viewed as research tools, the models could help to shed light on one of the most basic, policy-related problems in education, the relationship between school inputs and educational output. The process of developing the models could itself be very instructive. The results could add substantially to our knowledge of how teachers and schools make a difference to their pupils.

In sum, there are many potential uses of the proposed measures and models, some going well beyond what is generally understood by "accountability." If the development of a system is undertaken and carried through to completion, the by-products alone may well prove to be worth the effort.

Aaron Wildavsky *

A Program of Accountability for Elementary Schools†

The request for accountability in the sense of holding the school system responsible for the achievement of children in critical areas is a good one. Consumers of governmental services are entitled to know what they are getting. Truth in packaging applies just as much to government as to private industry. Indeed, the field of education may be on the verge of making a contribution to the general evaluation of governmental programs. The ability of ordinary citizens to appraise whether they are getting what they want is of critical importance in a system of democratic government. Yet no one today knows what citizens will do with this kind of information. In view of the inevitable tendency to oversimplify, it is desirable to add to public understanding through an assessment of what accountability means and what it will and will not do. The best way to get these ideas across is to set up procedures for accountability that embody them.

A student's ability to read is critical for later achievement. His ability in mathematics is indispensable for a whole range of occupations. Achievement in these two areas must be evaluated in terms of standardized tests. It is true that such a test does not by any means measure all that a teacher does or attest to all of his impact. No such test can be devised. Nor is it necessary to do so. To say that what a teacher does is so exotic that it cannot be measured is simply to say that he ought to do what he pleases, and that is not tenable. All the impalpable qualities of "growth" mean nothing if students cannot hold jobs as clerks in drugstores because they cannot make change correctly

*Aaron Wildavsky is a professor in the Graduate School of Public Affairs, University of California. This paper was originally prepared to assist in discussion of accountability in New York City.

†Reprinted from *Phi Delta Kappan,* 52 (December, 1970), pp. 212–216, by permission of the author and Phi Delta Kappan.

or cannot be messengers because they cannot read street signs. Before a student can do other things he must be able to read, and it is sufficient to say that he must develop in this direction as well as in others. The deprived child needs this skill more than other children.

It may be said that the standardized tests are culturally biased, but I think this is beside the point. Few doubt that if one took an article about the life of the Yoruba tribe in Africa or the city-state of Benin, equally remote from the experience of all students, those students who read well would be able to answer questions about the material and those who read poorly would have difficulty. The same would be true of a book directly concerned with the black man's experience in America. To say that one must wait until tests without cultural bias are developed is simply to say there will be no accountability. I should add that there is a great deal of difference between tests designed to help parents hold schools responsible and tests that work to exclude people from opportunity for high education and better jobs.

At this point I would like to add a word of caution about the problem of cheating on tests. As the pressure grows to improve student performance on standardized tests, teachers will be tempted to cheat. It is one thing for teachers to prepare students by giving them exercises similar to ones on the test; it is another for teachers to feed their students the exact words and phrases that will be used on the test. That practice should be discouraged. I find here an analogy with the New York State regents' examinations I used to take when I was a high school student in that state. One learned a great deal by going over previous examinations, and that was not considered a form of cheating. Rather than relying merely on negative sanctions I would suggest providing a length series of sample "previous" examinations, so that teachers will feel quite free to use them.

All standardized testing should be turned over to an extra-school organization—a state agency or a private business that will administer the tests and see that they are fairly conducted. Tests should not be brought into the schools until the morning of the testing day, and observers from the testing organization should be present. One drawback of this proposal is its expense, but if there is to be confidence in accountability, there must be assurance that the test scores mean what they say.

Teachers I know have told me that they fear spending most of their time gearing students to pass certain examinations. My reaction is: What is wrong with that, if the examinations are good indicators of what we wish students to learn? Learning a limited vocabulary by rote may be useless. If we wish to increase cognitive ability by enabling students to read material with understanding within a certain time, however, a test that measures that skill is a good idea. The ideal situation is one in which a student's ability to do well on this exam means that he can also pick up any other similar body of material and understand it well.

I am aware that reading ability may be affected by many things. Reading may be a function of the personality. It may be a result of motivation; children may not read because they see no reason to do so. It may be a function of certain high-level cognitive processes that are imperfectly understood. And so on. Let us say, then, that reading is a very complex matter, a product of many circumstances, most of which are badly understood and some of which may not be known at all. So what? Who said that one must know the causes before propounding the cure? The history of medicine has taught us that many diseases may be cured before their etiology is perfectly known. For present purposes it is sufficient that students be enabled to read a certain level of material with a certain degree of comprehension, whether or not the teacher or the researcher fully understands the processes by which this is done. No doubt more basic research should be conducted in reading. Surely, few would suggest waiting 20 years before we begin our efforts to improve performance through accountability.

There may be quick ways of getting at motivation to read by developing measures based on the amount of reading done by students. All the discussion of developing motivation would be beside the point unless the motivated student read more (or perhaps even a greater variety) of literature than his fellows. I would not wait until such a measure was perfected, however, before beginning a simpler use of accountability.

There are important conceptual difficulties with a program of accountability. Presumably we are after something like the economic concept of "value added." We want to know what impact exposure to a particular teacher or school has had on a child's reading or mathematical ability, compared to what it would have been in other circumstances. This requires some base-line knowledge of where a child would be expected to be, given his previous rates of achievement and those of other students similarly situated. Since reading and cognitive ability are not simple matters, the requisite talents may be developed in more than one class. How much of a student's progress (or lack of it) is due to his reading teacher versus other teachers would be exceedingly difficult to determine. How much is due to school versus home environment is a tricky question. Parceling out a single cause from many is never simple. I believe that rough and ready answers can be found to these dilemmas if the problem of causation is approached in a practical spirit.

To hold someone accountable is to assess how well he is performing. A program of accountability requires standardized tests on the one hand and significant norms on the other. Yet it is not easy to decide what these norms should be. The first that suggests itself is a national standard for reading or mathematics by grade. If this standard, however, is much higher than present performance, it will appear unrealistic to teachers and students alike. They may despair at ever achieving it and therefore not make the required effort.

Should an accountability group be performing above the national standard, they would have no way to measure their progress. Another way to handle the problem of setting the norm is to make it a subject for bargaining between local school boards, parent groups, teachers, and principals. This approach would have the advantage of allowing participation in setting norms and might have the effect of committing the participants more strongly to their achievement. Unfortunately, however, the negotiations may simply reveal who is more powerful or determined or aggressive. The result may be terribly low norms in some places and unfairly high ones in others. It would become impossible to determine either how the city as a whole was doing or how the various subgroups were faring. The level of conflict would surely rise without much hope of corresponding benefit.

A third alternative would be to divide all elementary pupils in the city into five or six groups based on the mean score by grade on the standardized tests. Students would be tested each September, and the focus would be on the rate of change during the year. Each school would then be rated on the basis of its ability to secure more rapid changes by grade in the mean scores of its students. Immediately we are faced with a major dilemma. One of the purposes of modern reform in education is to escape from the syndrome of helping those most who need it least. If the students who perform better initially are also the students who are capable of showing the greatest rate of change, teachers and principals will find it most efficient to concentrate attention on these students in order to improve total performance. We will be back again to the adage "To him that hath shall be given." One way of surmounting this difficulty is to require not only the mean but the median scores, so that schools are rewarded for securing improvement in the largest number of students as well as for the total rate of improvement. Another way of dealing with the problem is to use tests that have a "top" to them so that those who score the highest have difficulty in improving by a large percentage. Whatever the formula used, the principle is clear: The school gets rewarded more for improvements among those students who start out at the lower levels of performance than it does for the students who start out at the higher levels. The rational man will, therefore, exert his effort to bring forward those who need it most.

My preference is for a fourth alternative in which different norms would be set for different groups of students. It would be possible to compare groups of students with similar backgrounds. Groups can be defined largely in terms of previous opportunity. I would suggest working up a *short* list of the principal extra-school variables that appear, in terms of current knowledge, to be relevant to student performance, such as socio-economic level, rate of movement from one neighborhood and one school to another, and so on. It would then be possible to place each elementary school in one of five or six groups. Each group of schools could be rank-ordered according to student performance on standardized tests, with the result given three weeks after school starts and again sometime around the first week in June, so that progress during the school year could be measured. (The early tests are necessary because many students lose a lot of learning over the summer.) The norms against which progress is measured would not be the same for the entire city, but would differ for each of the five or six accountability groups.

The five top schools within each subgroup could be taken together and their current achievement and average growth used as the normative standard. In this way participants in each school's activity would know that the norm set for them had in fact been achieved by students in situations comparable to their own. Norms would be reasonably objective and realistic. Selection of these norms, however, is critically dependent on factual information about the degree of homogeneity within elementary schools. If the differences in achievement between schools are greater than the differences within schools, this proposal is feasible; if the heterogeneity within schools is great, however, it will be difficult to make sense out of the performance of the school as a whole, and it will be necessary to deal with different classes of students throughout the entire system.

Determination of the level of accountability with the school system is also a difficult problem Should it be a single teacher, a school, a district, or the entire school system? In a sense, all levels must be accountable and the efforts of all must be appraised. Determination of the center of accountability, however, cannot be avoided because if all are in some vague sense accountable it will be difficult to hold anyone responsible. Making a large geographical district or the entire system accountable will prove too imprecise. Nor will holding individual teachers directly accountable work. The problem of causality—how much does that teacher's effort contribute to the total result?—will prove insuperable. Teachers may also prove unable to cope with the pressures that come directly at them.

I recommend focusing accountability on the principal of the school because he is the one with the essential power in the system. My understanding is that the district superintendent, although nominally responsible for what the teacher does, usually gives him wide latitude. Local boards may change the situation, but it is too early to tell. The principal, therefore, is the one who is capable of limiting and usually does limit the teacher's discretion. The principal, moreover, could be assumed to have a longer-term commitment to the school system. If the work can be improved, or if he is replaced by others whose work is better, that is bound to have a profound impact throughout the system. If principals are to be held accountable, however, they must receive training in teaching. I do not believe that the concept of the principal as the master teacher is accurate today in view of the mechanisms of recruitment that obtain. For the moment it would be sufficient for principals to hire qualified people to assist them. Principals should also be given adequate administrative help or at least each one must have the same kind of help. In some school districts the amount of administrative help per pupil varies considerably from school to school. Either administrative help per pupil must be equalized or principals with a relative lack of administrative help must not be required to do as well. If accountability is to get support it must be as fair as we know how to make it.

However good a system of accountability is worked out, it will always have defects. Some teachers will find that their students are especially difficult to teach; others will find that their students make more rapid progress than they had thought. Some teachers may be especially gifted in dealing with children with special reading difficulties, while others do better with different kinds of students. If accountability is placed on the teacher it will be difficult to take account of their differing capabilities. By placing accountability on the principal, however, he will be able to take these special circumstances into account and not require the same level of performance from all his teachers regardless of the difficulty of their assignments. The requirement he must face is that the school as a whole show reasonable progress. While the principal is, in effect, charted with maximizing a kind of educational production, he may set different goals for his teachers in order to make the best showing for the school as a whole. In a different context a number of teachers could perform the same function by forming accountability groups with a school.

In order to envisage the problems encountered by making schools accountable through their principals, let us imagine that such a system were adopted. Everyone would presumably know which schools were performing better and worse than others. There would naturally be a tendency for parents to send their children to the schools shown to be performing better for children like their own. One way of handling this problem would be to prohibit movement from one school to another based on this criterion. Otherwise the normative basis of the school would change rapidly because those parents and students most interested in improving performance would go to the better schools. The result would be a reallocation of students, leaving certain schools worse off than they were before. A long-run solution, after accountability has been in force for a number of years, would be to treat the phenomenon as part of a market system and give the better school additional resources to accommodate new pupils. Here accountability would merge with some of the proposals for giving parents vouchers allowing them to send children where they hope to get better education. In the short run, however, it would be better to restrict movement and to place emphasis on improving the performance of schools that show the least progress in meeting the norms.

Realism compels us to recognize that there is more than one way to improve the performance of children: There are ways we would like, and there are ways we would hate. One of the easiest ways to improve school performance, for example, is to remove those children who are most troublesome and whose scores on achievement tests are likely to be the lowest. It would be sad to see accountability used to justify defining children as behavioral problems or as victims of mental disturbance just so they would be eliminated from the school population. Schools should be allowed only a very small proportion of transfers on these grounds; otherwise they will be in the same position as a football team that finally achieves a winning schedule by choosing only the weakest opponents. A trigger mechanism could be used so that any transfers on these grounds above a certain minimum would result in an investigation.

The problem of sanctions for failure to perform is an integral part of a system of accountability. If those who do badly are allowed to continue, the system will not work. If those who do well are not rewarded, there will be no incentive for them to continue. My preference is to accentuate the positive. Teachers and principals who show the greatest progress should receive recognition, promotion, and freedom. By "freedom" I mean that those who show excellent progress should be given the right to innovate in teaching methods and curriculum. Rather than attempt to control their behavior through prescription of detailed curricula, we should let them devise their own with broad limits. As a contribution to this effort, the superintendent of schools should make available a diverse number of curricula for various grades and of methods for teaching various subjects among which teachers might choose but to which they would not be limited if they performed well. One can choose to direct teachers by inputs—standard curricula and teaching methods—or by outputs—norms of achievement—but not by both. If the output norms are met, the inputs should be left to the teachers.

Before sanctions are applied, principals and teachers should be given supervisory help. Their administrative superiors should work with them to improve performance. Additional personnel and financial resources should be provided. The imposition of negative sanctions should be downgraded but cannot be entirely avoided. For the most part, teachers will simply have less freedom. Should a teacher or principal reveal consistently poor performance, it should be possible to transfer him, or ultimately, remove him from the system. Agreement should be sought with the teachers' union on procedures to be followed in this eventuality so that abuse will be minimized. If the union will not agree, then accountability is not possible.

In order to reduce anxieties and take cognizance of the difficulties of the enterprise, the procedure for accountability should be reviewed every two years. The groups that serve as the normative schools should be revised according to their performance.

No plan for accountability can succeed unless all the major participants in the educational process—parents, teachers, students, principals, superintendents, and board members—see something in it for themselves. It is worthwhile, therefore, to explore the advantages and disadvantages of this plan as the various participants might see it.

The hard part for teachers would be the fact of being judged on a rather narrow level of performance according to strict standards that may not be entirely valid. If they consistently fail to move their students toward the norm, teachers would be subject to sanctions. Under current conditions, however, teachers suffer psychological punishment due to a feeling of failure. Their ability to show progress, indeed even to know the direction toward which they and their students should be moving, may provide tremendous relief. Standards of accountability may also give teachers a mechanism for guarding against arbitrary action by principals. If a teacher can show that his students have made excellent progress toward the norm, or have even achieved it, he has prima facie evidence of competence. He should thus be entitled to a reward in the form of permission to work under less supervision with greater leeway to introduce his own ideas.

The initial reaction of principals to the idea of accountability may well be negative. It will be hard for them to see themselves as responsible for behavior of students and teachers as they find it difficult to control. As the most visible manifestation of the school authorities, principals are easy to blame and to pillory in public. Fear and defensiveness by principals would be understandable. Yet first thoughts are bound to give way to deeper considerations. Principals are already being held responsible according to vague standards and under rules that guarantee dissatisfaction. National norms are held up as appropriate by some and are condemned by others. Principals may come to believe they will be better off if they have a hand in shaping reasonable norms. If they are held to account by their administrative superiors and by parents they will also gain additional leverage in regard to recalcitrant teachers. If performance is poor; a principal can move to change teacher behavior with more than the ordinary amount of justification. He can also show his administrative superiors that he is doing a good job in a more convincing way than before. Accountability has its defects, but the norms it enforces on the principal are superior to "keeping out of trouble" or "pleasing the boss" or others one can think of.

Parents may be expected to give initial endorsement to a program of accountability. They should feel that at last they have a mechanism for appraising the performance of their children and the school in which they are taught. (Accountability not only means that the school is responsible to the parents, however, but that the parents are responsible for the school. They need to help teachers whose children fail to make adequate progress.) It is often difficult for parents to gauge the legitimacy of complaints made by their children or school critics; knowledge of whether their children are making progress with regard to the norms of accountability should help them decide where reality lies. When parents are asked to mobilize themselves concerning school policy, they may decide whether to become involved by consulting public information on school achievement.

Accountability, defined in terms of achievement in reading and math, will not satisfy those parental and neighborhood groups that are looking to schools to inculcate their cultural and/or political values. To them, accountability may be a barrier to control of schools, because it (in their view) falsely suggests to parents that schools are doing well. There is no escaping the fact that accountability is not a neutral device—it encapsulates a view of the educational function in which basic cognitive and mathematical skills are primary. Cultural, artistic, or political values would still receive expression (it could hardly be otherwise), but they would not be dominant.

The job of the superintendent of schools has become increasingly frustrating. He is placed at the very center of every controversy. At times he appears utterly surrounded by swirling clouds of controversey. Yet when all is said and done, he is too far from teaching and learning to know whether his efforts are worthwhile. Often he must feel that all he does is stay alive while the purposes for which he originally became an educator become increasingly remote. For such a man a program of accountability must have great meaning. It is his opportunity to affect education directly. It is his opportunity to participate in an innovation that could make his tenure in office worthwhile. The drawback is that progress, if it can be achieved at all, may be painfully slow. No one can be certain that the statement of educational goals will lead to their achievement. The factors that guide improvement in reading and mathematics for large populations may not be known to anyone. The special problems faced by deprived children may not respond to available techniques. While various schools and teachers may meet with notable success, average rates of growth may not change at all, or may even decline for reasons no one knows. Yet the superintendent may be regarded as a failure because a particular norm of accountability has been specified, when he might have escaped under the nebulous criteria which would otherwise exist. Still, he is unlikely to escape unscathed, and norms of accountability are as good a measure of progress as he is likely to get.

The board of education can find accountability of great use in defining problem areas and questioning the superintendent about them. The board can choose to hold the superintendent responsible for systematic performance or it can investigate problems according to the geographic area, grade, or level at which they occur. The board's greatest role, if it is so willing, will be to monitor the system of accountability and suggest revisions of it to the interested parties. It should take the lead in suggesting changes in the norms by which measurement is accomplished, the incentives and sanctions employed, and the test used.

Very young children are unlikely to question these arrangements. As they get older, students may well be the people most difficult to satisfy on the question of accountability. They may feel that no system of norms gives them sufficient freedom. They may dislike the idea that a single set of norms appears to define them when they know that each individual is much more than that. They may fear that they will be stigmatized if greater publicity is given to test results. They may not even want their parents to know how well or how badly they are doing. Part of the difficulty may be overcome by holding individual and class scores confidential except to parents. Another part will be dealt with by giving students special liberties in taking courses if they perform at an acceptable level. Ultimately, however, they must be persuaded that accountability is a useful mechanism for improving the performance of school children in general and that it is therefore of special benefit to those whose performance is now at a low level. Some students, like some teachers and principals will have to accept sacrifices for the common good. It will not be easy.

Henry S. Dyer

Discovery and Development of Educational Goals*

Since World War II most professional philosophers, with some notable exceptions, have backed away from rows over the goals of education and have stuck more or less consistently to analyzing the absurdities in all such forms of discourse(1). Before the philosophical silence set in, however, practically every major philosopher, from Confucius and Plato and Aristotle down to Whitehead and Russell and Dewey, has had a good deal to say about the aims of education and its functions in society. Since then there has been an increasing volume of writing on the subject by eminent nonphilosophers inside and outside the academic community. No less than two Presidential Commissions have taken a crack at the problem(2), and their efforts have been supplemented and extended by such documents as the Harvard report on objectives of general education (3), the Russell Sage reports on elementary and secondary school objectives (4), and the two taxonomies by Benjamin Bloom and his collaborators (5),

One would think that the accumulation of so much high-level verbiage on the subject of goals over at least two-and-one-half millenia would have exhausted the subject if not the discussants. One would suppose that by now the question of educational goals would have been fairly well settled, and the problem of how to define them would have found some useful answers. But the question is still very much open. The problem of goals is today, more than ever, a top priority and largely unsolved problem. It is symptomatic that a recent book on the preparation of instructional objectives starts off with an echo from Charles Dudley Warner's famous remark about the weather:

*From *Proceedings of the 1966 Invitational Conference on Testing Problems.* Copyright © 1966, 1967 by Educational Testing Service. All rights reserved. Reprinted by permission.

"Everybody talks about defining objectives, but almost nobody does any-thing about it (6)."

The trouble is that in spite of all the hard thinking and earnest talk about educational goals and how to define them, the goals produced have been essentially nonfunctional and I mean even when they have come clothed in the so-called "behavioral terms" we so much admire. They have had little or no effect on the deals and deliberations that go on in faculties and school boards and boards of trustees and legislative chambers where the little and big decisions about education are being made. As you watch the educational enterprise going through its interminable routines, it is hard to avoid the impression that the whole affair is mostly a complicated ritual in which the vast majority of participants-pupils, teachers, administrators, policy-makers-have never given a thought to the question *why*, in any fundamental sense, they are going through the motions they think of as education.

QUANTITY VERSUS QUALITY

In spite of the tardy recognition in a few quarters that there are some ugly situations in the schools of the urban ghettos and rural slums, the general attitude still seems to be that if we are spending 50 billion dollars a year on the education of 50 million children, and if over 40 percent of them are not getting to go to college, as compared with less than 20 percent a few years back, then "we must be doing something right," even though we haven't the remotest idea of what it is. This blind faith in quantity as proof of quality is precisely the faith that, in the long run, could be our undoing.

Perhaps in a simpler age a disjunction between educational purpose and educational practice was tolerable. A hundred years ago such a small part of the population went to school that the opportunities open to educators for inadvertently damaging the lives and minds of the generality of mankind were neither potent nor pervasive. The situation today, as the headlines hardly permit us to forget, is somewhat different. We have more knowledge than we know what to do with, more people than we know how to live with, more physical energy than we know how to cope with, and, in all things, a faster rate of change than we know how to keep up with. So we dump the problem on the schools and hope that somehow they can program the oncom-ing generation for the unforeseeable complexities of the twenty-first century, less than 34 years away.

Henry Adams as far back as 1905 had already figured out what we would be up against. As he saw it then, "Every American who had lived into the year 2000 would know how to control unlimited power. He would think in complexities unimaginable to an earlier mind (7)." This being almost 1967 rather than 1905, the near prospect of unlimited power in the hands of every

American (and European and Asian and African) has finally scared us into a rash of educational innovations that we hope will help the oncoming generation "think in complexities unimaginable" to us. But the rising curve of proposed innovations itself is adding to the burden of our complexities by swamping the schools with more untested devices, strategies, administrative arrangements, and curricular materials than those who run the educational system are prepared to absorb or evaluate. This is why it is more important than ever to reconsider the problem of goals.

Somehow we have to arrive at goals that are so clear and compelling that the movers and shapers of education can and will use them in deciding on the tradeoffs that are going to have to be made if the system is to be kept from stalling under the mounting load of new ideas and conflicting demands.

Why is it that the goals formulated in the past, even the recent past, have been largely nonfunctional? I think there are three principal reasons: (a) too much reliance on the magic of words, (b) too little public participation in formulating the goals, and (c) too great a readiness to suppose that the goals are already given and require only to be achieved.

WORD-MAGIC

In the 1947 report of the President's Commission on Higher Education there is the following paragraph:

> The first goal in education for democracy is the full, rounded, and continuing development of the person. The discovery, training, and utilization of individual talents is of fundamental importance in a free society. To liberate and perfect the intrinsic powers of every citizen is the central purpose of democracy, and its furtherance of individual self-realization is its greatest glory (8).

This is an example of word-magic. It is an expression of an ideal to which presumably the great majority of Americans would enthusiastically give verbal assent, without having the foggiest notion of what the words are saying. And this failure is not to be chalked up as a flaw in the thinking of the American people. For it is no mean task for anybody, however sophisticated in words and their ways, to translate into specifiable operations such metaphoric expressions as "full rounded, and continuing development of the person" or "liberate and perfect the intrinsic powers of every citizen." Phrases like these sing to our enthusiasms, but they don't tell us what to do about them. The difficulty is that the metaphors in which they are couched are extremely hard to translate in terms of what little we really know of human growth and functioning. How do you know, for instance, when you have liberated and perfected the intrinsic powers of a citizen? Or how do you calibrate the roundedness of his development?

To ask such questions is to suggest why the word-magic has not worked and why such goal statements leave school people with barely a clue for determining what the lines of progress ought to be or whether the system is making any headway in the desired directions. And this failure has led to more than a little disillusionment about the practical utility of any kind of goal statements and to a considerable degree of offhand cynicism about pious platitudes that have no relevance for practical operations beyond that of providing useful window dressing to keep the public happy.

PUBLIC PARTICIPATION INADEQUATE

A second reason that statements of goals generally fail to function is that there has not been enough genuine participation by the public in the goal-making process. The typical approach to working out educational objectives for pupils or schools or school systems is for a group of educators and academicians or psychometricians, or some mixture of these, to hole up and bring their combined expertise to bear on working out what they think should happen to people as a consequence of going to school. In the presentation of their findings they have often involved representatives of the citizenry at large, but this wider involvement has been usually little more than a series of gestures aimed at getting acceptance rather than participation. The result, again, is usually assent without understanding, and the goals produced turn out to be a dead letter.

The approach of the experts is back-end-to. It should not be one of trying to convince the public of what it ought to want from its schools but of helping the public to discover what is really wants; and among the public I include those who will be in charge in the next fifteen years or so—namely, the pupils themselves, as well as their teachers, their parents, their prospective employers, and behind all these, the school boards and legislators who make the ultimate decisions.[1] This is partly what I mean by the discovery and development of educational goals. By its nature this process of discovery will be necessarily tedious and often frustrating, and, most important, never-ending. So far as I know it has never been given a serious trial on any broad or continuous basis to the point where the actual needs and desires of individuals and of society become the determiners of such subsidiary matters as whether school budgets are to be voted up or down, whether school districts will be consolidated, or kindergartens shall become mandatory, or whether

[1]The goal-making efforts of the State Board of Education and interested citizen groups in the Commonwealth of Pennsylvania suggest the practical possibilities. See *A Plan for Evaluating the Quality of Educational Programs in Pennsylvania* (Harrisburg, Pa.: State Board of Education, 1965) Vol. 1, pp. 1–4 and 10–12; and Vol. II, pp. 158–161.

a foreign language shall be taught to all children or some children or no children at all in the third grade.

It is easy to dismiss the idea of the public search for goals as utopian. How can one possibly bring about genuine public involvement in the goal-making process or expect that anything really useful will come of it when everybody knows that 90 percent of what happens in and to the schools is determined by the power blocs and pressure groups and influence agents whose prime interest is keeping taxes down, or getting bus contracts, or simply gathering in the symbols that add up to prestige and power for their own sake? Nevertheless, in an essay on "Who Controls the Schools?" Neal Gross, who has looked these hard realities square in the eye, can still make the hopeful observation that:

> The control is ultimately, of course, in the hands of the people. If they really want it, they can have it any time, since it is they, after all, who elect the school boards (9).

The problem is to get them to take control and to know what they want their schools to deliver. The chances of a solution will be much improved when the experts stop talking exclusively to themselves and broaden their conversations to include the public.

GOALS ASSUMED AS ALREADY GIVEN

The third reason that educational goals have been nonfunctional is that too frequently they have been assumed as, in some sense, already given, and the only problem has been to figure out how to attain them. This assumption is as old as Plato and as recent as Clark Kerr. According to Plato the reason the guardians of the state must study geometry is that it forces "the soul to turn its vision round to the region where dwells the most blessed part of reality . . . for geometry is the knowledge of the eternally existent (10)." Clark Kerr's brief comment on the purposes of a university is in the same vein:

> The ends are already given-the preservation of the eternal truths, the creation of new knowledge, the improvement of service wherever truth and knowledge of high order may serve the needs of man. (11).

Interestingly enough it was Aristotle who wondered whether things were all that simple. He recognized that there could be diversity of opinion in these matters.

> Confusing questions arise out of the education that actually prevails, and it is not all clear whether the pupils should practice pursuits that are practically useful or morally edifying, or higher accomplishments-for all these views

have won the support of some judges, and nothing is agreed as regards the exercise conducive to virtue, for, to start with, all men do not honor the same virtue, so that they naturally hold different opinions in regard to training in virtue (12).

The fact that "all men do not honor the same virtue" is precisely what makes the structuring and conduct of education in a free society so complicated and frequently so frustrating. If schools are to keep at all, they must somehow accommodate themselves to the pluralism in the values of those whom they serve and from whom they derive their support. Any system that tries to operate on the assumption that there is one fixed set of goals to which all people must aspire is bound to be so far out of touch with the actualities of the human condition that such effects as the schools may have are likely to be altogether unrelated to the needs of the pupils in them or to the society they are expected to serve.

Each individual and each generation has to create its own truth by which to know the world of its own time and place, and, by the same token, it has to create its own goals for ordering its efforts to cope with the world. Thus, the discovery and development of educational goals have to be part of the educational process itself, starting with the child and continuing with the adult as he works his way through to the personal, social, and economic decisions that determine the shape of the free world he is to live in. This, as I understand him, is what John Dewey had in mind when he said that "freedom resides in the operations of intelligent observation and judgment by which a purpose is developed (13)." He was thinking in this particular instance of the child in the classroom trying to find goals that make sense for him, but the principle applies with equal force to such adult groups as school boards, where there is no authoritarian teacher hovering in the background ready to pounce in favor of the eternal verities, only superintendents, curriculum experts, and others who are equally sure they have all the answers.

I realize that there can be profound disagreement with this relativistic conception of educational goals, but I think it is time we stopped kidding ourselves that the misty absolutes we have inherited from the ancients can serve to unravel the ambiguities in education that are inescapable in our half of the twentieth century.

There is an inevitable dilemma in the business of goal-making that has to be faced candidly if we are going to make any headway in the process. On the one hand, as we have been saying for decades, we require goals that specify definite performance levels for pupils as they move through and out of the schools, so that we can gauge how the educational system is doing in its attempts to help them deal with the occupational, social, cultural, and moral demands of the world they are to enter. On the other hand, it is impossible to predict with much certainty anymore what the world is going to be like in 15 or 20 years, when the children now in elementary school will be taking over the social controls. Margaret Mead put the problem succinctly a few years ago. She said:

> If we can't teach every student . . . something we don't know in some form, we haven't a hope of educating the next generation, because what they are going to need is what we don't know (14).

The easy answer to this problem is that instead of teaching youngsters the substance of what they will need to know, we must teach them the "process of discovery" and express our goals in terms of the mastery of that, and its close relatives, flexibility, tolerance for ambiguity, adjustment to the environment, and the like. The danger is that we can still get caught in the word-magic. We can be too quickly satisfied that we know what we mean by the terms before we have worked out any more than a few "for instances" of the operations they might actually entail.

GOALS AND EDUCATIONAL MEASUREMENT

What is the way out? And what is the role of educational measurement in the search for educational goals?

I think the way out is to hold the search for long-term goals in abeyance for a while and concentrate on getting a clearer idea of what is happening in the schools right now and making up our minds about how much we like what we see.

Every morning, Monday through Friday, 50 million children leave 18 million homes and are funneled into the 120 thousand schoolhouses where they have an uncountable number of experiences affecting their thoughts, feelings, aspirations, physical well-being, personal relations, and general conception of how the world is put together. The extraordinary fact is, however, that in spite of the mountains of data that have been piled up from teachers' reports, tests, questionnaires, and demographic records of all kinds, we still have only very hazy and superficial notions of what the effects of the school experience actually are.

There are some things we are beginning to suspect that leave us more or less comfortable-mostly less. For instance, all but a very few children learn to read, at least up to the point where most of them can and do enjoy comic books.[2] It has been estimated that by the time students reach college, half of them will admit to some form of academic dishonesty (15), but the grade norms for this form of academic achievement are not yet known. According to the Project Talent data, the career plans most students make in high school

[2] A poll by the American Institute of Public Opinion, released February 20, 1963, estimated that 50 million adults (45 percent of the adult population) read comic strips. As a "cultural" diversion this activity ranked second in popularity to watching westerns on television.

are unrealistic and unstable (16), but nobody knows for sure whether this situation is good or bad or how far the schools can or should be held accountable for it.

In elementary school, according to the recent Educational Opportunities Survey conducted by the Office of Education, 10 percent of white children and 18 percent of Negro children have acquired an attitude that prompts them to agree with the proposition: "People like me don't have much of a chance to be successful in life." In high school, according to the same survey, 15 percent of whites and 19 percent of Negroes say that they have reached the conclusion: "Every time I try to get ahead, something or somebody stops me (17)." To what extent can attitudes like these be attributed to school experiences and how much to the education supplied by the city streets? Again, we don't know, but information of this sort seems indispensable to the process of arriving at educational goals and deciding on priorities among them.

WHAT THE OUTCOMES ACTUALLY ARE

The point I am trying to make is very simply this: People are more likely to get clear in their minds what the outcomes of education *ought* to be if they can first get clear in their minds what the outcomes actually *are*. To know that a considerable number of pupils are learning to cheat on examinations or learning that the cards are stacked against them should help to suggest, if only in a negative way, what educational outcomes are to be preferred.

It has been customary to take the view that before one can develop measures of educational outcomes, one must determine what the objectives of education are. What I am suggesting is that it is not possible to determine the objectives until one has measured the outcomes. This sounds more like a paradox than it really is. Evaluating the side effects of an educational program may be even more important than evaluating its intended effects. An up-to-date math teacher may be trying to teach set theory to fourth graders and may be doing a good job of it, but one wants to know whether he is also teaching some of the youngsters to despise mathematics.

In a recent essay on "Education As a Social Invention," Jerome Bruner makes the cogent point "that however able psychologists may be, it is not their function to decide upon educational goals," but it *is* their function to be "diviner(s) and delineator(s) of the possible. "And he goes on to say that if a psychologist "confuses his function and narrows his vision of the possible to what he counts as desirable, then we shall all be the poorer. He must provide the full range of alternatives to challenge society to choice (18)."

The same argument holds with equal if not greater force for the educational tester who is intent on doing his full duty to society. He must provide instruments and procedures for displaying and accurately ordering as many of the behavioral outcomes of the educational process as he, with the help of everybody involved, can imagine, regardless of whether these outcomes are to be judged good or bad, helpful or harmful, desirable or undesirable. The educational tester may not allow his thinking to become trapped in the traditional categories of the curriculum such as English, mathematics, and science; he must be concerned with the whole spectrum of human behavior as possible outputs of the educational process and he must try to find ways of categorizing it and measuring it that will make sense to the general public that decides on what schools are for.

In the *Taxonomy of Educational Objectives, Handbook II: Affective Domain,* David Krathwohl and his collaborators have made an enormous contribution to this effort if for no other reason than that they insist one must attend to human functioning beyond the cognitive. Their focus, however, is on "classifying and ordering responses specified as *desired* outcomes of education." (19)." What is now required, it seems to me, is a taxonomy of all possible educational outcomes without reference to whether they are desirable or undesirable, good or bad, helpful or hurtful.[3] Only as this requirement is met are we likely to approximate testing programs that will begin to tell us all we need to know for evaluating educational programs.

BROADER TESTING SPECTRUM NEEDED

Any achievement testing program that is limited to measuring performance in the basic skills and mastery of academic subject matter, and this, I suspect, is the pattern of most such programs, is almost certain to do more harm than good by not raising the question of whether excellence in performance in such things as reading and mathematics and science and literature is not being bought at the expense of something left unmeasured, such as academic honesty and individual sense of self-worth. Granted the tremendous importance of mastery of the basic intellectual tools for these times, it seems axiomatic that they hardly compare in importance with common honesty and mutual trust as the indispensable ingredients of a viable free society.

It is easy to argue that the present state of the art leaves much to be desired in the measurement of the affective and social outcomes of the educational system. It is easy to argue that such instruments as we have for these purposes are productive of soft data, full of superficialities and pitfalls that can lead people astray in assessing what the educational system is really doing to students. This is all too true, and anyone with a conscience rooted

---

[3]Krathwohl and his collaborators hint at this possibility in a footnote on p. 30.

in sound measurement knows it only too well. But such arguments only point to the need for firming up the soft data by going after the correlates of behavior that get beneath the semantic confusions inherent in self-report devices.[4] They also point to the need for keeping a spotlight on the limitations of the data we have, when, for want of anything better, such data have to be consulted. Not to consult them at all is to keep our eyes shut to many of the products of schooling that most need attention.

Finally, educational measurement has its uses not only in the discovery but also in the development of the goals. In an ideal world, this developmental process is a continual series of approximations an unending iterative process for constantly checking the validity of concepts against the behavior of the measures derived from them, and checking the validity of the measures against the concepts from which they have been derived. The back-and-forth process begins in the vague concerns of the public for what it wants but has not defined-personal fulfillment, effective citizenship, the good life, the open society, and so on. All of which terms are still word-magic. They are no good in themselves as goals. But as symbols of human hope, they cannot be neglected in the *search* for goals. They have an extremely high heuristic value in getting the search started.

The first practical approximation in the search, however, is some combination of tests and other measures that can begin to delineate for all to see, the dimensions along which we think we want to progress. This is to say that, in the last analysis, an educational goal is adequately defined only in terms of the agreed upon procedures and instruments by which its attainment is to be measured. It is to say that the development of educational goals is practically identical with the process by which we develop educational tests. It is to imply what in some quarters might be regarded as the ultimate in educational heresy: *teaching should be pointed very specifically at the tests the students will take as measures of output;* otherwise, neither the students nor their teachers are ever likely to discover where they are going or whether they are getting anywhere at all.

A great problem, probably the greatest problem, in the development of meaningful goals is that of making sure that the tangible tests that come out of the process bear a determinable relationship to *all* the vague individual and collective concerns that go into it. The only way this relationship can be assured is through some sort of continuous dialogue among testers, students, educators, and the public bodies that control the educational enterprise. As anyone who has tried it knows, this is not an easy dialogue to get going or

[4]See Pauline S. Sears and Vivian S. Sherman, *In Pursuit of Self-Esteem* (Belmont, Calif: Wadsworth Publishing Company, 1965); also the approach of Sandra Cohen in her study of the attitudes of primary school children to school and learning: "An Exploratory Study of Student Attitudes in the Primary Grades," in *A Plan for Evaluating the Quality of Educational Programs in Pennsylvania,* Vol. II, pp. 61–130.

keep going in fruitful directions, but without it there is small likelihood that anyone will be able to figure out where American education is, or where it ought to be headed, or how it must tool up to get there.

Educational measurement, in the full sense of the term, is one field in which insulation of the experts is intolerable, for measurement in education is the only process by which a society can externalize and give effect to its hopes for the next generation.

REFERENCES

1. Walter Kaufmann, "Educational Development from the Point of View of a Normative Philosophy." *Harvard Educational Review* (Summer 1966), pp. 247–264.
2. The President's Commission on Higher Education. Higher Education for American Democracy, Vol. I, *Establishing the Goals.* Washington, D. C.: U. S. Goals. *Goals for Americans,* Chapter III, "National Goals in Education" by John W. Gardner (New York: Prentice-Hall, Inc., 1960).
3. Harvard University Committee on the Objectives of General Education in a Free Society, *General Education in a Free Society* (Cambridge, Mass: Harvard University, 1945).
4. Nolan C. Kearney, *Elementary School Objectives* (New York: Russell Sage Foundation, 1953); Will French and Associates. *Behavioral Objectives Of General Education in High School* (New York: Russell Sage Foundation, 1957).
5. Benjamin S. Bloom (ed.), *Taxonomy of Educational Objectives,* Handbook I: *Cognitive Domain* (New York: Longmans, Green and Co., 1956); David R. Krathwohl, et al. *Taxonomy of Educational Objectives, Handbook II: Affective Domain* (New York: David McKay Co., 1964).
6. John B. Gilpin, in the Foreword to Robert F. Mager, *Preparing Objectives for Programmed Instruction* (San Francisco: Fearon Publishers, 1962).
7. Henry Adams. The *Education of Henry Adams: An Autobiography* (Boston: Houghton Mifflin Co., 1930) p. 496.
8. The President's Commission on Higher Education, Vol. 1 (1947), p. 9.
9. Neal Gross, "Who Controls the Schools?" in Seymour E. Harris, (ed.), *Education and Public Policy* (Berkeley, California: McCutchan Publishing Corporation, 1965) pp. 19–29.
10. *The Republic,* Book VII, paragraph IX.
11. Clark Kerr. *The Uses of the University* (Cambridge, Mass.: Harvard University Press, 1963) p. 38.
12. *Politics,* Book VII, paragraph I.
13. John Dewey. *Experience and Education* (New York: Collier Books, 1963) p. 71.
14. Margaret Mead "Changing Teachers in a Changing World." The Education of Teachers: *New Perspectives,* Official Report of the Second Bowling Green Conference (Washington, D. C.: National Education Association, 1958) pp. 121–134.
15. William J. Bowens, *Student Dishonesty and Its Control in College.* (Mimeo-

graphed. New York: Bureau of Applied Social Research, Columbia University, 1964) p. 44.

16. John C. Flanagan and William W. Cooley. *Project Talent One-Year Follow-Up Studies* (Pittsburgh, Pa.: University of Pittsburgh, 1966) p. 179.

17. James S. Coleman et al. *Equality of Educational Opportunity* (Washington, D.C.: U. S. Office of Education, 1966) p. 199.

18. Jerome S. Bruner. *Toward a Theory of Instruction* (Cambridge, Mass.: Harvard University Press, 1966) pp. 23–24.

19. David R. Krathwohl, *Taxonomy of Educational Objectives, The Classification of Educational Goals, Handbook II: Affective Domain* (New York: David McKay Company, 1964) p. 4.

Brandon B. Smith and David J. Pucel

Goal Structure and Change Definition in the Process of Curriculum Development[*]

Persons who undertake curriculum development efforts quickly find themselves faced with the problem of adequately developing and precisely defining sets of instructional goals and/or content. Faced with this problem, theorists frequently begin to search for an appropriate model or strategy or they resort to relying on the opinions of subject matter experts. Although most educators are well informed about the use of and need for having instructional objectives and are accustomed to developing behavioral statements of objectives, relatively few educators are aware of the various problems encountered in identifying and evaluating instructional programs. As educators become more conscious of the need to evaluate and improve existing programs, the inadequacies of current methodologies for identifying the goals and structure of goals for various subject matter disciplines will become even more evident.

The position taken in this article suggests that there are two basic procedures currently used to identify and organize the instructional goals (objectives) for a curriculum. First, subject matter scholars can be used to study the problem and suggest the most appropriate organization of instructional content for a particular subject matter area. Implicit in this procedure are the assumptions that subject matter "experts" are able to accurately and precisely define instructional goals-behaviors and they are able to develop an efficient structure for teaching the behaviors. A second approach to the problem, and the one advocated in this article, is to use an objective, empirical procedure

*Reprinted from *The High School Journal,* 53 (April, 1970), pp 401–410, by permission of the author and editor.

to identify the structure of goals (behaviors) possessed by a criterion group of people (subjects). These behaviors, besides representing the instructional goals and content of a curriculum, also represent the criteria against which to evaluate the impact of the program.

The purpose of this article is to review selected techniques for identifying the criterion structure of goals. The techniques discussed have relevance to both curriculum development and evaluation since the criterion behaviors can be used as a standard against which to assess goal definition and student behavioral changes. Emphasis is placed on the rationale underlying each technique, together with the use of the technique rather than providing information about developing behavioral statements of objectives. While much of the material presented deals with vocational education and military service training, an attempt is made to illustrate that each of the techniques may be applicable to a wide range of educational situations.

TRADE AND JOB ANALYSIS

One of the most widely used and accepted techniques for identifying and organizing the instructional goals for occupational training programs is the trade and job analysis (FRYKLUN, 1956). The basic rationale of the job and analysis technique is to identify and then teach to students, the manipulative skills (doing operations) and knowledges (technical information) possessed by on-the-job workers. Operationally, this means that subject matter experts observe the performances of on-the-job workers and record the type and frequency of each psychomotor behavior. Cognitive knowledges possessed by each workman are then inferred from specific psychomotor tasks which were previously identified.

The structure of the criterion behaviors of the workers is obtained by developing a rank order listing of the psychomotor behaviors bases on the frequency and complexity of each. The most frequent, less complex operations and knowledges are taught to students first and are followed by less frequent, more complex operations, until all of the on-the-job psychomotor behaviors have been mastered.

Although the trade and job analysis technique is a relatively useful technique for identifying the criterion behaviors (goals) of on-the-job workers, it is very subjective. Cognitive objectives are identified and organized according to the judgements of expert observers who infer what workers "need to know" from what workers "do" on the job. Furthermore, the technique provides little information concerning the interrelationships among the tasks and between the prerequisite technical knowledges and tasks. Evaluation is typically conducted by determining whether or not students can perform each of the criterion manipulative tasks which have been identified. It is, therefore, not possible to accurately determine the degree to which students have a similar level of understanding of the tasks as compared with persons performing on-the-job nor is it possible to ascertain the degree to which students are aware of the interrelationships among the tasks. In general, trade and job analysis is a useful technique for identifying a criterion structure of goals, but is of limited utility for developing an optimal instructional sequence of goals or for accurately defining goal change.

TASK ANALYSIS

Recently, psychologists working with military training research, have studied and written extensively (Ammerman and Melching, 1966; Ammerman, 1966; Smith 1964; Melching, 1966) about using task analysis to identify, analyze and classify the instructional objectives. Because of the wide range of jobs and the large number of servicemen who must receive specific occupational training, the military services have spent considerable time and effort in developing task analysis as the single, most generalizable technique for identifying the criterion performance standards for military courses of instruction. While there are similarities between trade and job analysis and task analysis, task analysis strongly reflects the military services' increasing concern with the problems of (a) identifying the major criterion behaviors for each job, (b) developing the optimal sequence of instructional elements and (c) writing standards of performance to evaluate each objective.

Task analysis is predicated on the principle (Gagné, 1964) that any human task can be analyzed into relatively distinct component behaviors which are mediational, instructional links that are prerequisite to the mastery of the task. Thus, besides identifying various types of instructional objectives (tasks), task analysis also yields a hierarchical structure (sequence) of instruction elements. Task analysis is typically accomplished by having subject matter experts critically analyze the actual and/or anticipated behaviors of on-the-job workers and then classifying the behaviors into one of three types of instructional objectives: (1) general objectives, (2) terminal objectives, or (3) enabling objectives. General objectives are broad statements of instructional intent or purpose, while terminal objectives are defined as specific behaviors which can stand alone as a particular instructional unit. Enabling objectives, on the other hand, derive their instructional values from the referent terminal behaviors by establishing a state of readiness for learners and by providing mediational prerequisites for effective instruction. In general, a program consists of one or more general objectives and numerous terminal tasks which are capable of being analyzed into a hierarchical series of subordinate component tasks (enabling objectives). Each set of component tasks is organized into a psychologically relevant instructional sequence with the most fundamental component tasks appearing first (lowest level) in the structure and systematically leading to the mastery of higher order tasks until mastery of the respective terminal task is achieved.

Although task analysis has been used most frequently and successfully by the military services to identify and organize criterion psychomotor behavior, its application to academic subjects (e.g. reading, English, science, mathematics, etc.) has also been documented (Gagné, 1965) and its basic instructional rationale has been tested (Gagné, Mayor, Garstens and Paradise, 1961; Gagné and Paradise, 1962). For example, it has been shown that task analysis can be used to identify and develop a hierarchical structure of terminal and component tasks in mathematics. The results of the experiment further revealed that the level of final task performance for students was largely dependent upon mastery of lower level, prerequisite component tasks. In addition, it was also found that the instructional sequence was effective for both high and low ability students, although, as expected, lower ability students required more time to master the terminal tasks than the high ability students.

A procedure for evaluating curriculums based on task analysis has also been discussed (Gagné, 1968). The logic suggests that since it is possible to identify and organize a series of terminal and component behaviors through task analysis, it is also possible to assess the validity of the content and structure of content in terms of the ability of each student to achieve mastery of the terminal tasks. By analyzing the ability of students to perform each task, it is possible to determine where curriculum revisions must be made such that the optimal sequence of terminal and subordinate component tasks can be developed. This suggests that when task analysis is used to develop an instructional program, it is possible to systematically and empirically evaluate and revise specific parts of a program or to revise the content and organization of the whole program. Revisions may involve changing the content or simply changing the sequence of content to allow students to achieve the goals or objectives set forth in the program.

Although the task analysis has been used effectively as a generalizable technique to facilitate the development and evaluation of instructional goals, there appear to be at least three major limitations. First, task analysis is a relatively subjective, time consuming procedure. The results of a survey of military instruction indicated that the procedure requires an average of 17.6 hours of instructional personnel time to decide what to teach for each hour of nonequipment instruction (Ammerman and Melching, 1966). In other words, to develop an eight week career course for officers using the task analysis approach would require about three man years. Second, because the analysis is conducted by subject matter experts, it is doubtful whether two independent analyses of a job would be identical (or very similar) in terms of instructional objectives, content, and organization of content. Lastly, task analysis appears to be most readily adapted to content areas which deal primarily with the development of well defined, identifiable psychomotor behavior (mathematics, skilled trades, etc.). In general, for training situations which involve definable psychomotor behavior, the task analysis represents a powerful, internally consistent technique for identifying the structure of instructional objectives. However, for training situations where terminal behaviors are relatively complex, abstract or ill defined (e.g. NCO training, leadership development, etc.) it has been shown (Powers, Kotses and Deluca, 1967) that modifications in the analysis and instructional process were necessary. In these situations, the terminal behaviors (tasks) were primarily complex cognitive behaviors and success in the training program was predicated on mastering concepts which (a) required large amounts of time to develop (b) needed to be retained over long periods of time and (c) were generalizable to a wide range of other terminal tasks. Thus, in these situations, emphasis was placed on identifying and teaching durable, generalizable knowledges rather than developing specific manipulative skills.

COGNITIVE STRUCTURE ANALYSIS

A third approach to goal definition has been developed and tested in a series of three studies conducted through the Minnesota Research Coordinating Unit for Vocational Education, University of Minnesota (Moss and Pucel, 1967; Smith, 1968; and Pratzner, 1969). This third approach, "cognitive structure analysis," is concerned with identifying what persons must know and the structure of that knowledge in order to perform optimally in a given subject matter area. In other words, the studies experimented with an empirical procedure for producing "psychological maps" of cognitive concepts which provide clues and guidelines for developing and evaluating curriculums.

The theoretical basis for the method is predicated upon theories proposed by various cognitive psychologists such as Bruner (1960) and Ausubel (1963). The operational procedures, however, are bases upon the work of verbal learning theorists like James Deese (1964, 1967), Garskoff and Houston (1963), Johnson (1964, 1967), and Nobel (1952). The assumptions underlying the method are: (a) concepts related to occupations and subject matter areas are represented in the minds of persons in the form of words which can be viewed as verbal labels for these underlying concepts, (b) associative meanings for each word concept can be empirically defined as the total free-associative response distribution which the word elicits from an individual or group of individuals, and (c) the hierarchical structure of concepts can be identified by systematically examining the overlap in the response distributions of different words representing concepts in the area under study. By using the free-association methodology with a defined criterion group of subjects, it is possible to identify the psychological (associative) structure of concepts for a particular subject matter area which produces a "map" of the cognitive goals of instruction. Since these "maps" represent the optimal, criterion structure of cognitive concepts for a program, it is possible to evaluate programs on the basis of how effective they are in teaching students the relationships between and among concepts. In other words, goal change is defined as the degree to which students are capable of recognizing, using and demonstrating the functional relationships among concepts within a particular subject matter area. In this case, the goal of instruction is to teach the interrelationships among concepts, rather than to develop specific responses to independent questions (stimuli).

The method used to conduct the three studies involved the following activities: (a) identifying pairs of flexible (persons performing optimally) and inflexible (persons not performing optimally) workers for each of two electronic repair occupations, (b) identifying a random sample of approximately 180 major technical words representing concepts from the knowledge base of these occupations and developing associative test booklets, (c) administering the free association test to each worker and pooling associative responses for groups of flexible and inflexible workers respectively and (d) computing and factor analyzing associative matrices to yield a hierarchical structure of concepts for each group of workers.

The findings of the first study (Moss and Pucel, 1967) suggested that cognitive structure analysis could be used to identify an optimal hierarchical structure of cognitive goals for persons in a given occupation. The second study (Smith, 1968) demonstrated that besides being able to identify cognitive maps, the procedure was both reliable and sufficiently sensitive to discriminate between pairs of flexible and inflexible workers within an occupation. In other words, cognitive structure analysis appeared to be a valid technique for identifying the optimal criterion structure of cognitive concepts for an occupation. The third study (Pratzner, 1969), besides replicating the results of the first two studies, found that there were commonalities between the hierarchical structures of flexible workers from two different, but related electronics occupations. This suggests that there are common cognitive goals (content) which may be used to develop and evaluate clusters of electronics training programs.

While the results of the three studies are encouraging, there are several basic research problems which must be investigated before the technique will be ready for practical use. Larger samples of stimulus words must be obtained; methods of selecting criterion groups of workers (students) must be improved; more efficient ways of handling associative data must be developed; procedures for labeling concepts must be validated. At this point, it seems safe to say that additional experimentation is necessary before cognitive structure analysis is ready for wide educational applications.

SUMMARY AND CONCLUSIONS

There are many complex problems involved in developing goal structures for curriculum development efforts and evaluating programs based upon these goal structures. However, regardless of program or discipline area, it is essential to first develop and/or adopt a generalizable technique to identify the criterion structure of goals-objectives. While there are numerous techniques which may be used to accomplish this task, each technique has certain advantages and disadvantages depending upon the intended purpose. The purpose of this article was to review and briefly discuss the advantages and disadvantages of three different techniques for identifying the structure of goals.

First, the trade and job analysis was discussed as a subjective methodology for identifying and organizing the psychomotor behaviors of on-the-job workers. The resultant structure or organization of these behavior is based on the frequency of occurrence rather than on any psychological or logical relationships between the behaviors. The curriculum is, therefore, evaluated on the basis of whether or not students can master each of the tasks or operations typically performed by on-the-job workers. Relatively little emphasis is placed on developing instructional techniques which illustrate the interrelationships among manipulative operations and between manipulative operations and cognitive knowledges.

While there are some similarities between the trade and job analysis and the task analysis procedure, task analysis is a more detailed, complex procedure for identifying, classifying, and organizing the instructional objectives for a particular subject matter area. The results of task analysis yield a hierarchical structure of general, terminal and enabling objectives. Lower level, enabling objectives are conceived as prerequisite mediational links to final task performance. Through a systematic procedure, it is possible to evaluate the effectiveness of the sequence for teaching the tasks of a total curriculum or for parts of the curriculum by evaluating the students' proficiency at performing both component and terminal tasks.

Lastly, cognitive structure analysis was discussed as a method for identifying the cognitive behaviors of a particular discipline. It represents an experimental method for producing psychological maps of concepts which provide clues for both curriculum development and evaluation. The methodology represents one of the few techniques which is specifically designed to deal with the structure of cognitive objectives rather than the structure of psychomotor behaviors. Curriculums can be evaluated on the basis of how well students develop optimal relationships between key concepts in the subject matter area. This latter approach overcomes the limitations associated with other methods which rely on the overt manipulative performances of students to evaluate the effectiveness of instruction.

Although three alternative methods have been presented, it is likely that none represents the final answer to defining goals and evaluating change. It is likely that some combination of the techniques discussed is more reasonable than any one in isolation or that new techniques-methodologies must yet be developed.

Bibliography

1. Harry L. Ammerman and William J. Melching. *The Derivation, Analysis, and Classification of Instructional Objectives,* Technical Report 66–4 (Alexandria, Virginia: HumRRO, George Washington University, May, 1966).
2. ————. *Some Important Ways in Which Performance Objectives Can Vary* (Alexandria, Virginia: HumRRO, George Washington University, 1966).
3. David P. Ausubel, "A subsumption Theory of Meaningful Verbal Learning and Retention." *J. Gen. Psychol.,* 66 (1962), pp. 213–224.
4. ————, "Some Psychological Aspects of the Structure of Knowledge." (In) *Education and the Structure of Knowledge,* Stanley Elam, ed. (Chicago: Rand McNally and Company, 1964), pp. 221–262.
5. Jerome S. Bruner, *The Process of Education* (Cambridge, Massachusetts: Harvard University Press, 1960).
6. James Deese, "On the Structure of Associative Meaning." *Psychol. Review,* 69, (1962), pp. 161–175.
7. ————. *The Structure of Associations in Language and Thought* (Baltimore: The Johns Hopkins Press, 1965).
8. Verne C. Fryklund, *Analysis Technique for Instructors* (Milwaukee: The Bruce Publishing Company, 1956).
9. Robert M. Gagné, *The Conditions of Learning* (New York: Holt, Rinehart and Winston, Inc., 1965).
10. ————, "Curriculum Research and the Promotion of Learning," (In) *Perspectives of Curriculum Evaluation,* Ralph Tyler, Robert Gagne, and Michael Scriven, Monograph writers (Chicago: Rand McNally and Company, 1967), pp. 19–38.
11. ————, and Noel E. Paradise, "Abilities and Learning Sets in Knowledge Acquisition," *Psychol. Monogr.,* 76, No. 7 (Whole No. 526, 1962).
12. ————, "Training and Principles of Learning." (In) *Readings for Educational Psychology,* Ellis Batten Page, ed. (New York: Harcourt, Brace and World Inc., 1964), pp. 86–104.
13. ————, John R. Mayor, Helen L. Garstens, and Noel E. Paradise, "Factors in Acquiring Knowledge of a Mathematical Task. " *Psychol. Monogr.,* 75, No. 14 (Whole No. 518, 1961).
14. Bertram E. Garskof, and John P. Houston, "Measurement of Verbal Relatedness: An Ideographic Approach." *Psychol. Review,* 70 (1963), pp. 377–388.
15. Paul E. Johnson, "Associative Meaning of Concepts in Physics." *J. of Educ. Psychol.,* 55 (1964), pp. 84–88.
16. ————, "Some Psychological Aspects of Subject Matter Structures." *J. of Educ. Psychol.,* 56 (1965), pp. 217–224.

17. George Mandler, "From Association to Structure." *Psychol. Review,* 69 (1962), pp. 415–427.
18. William H. Melching, et. al. *Deriving, Specifying and Using Instructional Objectives.* Professional paper 10–66 (Alexandria, Virginia: HumRRO, George Washington University, 1966).
19. Jerome Moss, Jr. and David J. Pucel, "Identifying the Associative Structure of Technical Concepts for a Group of Flexible Radio and Television Repairmen" (Unpublished Staff Study: Department of Industrial Education, University of Minnesota, 1967).
20. Clyde E. Nobel, "An Analysis of Meaning." *Psychol. Review,* 59, 1952, pp. 421–430.
21. Theodore R. Powers, Harry Kotses, and Arthur J. DeLuca. *Training Requirements for the General Military Science Curriculum of the Army ROTC Program.* Technical Report 67–17 (Alexandria, Virginia: HumRRO, George Washington University, 1967).
22. Frank C. Pratzner, "Testing an Empirical Procedure for Identifying Technical Associative Conceptual Structure: Discriminating Between Workmen Within and Between Two Occupations." Unpublished Dissertation (Minneapolis, Minnesota: University of Minnesota, 1968).
23. Brandon B. Smith, "Testing an Empirical Procedure for Identifying Technical Associative Conceptual Structure: Discriminating Between Flexible and Inflexible Radio and Television Repairmen," Unpublished Dissertation (Minnesota: University of Minnesota, 1968).
24. Robert S. Smith, Jr. *The Development of Training Objectives.* Research Bulletin No. II (Alexandria, Virginia: HumRRO, George Washington University, 1964).

Herbert J. Walberg, The University of Wisconsin

Curriculum Evaluation: Problems and Guidelines*

Thomas Kuhn[1] termed underdeveloped fields of science as "pre-paradigmatic." He defined "paradigms" as "universally recognized scientific achievements that for a time provide model problems and solutions to a community of practitioners." In distinguishing "pre-paradigmatic" and "normal" science, Kuhn writes:

> No natural history can be interpreted in the absence of at least some implicit body of intertwined theoretical and methodological belief that permits selection, evaluation, and criticism. If that body of belief is not already implicit in the collection of facts—in which case more than 'mere facts' are at hand —it must be externally supplied, perhaps by a current metaphysic, by another science, or by personal or historical accident. No wonder, then, that in the early stages of development of any science different men confronting the same particular phenomena, describe and interpret them in different ways.

By this characterization of nascent disciplines, then, educational research and evaluation are in an early stage of development. Gage,[2] for example, has summarized some paradigms for research on teaching, but none would meet Kuhn's criterion of universal recognition. While these and other paradigms in education have been useful in isolated research efforts, none has led to a progammatic, cumulative series of studies. Much of educational research is atheoretical, and what theoretical work that has been accomplished is largely derived from the physical, biological, and social sciences, from philosophy, or from personal idiosyncrasies. Even aside from theory, fundamental and

---

*Reprinted from *Teachers College Record,* 71 (May, 1970), pp. 557–570, by permission of the author and the editor.
    [1]Thomas S. Kuhn. *The Structure of Scientific Revolutions* (Chicago: University of Chicago Press, 1962).
    [2]N. L. Gage, ed., "Paradigms for Research on Teaching." *Handbook of Research on Teaching.* (Chicago: Rand McNally, 1963).

unresolved methodological problems of gathering "facts" plague educational research and evaluation. Research workers and schoolmen alike have been disappointed in the practical results of experimental methods in education.[3] Experimenters argue that more precise measurement and rigorous research designs are likely to bear fruit eventually. But other investigators question the appropriateness of quantitative methods and use in their place methods of anecdotal descriptions of classroom events, like those of the social anthropologist, or observation and intuition, in the manner of the clinical psychologist. The point is not to bewail the inadequacy of various methods of gathering "facts," but to illustrate the necessity for a reassessment of educational evaluation, its theory, practice, and their interdependencies.

TYLER'S STRATEGIES

The writings of Ralph Tyler have been the basis of much of the major work in educational evaluation and offer a constructive starting point for conceptualizing work in this field. Tyler[4] proposed a three stage process in curriculum development: (1) stating objectives in terms of student behavior, (2) specifying learning experiences likely to contribute to student attainment of objectives, and (3) evaluating learning experiences in terms of attainment of objectives. (This rationale arises from the means-ends distinction emphasized by the pragmatic philosophers Charles Peirce, William James, and John Dewey.)

The next two sections identify the problems of Tyler's strategies in stating objectives and specifying learning experiences in course evaluation. By no means is this discussion intended to belittle the work of Tyler, his former colleagues, and students at the University of Chicago. Indeed, their fundamental contribution to both the theory and practice of evaluation can hardly be overestimated. However, Tyler himself might be the first to admit that this is not a time for orthodoxy, even his own. He writes:

> The accelerating development of research in the area of educational evaluation has created a collection of concepts, facts, generalizations, and research instruments and methods that represent many inconsistencies and contradictions because new problems, new conditions, and new assumptions are introduced without reviewing the changes they create in the relevance and logic of the older structure.

[3]See Donald T. Campbell and Julian C. Stanley, "Experimental and Quasi-Experimental Designs for Research on Teaching." *Handbook of Research on Teaching, op. cit.*; J. M. Stephens. *The Process of Schooling: A Psychological Examination* (New York: Holt, Rinehart and Winston, 1967); H. J. Walberg, "Can Educational Research Contribute to the Practice of Teaching?", *Journal of Social Work Education*, Vol. 9 (Fall 1968), pp. 77–85.

[4]Ralph W. Tyler. *Constructing Achievement Tests* (Columbus, Ohio: Ohio State University Press, 1934).

Therefore let us examine the "relevance and logic of the older structure."

CONTROVERSY ON OBJECTIVES

During the past few years a controversy has centered on the specificity of the statement of objectives. Gagné[5] and Mager[6] hold that the objectives must be precise, detailed descriptions of student behavior exhibited on attainment of the objective. Others have argued that behavioral objectives constrict education to the trivial kinds of behavior that can be described precisely. Eisner[7] warned that adherence to precise behavioral objectives may prevent the teacher from spontaneously deriving new objectives from on-going learning activities, especially in the arts where creative expressions are most clearly valued. Moreover, even the behaviorists would have to admit that it is often time-consuming and frustrating, if not impossible, to get curriculum workers and teachers to state precise behavioral objectives. Nor have evaluations employing behavioral objectives proved to be conspicuously successful.

Bloom[8] takes a reasonable position on this controversy: "It is virtually impossible to engage in an educational enterprise of any duration without some specification to guide one." Further, "Insofar as possible, the purpose of education and the specifications for educational changes should be made explicit if they are to be open to inquiry, if teaching and learning are to be modified as improvement or change is needed, and if each new group of students is to be subjected to a particular set of educative processes." Hopefully, further work in evaluation will reveal the efficacy of explicit objectives in instruction and evaluation.

Another point made by Bloom also seems constructive: less specific objectives may be more appropriate for educational media designed for teacher use. Indeed, it may be that a teacher's rigid adherence to pre-determined, specific objectives may impede student learning in much of education. Now in training, as opposed to liberal education, a number of explicit criteria are set forth; they can be "covered" by the teacher, programmed materials, or, probably just as effectively, by a textbook. Training is most effective when the objectives are explicit and when adequate motivation or reinforcement can be assumed as in military or industrial settings. Such

[5]R. M. Gagné, "The Analysis of Instructional Objectives for the Design of Instruction," in Robert Glaser, ed., *Teaching Machines and Programmed Instruction* (Washington, D.C.: Department of Audiovisual Instruction, National Education Association, 1965).

[6]R. F. Mager. *Preparing Instructional Objectives.* Palo Alto, Calif.: Fearon Publishers, 1962.

[7]Elliott W. Eisner, "Educational Objectives: Help or Hindrance?" *School Review*, Vol. 75 (Winter 1967), pp. 250–62.

[8]Benjamin S. Bloom, "Some Theoretical Issues Relating to Educational Evaluation." *Educational Evaluation: New Roles, New Means.* Sixty-eighth Yearbook, Part II, National Society for the Study of Education (Chicago: University of Chicago Press, 1969).

training is characterized by its emphasis on the acquisition of basic skills, which can often be defined behaviorally.

On the other hand, curriculum makers, school boards, and teachers aspire to inculcate ideals, values, social skills, and other intangibles. They are concerned with higher-order cognitive processes such as analysis and critical thinking. Moreover, both the teacher and the students bring important, though vague objectives, ideas, and interests to class, some permanent, others transient. Paradoxically, these random elements lend caprice and serendipity to the class that may be far more important to the attainment of general ideals than predetermined specific objectives and lessons. Or certain events of the day may conjoin unexpectedly with the teachers' planned objectives and activities. These occurrences inject relevance, suspense, humor, and other human qualities to learning that are impossible with a programmed machine, a programmed course, or a programmed teacher.

THE PROBLEM WITH PROGRAMMING

Though the word "programmed" has a modern ring, in education it is an essentially medieval idea. It stems from the time before printing when professors literally dictated Aristotle and exegeses to their students. The lecture method is still prevalent in modern times, and is bound up with the objective of "covering" a subject or a text through lectures and recitation. This is not to say that lectures always are inappropriate. There are a few teachers who can occasionally muster a beautiful lecture and create excitement in their students. But in the main it is overused: writing is generally more organized and comprehensive than speech, and reading normally proceeds at three times the speed of speech. Moreover, the reader may skip or skim parts of the work he knows and actively concentrate on what gives him difficulty.

Not only are programmed methods inefficient in "covering" material, they may be harmful to the social environment of learning.[9] Classroom groups have at least two tasks: attaining instructional objectives through learning and developing a viable, if not cohesive, social structure. Paradoxically, if the course or teacher specifies the purposes and procedures of instruction too emphatically, the group may resist and learning may not proceed. This phenomenon may be observed on the university campus particularly in

[9]See Gary J. Anderson, Herbert J. Walberg, and Wayne W. Welch, "Curriculum Effects on the Social Climate of Learning: A New Representation of Discriminant Functions." *American Educational Research Journal*, Vol. VI, No. 3 (May, 1969). Herbert Thelen, "The Evaluation of Group Instruction." *Educational Evaluation: New Roles, New Means.* Sixty-eighth Yearbook, Part II, National Society for the Study of Education (Chicago: University of Chicago Press, 1969); and Herbert J. Walberg, "The Social Environment as a Mediator of Classroom Learning." *Journal of Psychology,* Vol. 60, No. 6 (December, 1969).

the lists of demands for greater student participation in the formulation of objectives, activities, and evaluation of learning. The little available objective evidence (cited above) suggests that the social environment has greater effect on important affective learning than on cognitive achievement.

If explicit programmed objectives have been slighted in this discussion, it may be a reaction to their current vogue. Federal funding agencies have required their use in new educational projects; persuasive exponents have sold them to schools. Their rhetoric seems to insist that what is not objectively specified and precisely measured does not exist or is not important, and further, that what is most measurable is most important. Taken to an extreme, the argument holds that social and affective learning may be ignored since it is difficult to measure; that, in the cognitive domain, essay examinations are undesirable because they lack technical standards of reliability; and that hope lies in multiple-choice tests because they are efficient and require no judgment in scoring. And this may be right; it remains to be seen. But until there is convincing evidence to support these kinds of assertions, it is dangerous to force such an orthodoxy on the schools.

THE NEED FOR INDICATORS

In the meantime, the evaluator is often supplied with vague, general objectives or no objectives at all. Obviously these conditions make his work more difficult—but not impossible. His job is to elicit more explicit objectives from the curriculum maker, or, failing this, he has other alternatives. He may be able to derive explicit objectives from the general; he may infer objectives from the learning materials themselves; and he may administer a general battery of indicators to find out what objectives the materials accomplish.

These alternatives may be used in combination, but in any case, a general battery should be employed for at least two reasons. Many different kinds of learning may occur in a course; by emphasizing one, others may be sacrificed. Also, the evaluator cannot assume that schoolmen will value the same objectives for the subject as the course developer; therefore, he must include indicators that may be of interest to a variety of consumers. Metfessel and Michael[10] provided a comprehensive, seven-page list of about 105 suggested criteria. While it would not be feasible to include all these in most projects, it would seem necessary in any educational evaluation to use indicators of the following: factual and conceptual mastery of the general subject; higher-order cognitive mastery such as understanding and analysis; and affective learning such as values, interests, and attitudes brought about by the course. It would also be desirable to include other indicators even if they are only

[10]Newton S. Metfessel and William B. Michael, "A Paradigm Involving Multiple Criterion Measures for the Evaluation of the Effectiveness of School Programs." *Educational and Psychological Measurement,* Vol. 27 (Winter 1967), pp. 931–44.

in experimental stages of development. One of these is the induced flavor or projected image of the subject, for example, the relative emphasis on developmental, logical, or intuitive aspects. For reasons discussed earlier, indicators of the social environment of learning might reveal unintended consequences of the course. Systematic observations in classrooms might show changed patterns of teacher behavior; casual visits would at least reveal whether or not the teachers are using the course materials. Since these indicators are by no means comprehensive, teacher and student comments might be solicited. Although it is difficult to code comments objectively, presumably any expected or unexpected sterling qualities or glaring inadequacies would be salient enough to detect.

LEARNING EXPERIENCES

Let us now turn to another difficulty of Tyler's strategy—designing and selecting the most appropriate learning experiences to attain general or specific objectives. Stephens[11] has taken a fresh look at educational research over the last fifty years and produced some humbling conclusions. The results of his survey indicate that the things commonly believed to promote learning make no difference at all. Research on teaching, for example, has consistently concluded that different teaching methods make little or no difference in student learning and attitudes. These conclusions apply to television and traditional instruction, team teaching and ordinary teaching, teaching in large and small classes, homogenous and heterogenous group, core and traditional curricula, lecture classes and discussion classes, teacher-centered and group-centered approaches, in small schools with indifferent facilities and large with lavish facilities. Thus, it has proven impossible to specify instructional activities which optimize the general performance of students.

Perhaps as a consequence, some theorists have proposed sub-optimizing learning for groups of students with different aptitudes. This proposal is at least 25 years old and can be traced to Plato's *Republic* where he describes children of brass, iron, and gold and the different learning experiences required for each group. This concept is now known as "individualizing" instruction. Technically it depends upon the presence of "aptitude-instruction interaction," i.e., the tendency for different students to benefit unequally under different methods of instruction. For example, student A performs better under instruction A; whereas student B performs better under instruction B. Unfortunately, it is extremely difficult to find consistent evidence for the aptitude-instruction interaction. Bar-Yam,[12] in a 231-item review of

[11]J. M. Stephens. *The Process of Schooling: A Psychological Examination, op. cit.*

[12]Miriam Bar-Yam. *The Interaction of Student Characteristics with Instruction Strategies: A Study of Students' Performance and Attitude in a High School Innovative Course.* Doctoral thesis (Cambridge, Mass.: Harvard University, 1969).

aptitude-instruction interaction research, has found a little evidence that bright students and independent, assertive, flexible students perform better with flexibility and independence in the classroom; whereas dull students and dependent, anxious, rigid students do better under directive, highly structured conditions. While a balance of evidence shows that the two types of students perform better under these two conditions of learning, there are a number of studies which do not support this notion. Moreover, these interactions account for little variance compared to that accounted for separately by intelligence, socio-economic status, and prior achievement. It is likely that if there were powerful interactions of student aptitudes and instruction, they would have been found by now. Moreover, Bracht and Glass[13] point out that it might be fruitless to look for these kinds of interactions in courses because they are complex and contain many instructional and content elements.

THE ENVIRONMENT OF LEARNING

Perhaps a more fruitful area of optimization and sub-optimization research lies in the social environment of learning brought about by different courses. Exploratory research has already shown significant differences in environments attributable to randomly assigned courses.[14] Moreover, with relevant factors held constant, the social environment is an optimizer of cognitive and affective learning;[15] and environmental characteristics sub-optimize student learning, i.e., students of different levels of intelligence, personality, and other characteristics differ sharply in their performance in different environments.

The discussion in this section is not to depreciate basic instructional research in curriculum evaluation; indeed, curriculum projects offer an ideal setting for the educational psychologist to test his ideas against instructional realities. Moreover, courses are superseded; whereas instructional research, if it becomes an applied science, could develop empirical laws of learning that would have continuing relevance for courses in the future.

For the time being, however, Tyler's second stage must be based on common sense and guess work. Educational psychology offers no satisfactory method of designing learning experiences to attain given objectives. In view of the multiplicity of vague course and teacher objectives, the problem of specifying learning activities, and the possibilities of aptitude-instruction and aptitude-environment interactions, the course developer might do well to

[13]Glenn H. Bracht, and Gene V. Glass, "The External Validity of Experiments." *American Educational Research Journal*, Vol. 5 (November, 1968), pp. 437–74.

[14]Anderson, Walberg, and Welch, "Curriculum Effects on the Social Climate of Learning: A New Representation of Discriminant Functions," *op. cit.*

[15]H. J. Walberg, "The Social Environment as a Mediator of Classroom Learning," *op. cit.*

avoid trying to optimize and instead, include many diverse concepts and learning materials in the course. These elements, with a guide to their possible organization and use, may enable supervisors, teachers, and students to optimize and sub-optimize according to their own needs and objectives. If this is done, there is all the more need for a general battery of indicators in the evaluation of the course. A second consequence is the necessity of studying sub-groups of students who are likely to perform especially well or poorly under varying conditions of course use.

Having examined the difficulties of the Tyler strategies of stating objectives and specifying learning activities, and offered some provisional solutions that seem workable, let us turn to the problem of generalizing curriculum research.

GENERALIZABILITY

That evaluation should be generalizable to specified populations of students seems an obvious objective; yet most evaluations must be faulted on statistical grounds. Certain well-known but little employed statistical procedures relating to randomization bear repeating here. Let us first consider the two traditional uses of randomization. As R. A. Fisher[16] showed, the assumption underlying statistical inference is that the experiment to which it is applied meets the following conditions: (1) there has been a random selection of units from the population under study, from which population parameters can be estimated, and (2) for the estimation of experimental effects, there has been a random assignment of experimental units to treatments (and nontreatment to control groups). The first assumption allows estimation of population parameters with a known probability of error; the second allows the estimation of treatment effects with a known probability of error. It would hardly seem necessary to point out these assumptions again in 1970; but educational researchers (and social and biological scientists, for that matter) have continued to ignore them and resorted to "convenient" samples, "matched" groups, and "quasi-experiments." While descriptive statistics may be calculated for nonrandom samples, it is misleading to infer population parameters for them.

Only random samples of the population permit valid estimates of population parameters. Actually the sample defines the population, and statistical inference must be limited to that population from which the sample has been drawn. Unfortunately, this means that in a typical curriculum study, the sample, even if it is random, unnaturally constrains inferences to volunteer teachers or local schools or school systems with cooperative administrators.

[16]Ronald A. Fisher. *Statistical Methods for Research Workers* (Edinburgh: Oliver and Boyd, 1925).

There is a great need for national random samples in educational research. To our knowledge, there has never before been a curriculum project to employ a truly random national sample of teachers with random assignment to control and experimental treatments.

A related statistical point often overlooked or misunderstood concerns the units of analysis, which must be independent observations. If a sample of teachers is drawn and the comparative progress of their students in different courses is to be studied, the proper unit of analysis is the mean of the students under each teacher. The "degrees of freedom" used in statistical significance tests is the number of teachers, not the number of students since students within the same class are not independent sampling units. This is not to say that non-inferential research studies with students or classes as the units of analysis are invalid; indeed, they are necessary to examine certain questions, for example, the comparative progress of bright and dull students in two courses. However, these studies do not permit generalization to the population.

THE LONG HAUL

Another problem of generalizability has to do with changes in the course and students across time. To what extent does a course remain unchanged while undergoing evaluation? The intent of formative evaluation, of course, is to suggest ways that course materials might be improved. But even at the stage of summative evaluation, the course may still be evolving. If this is so, it may be well to recycle the formative evaluation each year from the beginning to the end of the project, and to begin yearly cycles of summative evaluation during the last few years of the project and extend them for a few years after the course is completed. Evaluation of this scope and duration would require much labor and coordination, but it may be the most effective, if not efficient method of valid, comprehensive assessment.

If a project would continue evaluating for several years, it would allow follow-up studies of the students several years after they have taken the course; evaluation "over the long haul," as Carroll[17] has put it, might be quite valuable. Ebbinghaus's classic studies of memory curves have shown the rapid rate of forgetting immediately after learning and the retention of the residual for long periods. Thus, an important topic for extended-term evaluation is the student retention over long periods after completing the course. Another question that may be answered by long-term evaluation is: Has the course aroused the student's motivation and interest enough for him to continue learning as evidenced by pursuing a career in the area of the

[17]John B. Carroll, "School Learning over the Long Haul" in J. D. Krumboltz, ed., *Learning and the Educational Process* (Chicago: Rand McNally, 1965).

course, taking more courses, or continuing his interest through independent study?

Still another problem of generalizability across time is the changing state of society and the possible irrelevance of courses developed before relevant changes. A vast complex of waxing, waning forces bear upon the content and methods of the curriculum. Dewey held that the schools reflect society, which seems obvious enough; but because the reflection is screened, distorted, and delayed, it would be difficult to specify and quantify the characteristics of society that brought about a given curriculum change. Many of the forces are, like social class, hypothetical constructs difficult to measure and weakly related to a host of other constructs in an uncertain direction of causality. Consider the changing character of high school physics: in 1949, applied, technical aspects were given primacy; 1959 marked the era of waxing scientific modernity and rigor; and 1970 seems to exemplify concern for the humanistic, social, and moral relevance of science. Many factors come to mind that may have led to these changes, but who is to say which and to what extent? The point is that social conditions change rapidly, and the curriculum reflects the changes. Ironically the course that appears to be relevant to specific conditions at one period may likely be outdated quickly. Until social indicators of the *Zeitgeist* are developed, the course evaluator will have to duck these issues or assert subjective judgment.

EXPLICITNESS, OBJECTIVITY, AND JUDGMENT

Explicitness in evaluation means that the methods employed are described in enough detail that the reader may assess their validity and attempt to replicate them. Objectivity is the independence of results from the individual characteristics of the evaluator. Meeting the standard of objectivity will increase the likelihood of making evaluation an applied science. Yet neither science nor evaluation are value-free: subjective factors have enormously influenced the progress of science (the root of the word "evaluation" connotes human judgment and possible personal bias). The interplay of these factors warrants more careful consideration.

The need for objectivity is most apparent in summative evaluation, for its purpose is to assess the comparative or absolute effectiveness of the finished course in attaining objectives. Many projects have sampled a highly selected group of teachers with able students, administered achievement test items based upon the course text, and concluded that the resulting scores demonstrate the effectiveness of the course. A few projects have employed pretests and posttests to show student growth in achievement during the course; and still fewer projects have contrasted the achievement of students in their course with a contrast or control group of students in other courses. If these methods are made explicit, the evaluator and his readers are able to judge the value of the evaluation design. While the readers, if not the evaluator, may conclude that the evaluation is trivial, biased, or invalid, these judgments can only be made if the methods and results are explicit.

Objectivity and judgment are also important in formative evaluation. It is extremely difficult for course developers to be objective and critical of their own work, yet it is absolutely necessary. As in any creative work, there must be a continuous, balanced re-cycling of productive and critical phases. The first and most severe critic must be the developer. But his own criticism is not enough, for inevitably he will be biased and unable to see all the weak points of his work. Therefore, he must solicit critical opinion from his immediate colleagues and various outsiders—specialists in educational media and evaluation, university professors of the subject, and school teachers and students using trial versions of the course. Yet here a balance is needed for critical capacity often outruns the productive with the result that work is never finished. Too much criticism, doubt, and revision may prevent bringing work to fruition. No amount of revising and polishing of a course or evaluation will result in a perfect product. One can hope for a reasonably good job given the inevitable constraints of time, energy, and funds. After this, remaining creative energy might well be channeled into objectivity and judgment in identifying the strengths and weaknesses of the finished course and evaluation and their implications for future projects.

Perhaps the role of judgment has been underestimated; the evaluator must judge. Bias can enter the "objective" methods and results through the choice of groups and instruments employed in the evaluation. Therefore, judgments and decisions regarding technical methods must stem from an explicit rationale for the evaluation so that the reader may judge its validity. A rationale is needed for the interpretation and judgment of the results; these processes must be explicit, couched in interpretive rather than objective language, and should err on the side of caution.

Education requires rigor and relevance, social and moral passion; but these very factors may be the downfall of research and evaluation. The history of "scientific breakthroughs" in education reveals a discouraging series of inadequate experiments which could not be replicated.[18] The technical inadequacies went unrecognized by educational policy makers and did not deter them from attempting to reform the schools. Contemporary examples may be found in critical reviews[19] of two recent books on "creativity" and "teacher expectancies and blooming students." The rather devastating

---

[18]Gene V. Glass, "Educational Piltdown Men." *Phi Delta Kappan,* Vol. 50 (November, 1968), pp. 148–51.

[19]Lee J. Cronbach, "Intelligence? Creativity? A Parsimonious Reinterpretation of the Wallach-Kogan Data." *American Educational Research Journal,* Vol. 5 (November, 1968), pp. 491–511; Robert L. Thorndike, a review of Robert Rosenthal and Lenore Jacobson. *Pygmalion in the Classroom. American Educational Research Journal,* Vol. 5 (November, 1968), pp. 708–11.

reviews were probably read by only a handful of educational researchers concerned about the methodology. Yet these books or newspaper summaries of them reached the public and professional educators, and policy decisions based upon findings have already been made. The implication for evaluation is clear: it is not enough to present objective results and judgments; the evaluator must make clear to the nontechnical reader the possible inadequacies of this methods and the weaknesses of his conclusions. An authoritative, referred journal of educational evaluation would serve as an excellent vehicle for such studies.

There is also the problem of the evaluator's allegiance. An evaluator on a project staff may have conflict of interests which bias his judgment. Since he is paid by the project, his job or even the project may be at stake if he publishes an uncomplimentary report. On the other hand, nonstaff evaluators may lack appreciation of the special qualities of a project or the interest and wherewithal to do a comprehensive job. It is difficult to imagine how a federal bureau modeled on the Food and Drug Administration or the National Bureau of Standards could take on this work especially in view of the traditional fear of national control of education. An independent group modeled on Consumer's Union may seem even more farfetched. Yet the massive amount of evaluation needed in education may require such steps. In the meantime, curriculum groups will probably continue their own evaluation, and there are a few ways that conflicts of interest may be lessened. Developing a critical climate and involving outside critics have been mentioned. Another alternative is to commission outsiders to carry on parts of the evaluation. This practice would be especially useful when the project lacks the facilities or specialized competence for certain aspects of the work, for example, the data files from national testing agencies or the techniques of quantifying teacher observations. Still another alternative is to separate the evaluation group to some extent from the rest of the project staff and give them no responsibilities for course development.

The evaluation group should have autonomy and authority to carry out their work. Presumably they would be sympathetic to the goals of the course and perhaps identified with them, but would be expected to reach their own decisions regarding evaluation. They would serve as a kind of "loyal opposition" as in the British Parliament. None of these methods, however, can insure complete objectivity and valid judgment.

Nor can the alternatives described above make educational evaluation a science in the same way physics or chemistry is a science. Like the social sciences, educational research is inevitably subjective in known and unknown ways. And this is as it should be, for education is committed to social and moral values. The general goal is making explicit these values and the "objective" methodology so that other workers can assess their validity from their own viewpoint.

USEFULNESS OF EVALUATION

Finally, evaluation should be useful. Obviously, formative evaluation should be useful in improving the course and is of concern mainly to the course makers before releasing the final product. On the other hand, others will be interested in the summative evaluation. Who should it be useful for —the curriculum maker, the subject-matter expert, the supervisor, the teacher or the student? Or should it be designed for a technical research audience or school purchasing officers in large city school systems?

In line with earlier discussion, an evaluation report should be appropriately explicit concerning sampling, research design, measurement, statistical analysis and interpretation. Such a report would enable other evaluators to judge the merits of the evaluation. On the other hand, this kind of detailed analysis may make the report dull and restricted to a technical audience. Therefore, many teachers and supervisors would not read it in its entirety or at all. They would be more interested in a description of the course and only the results of the evaluation. These problems can be resolved by writing at least two reports, one a technical substantive report for the research audience, the other a shorter substantive report for schoolmen. Part of the results might well be published in journals for the teaching audience or reported orally and graphically at various regional conferences so that teachers and supervisors may react to their results, ask questions, and make comments about the usefulness of materials and raise further questions for the evaluator to pursue.

Some of these points would hardly seem in need of saying. But there is a danger of evaluation becoming an isolated professional specialty. Already at educational research meetings, presented papers often appear to be displays of methodological virtuosity rather than educationally relevant. If educational evaluation is to become a useful applied science, it must develop theory, rigor, and relevance; and it has a long way to go on all three counts.

In conclusion, the recommendations made earlier in this paper may also make evaluation useful. Stating the special objectives of the course as best one can will enable others to judge its effectiveness on these criteria. Including both special indicators and those of interest to various groups will enable others to form a judgment of the course on the basis of their own priorities. Studies of sub-groups of students will enable those working with similar groups to judge the adequacy of the course for their students. Basic educational research might reveal better instructional methods and media. Including a random sample would allow generalizing the results to specified populations. Explicitness, objectivity, and critical judgment in formative evaluation are likely to improve the course. And finally, an objective reporting of the results and possible sources of bias will enable both other evaluators and potential consumers to judge the effectiveness of the evaluation itself.

David Engler *

Instructional Technology and the Curriculum†

There is a widespread and unfortunate tendency in education these days to regard instructional technology as being synonymous with such things as computers, teaching machines, and audio-visual devices of all sorts, and to express concern about the possibility that the advent of such machines will mechanize and therefore dehumanize education. The image of the machine, cold and impersonal, manipulating our children as it manipulates rats and pigeons in the laboratory, is a haunting reminder of Huxley, Orwell, and others who have painted for us the frightening picture of the demise of humanization.

This is an unfortunate tendency, because in focusing on the machine as a threat to humanistic education, it is pursuing the scent of the red herring and ignoring the real problems of technology, humanism, and their relationship to each other.

Our thesis here is that the conflict between a humanist curriculum and instructional technology is more apparent than real; that it is, in fact, the product of semantic confusion and fuzzy definitions; that it is based on the assumption that we now have a humanistic curriculum but do not utilize instructional technology, an assumption which on both counts is at best debatable and at worst fundamentally erroneous; that, in fact, we must deal with a problem that is not technological but rather is ecological.

Let's consider first our definitions. Instructional technology is defined in two rather different ways. First, and most commonly, it is defined as hardware

*Mr. Engler is group vice president for instructional technology, McGraw-Hill Book Company, largest publisher of instructional materials in the U.S.

†Reprinted from *Phi Delta Kappan 51* (March, 1970), pp. 379–381, by permission of the author and Phi Delta Kappan.

—television, motion pictures, audio-tapes and discs, textbooks, blackboards, and so on; essentially, these are implements and media of communication. Second, and more significantly, it is defined as a process by means of which we apply the research findings of the behavioral sciences to the problems of instruction.

Defined either way, instructional technology is value-free. Gutenberg technology, which is widely used but not often recognized as a technology in schools, can produce the Bible, *Mein Kampf,* and *Portnoy's Complaint* with equal indifference. Television can present brilliant insight into the human condition as well as mindless and brutalizing violence with equal clarity. Technology as hardware is neutral. Notwithstanding Marshall McLuhan's preachments to the contrary, the mesage is the message.

The process of instructional technology is similarly value-free. It can be used to achieve good objectives or bad objectives; it can help to better define objectives and to better measure the achievement of those objectives, but it will work equally well for almost any objective. It is a tool, and like all tools, it is morally and philosophically neutral.

Historically, curriculum, by which we mean the sum total of the content of education, has been largely unaffected by any changes in technology. Motion pictures, radio, phonographs, television, and other widely used hardware have had no significant effect on the curriculum. Where they have been used, it has been to deliver the existing curriculum.

On the other hand, changes in curriculum have rarely required any changes in instructional technology. The vast curriculum reform movement of the past decade led to substantial changes in the goals and the content of many subject matter areas, but virtually all of these reforms relied on the traditional technology. Modern mathematics was taught through the same technology with which traditional mathematics had been taught.

In retrospect, one would be hard put to cite an example of significant curriculum change that was the result of any new technology. This is because decisions about curriculum are largely value judgments, and technology, being value-free, is simply not very meaningful in making such value judgments.

Thus, to raise questions about the conflict between humanism and technology is to tilt at windmills. There can be no curriculum, humanist or otherwise, without some means of delivering instructions to the learner and some strategy that will facilitate learning on his part. There can be no curriculum without an instructional technology. The real question is: Can we devise an instructional technology that will further humanize our curriculum?

To answer this question we must first consider the extent to which our curriculum is now humanistic, as well as the extent to which our prevailing instructional technology facilitates the transmission of that humanistic curriculum from school and society to each individual.

In fact, our society, our times, offer abundant symptoms of a widespread failure of humanism in our educational system. Song My may turn out to be one of the most shattering of these symptoms, but others abound in the crime, racism, alienation, and other sociopathic behavior produced by individuals who are the products of our educational system. If humanism is a significant aspect of our curriculum today, it is not succeeding in humanizing massive numbers of our citizens.

Beyond these social manifestations of the failure of our schools to humanize a significant segment of our population, there is the question of whether or not this failure is the result of an inadequate emphasis on humanism in our curriculum, or an inadequate method of transmitting that humanism to all of our population, or both.

However, to answer the question of whether or not our curriculum is humanistic enough requires one to make value judgments about ideas on which there are many philosophical and ethical differences of opinion among people. That task we shall leave to each individual reader.

The students, who picket their university with signs saying, "Do not fold, spindle, or mutilate" bear witness not to the cold impersonality of computers but to the dehumanization that characterizes an educational system which does not value their human individuality. The ghetto dropout bears witness to the same problem. So, in fact, does virtually every youngster who experiences failure in school. Thus, to attempt to transmit a humanistic curriculum by means of a technology that fails to accomodate human individuality is to negate the essence of humanism.

The assumption that our traditional methods of instruction do not constitute a technology seems utterly indefensible. This is so whether one defines technology as a process or as hardware. The most accurate statement one can make about our present methods is that they are an old technology. The basic media of instruction, such as textbooks, chalkboards, and teachers, have been used for many years. Today, teachers are better prepared, textbooks are better written and better designed, and chalkboards have changed color, but their functions and their relationships to learners have not changed essentially in over a hundred years. Moreover, the process by means of which instruction is carried on has not changed in any fundamental respect during this period. It remains teacher-centered, group-oriented, and textbook-based.

It is a technology derived from the impact of an industrial society on the role and methods of education. In its time, it was a technology that contributed enormously to humanizing education by making education accessible to vast numbers of children who had never before had such opportunities.

It was a technology designed to implement a curriculum which had as two of its major objectives to raise the level of literacy and to prepare youngsters to function in society as workers and citizens. Its prototype was the Lancasterian model of large-group instruction which developed and spread in Britain and the United States early in the nineteenth century; and while this model has undergone many modifications over the past century and a half, the general configuration of mass-production education remains fundamental to this technology.

The industrial revolution ended in our society many years ago, however, and we are becoming increasingly aware of the fact that we live in a postindustrial society. Our curriculum is changing and will continue to change as our awareness of this reality increases.

What are the factors that lead people to question our present curriculum and its related technology? They include the dwindling social demand for semiliterate and functionally illiterate workers; the concomitant increase in the need for citizens who can cope with the accelerated rate of change that characterizes modern technological society; the emerging realization that there no longer exists a finite body of knowledge constituting at any level what an "educated" individual should know, but that, on the contrary, the so-called knowledge explosion has rendered such a view completely obsolete; the growing recognition that for all citizens education is the *sine qua non* of economic and social adjustment, to say nothing of success; the need for citizens who are capable of bringing critical analysis to bear upon the information aimed at them by government and industry through the powerful and pervasive mass media of communications.

The new curriculum as it develops today and in the years ahead will have to reckon with these factors. It will have to assume responsibility for the successful achievement of its objectives by every individual in school. It will have to concentrate on developing the ability to learn instead of imparting a fixed schedule of knowledge. It will have to nurture an independence of mind and related skills of analysis that are all too often missing in the products of our present curriculum.

All of this brings us, at last, to the question of ecology. If we view the ecology of education as the web of relationships between and among learners, teachers, and the environment in which.they operate, then it becomes apparent that these relationships are largely defined by the prevailing technology of instruction. Certainly these relationships are not inherent in the individuals or things that are the component parts of education; rather, they are conventions that attach to the traditional goals of education and the methods that are associated with the achievement of those goals.

In the past, many attempts to change education, particularly those attempts to individualize instruction and to develop skills of independent inquiry, have failed because they did not include any mechanism for changing the ecological balance between teachers and learners. Usually, these changes were imposed on the existing ecology in which the teacher leads a group-based lockstep progression through the course of study. This ecology is inevitably characterized by a high degree of active involvement on the part of the teacher and a comparably high degree of passive involvement on the part of the learner. It accepts as normal a distribution of success and failure that can be described by a bell-shaped curve; in fact, results which do not produce a bell-shaped curve often lead teachers to wonder whether or not their objectives and/or tests are too easy or too difficult.

This ecology more often than not results in a fair amount of boredom in students because it often attempts to teach them things they already know; it results in a high degree of frustration in students because it often attempts to teach them things they are not prepared to learn; finally, it tends to produce among the students with whom it is successful the habit of conformity, since that is what produces the highest payoff in grades.

To change the ecology so that each individual can receive the attention and instruction that he needs is obviously no small task. For the institution of the school and for the teacher in particular to assume responsibility for the success for each and every child is to go beyond the scope of the resources presently allocated to education. To transform millions of students who have been well-trained to pass their tests, get their grades, and move on to the next subject into millions of independent learners whose most important rewards come from the pleasures of learning is an undertaking of staggering dimensions. It should be clear to us by now that our present strategies and instruments of instruction, the prevailing instructional technology, cannot provide us with the means for effecting these changes.

Only a new instructional technology can change the existing ecological balance in education. The state of the art in instructional technology is such today that many of the tools and techniques needed to effect such change are available and feasible. We can, for example, by individual, specific diagnosis and instruction eliminate the practise of teaching youngsters what they already know or of teaching them what they are not prepared to learn. We can devise the means and organize the instructional environment to permit individuals to master the basic skills and acquire the basic information that are necessary ingredients of analytical or problem-solving work in most subjects. We can leave to the teacher the functions of diagnosis, evaluation, decision making, and direct, individual interaction with the learner on the level of the higher order intellectual, esthetic, and ethical objectives that are the essential ingredients of a humanistic curriculum.

This technology will require significant changes in how space is utilized in schools, in how time is allotted for each individual, in how progress and achievement are measured, in how materials of instruction are designed and used, in how teachers and learners relate to each other, and, above all, in how learners relate to the process of learning. Instructional technology in the form of hardware will obviously be an ingredient of this ecology, just as it is today;

but only instructional technology as process will have the power to alter the ecology of education so that it is more responsive to individual human differences.

The problem is to get off the pursuit of the red herring of conflict between humanism and technology and get on to the task—huge and long-term though it be—of using technology to further humanize education.

Leon M. Lessinger *

Four Key Ideas to Strengthen Public Education†

Those of us in the business of keeping school these days may be excused a certain amount of annoyance and just plain anger at the flat-out statement reechoing through an army of critics—"the schools have failed."

A number of well known public officials have told me that it is now politically popular to be *for* Education but to be *against* the public schools.

The Education Establishment is much maligned in Washington and state capitals. When educators appear before committees of the Congress and Legislatures to make claims for quality education conditioned on major infusions of new money, the credibility gap assumes cavernous porportions. For the first time leaders in the education profession are challenged to produce facts about actual student accomplishment as well as rational arguments to justify their claims for still larger bites of the tax dollar. Credentials, resource allocations, traditional slogans and even vivid portrayals of neglected children are no longer enough. Foolishness, waste, outmoded practice—the inevitable by-product of any huge bureaucratic enterprise with large amounts of money to spend is continually under attack. The signs are that the level and intensity of the attacks will grow.

It is tempting to try to explain how we got into this situation. But that would take too much time and would probably serve little productive purpose.

"The great thing in this world" said Oliver Wendell Holmes, "is not so

*Leon M. Lessinger, Callaway Professor of Education, Department of Educational Administration, Georgia State College, Atlanta, Georgia. Former Associate Commissioner, Elementary and Secondary Education, U.S. Office of Education, Washington, D.C.

†Reprinted from the *Journal of Secondary Education,* 45 (April, 1970), pp. 147–151, by permission of the author and editor.

149

much where we are, but in what direction we are moving." This is *not* the time to be too defensive, too complacent, too eager to ward off attack. For despite all the difficulties and disappointments, despite all the clamor and loss of credibility, the American people support formal education and have a large residue of faith in the educational practitioner. This *is* a time for constructive solutions—the needs and the opportunities were never greater.

I have some suggestions to make about the nature of those needs and the shape of the solutions to the problems of meeting those needs. My suggestions grow out of a careful review of the programs which I administered in the United States Office of Education. Four years and billions of dollars later there are successes to illustrate and directions to travel. Let us begin.

First of all let us deal with the statement "the public schools have failed." The vast, decentralized, locally-controlled system of America's public schools has helped to produce the most efficient, affluent, technologically advanced society in the world. It reaches more people for longer periods of time than any other country's educational system. Its twin ideals of equality of opportunity and concern for each individual's competence are unsurpassed and unexcelled. In many respects the situation in formal education is strangely akin to that of poverty. Three decades ago, an American President claimed that "one third of the Nation are ill-housed, ill-fed, and ill-clothed." Now we have reduced that poverty figure more than half but we are more incensed about the problem. So it is in education. But the public schools have not been successful in educating the poor and disadvantaged. They have not responded to the increased and changing expectations of a more impatient and well-informed citizenry.

So the most appropriate statement is not that the schools have failed; rather it is more correct to say that the burdens placed upon the organizations charged by the public with delivering educational services—the school districts, State departments of education, professional societies, and universities—now exceed the capabilities of those organizations to meet those burdens. Looked at from this vantage point, the effectiveness of the formal educational system is a ratio between burdens and capabilities.

When burdens or responsibilities or demands increase the effectiveness of a system will also increase if there is a sufficient increase in its capability. Similarly, even if there is an increase in capability, the effectiveness of a system in meeting its responsibilities will decrease if there is a more commensurate increase in burdens. This suggests that the most productive study of solutions probably lies in a search for clear definitions of burdens placed upon the schools, techniques designed to meet those burdens and resources allocated against the demands generated by the burdens. This precisely is what is available in a study of the results of expenditures of money in the administration of the Elementary and Secondary Education Act of 1965. What have we learned?

1. Programs are successful when the people responsible for them have a "Can-Do" or success oriented set of attitudes.

In principle, the American educational commitment has been that every child should have an adequate education. This commitment has been translated into resources available such as teachers, books, space, equipment, tax-bases. When a child has failed to learn school personnel too often have assigned him a label—slow, unmotivated, retarded, or culturally deprived and acted in terms of the label with a sense of the futility of real success. Where school personnel have assumed a revised commitment—one that insists that every child can and will learn, these actions have resulted in a willingness to change a system which does not work, and find one which does; to seek causes of failure in the system and in the training of its personnel and not solely in the students. And the results have been striking!

2. Program descriptions are available which, if followed carefully, improve student learning. The following set of seven illustrate favorable opportunities for improving school productivity:

(a) Elementary schools, where children are allowed considerable individual choice of what they study within an educationally rich environment (animals, maps, typewriters, calculating machines, scientific equipment, paints, etc.); and the program is designed to insure that the children enjoy school while achieving results.

(b) Schools where great emphasis is placed on older children tutoring younger ones, and where community service is encouraged and properly managed.

(c) Schools with strong emphasis on individually prescribed instruction so that each child can progress at his own rate within the curriculum.

(d) Work-study schools—where students go to school part-time and have part-time jobs—to provide a link between education and the world outside.

(e) Schools with emphasis on learning outside of the schoolroom with visits to and study in museums, factories, libraries, farms, and hospitals. Schools where greater use is made of instruction by TV at home or in school.

(f) Schools, where a student uses a particular school only as a home base for his activities and may pick and choose in a competitive system among various schools for various activities.

(g) Schools, where parents or members of the community or all of them actively participate in planning the school and in all its activities.

3. Programs are successful when their objectives are clearly defined and resources are placed against the objectives.

Over and over again one finds the same kind of statement as written in the Fourth Annual Report of the National Advisory Council on the Education of Disadvantaged Children.[1]

The successful pre-school programs all had certain features in common: careful planning, including the definition of academic (cognitive) objectives; teacher training (usually including frequent reviews of the program); and much use of small groups.

Materials were selected carefully for their relevance to program objectives. Two programs stressed diagnosis of individual pupils' needs, three limited their curriculum and methods strictly to what was needed to achieve the objectives and meet the needs, and one removed competing stimuli from the classroom. Parental involvement featured as important in only one of the successful programs. *To summarize the comparisons, success in pre-school programs seemed to be found upon:*

—careful planning, including statement of objectives;
—teacher training in the methods of the programs;
—small groups and high degree of individualization; and
—instruction and materials closely relevant to the objectives.

At the elementary level, ten comparisons were drawn. *Instruction irrelevant to the stated objectives of the programs seemed to be the most frequent reason for failure at this level.* No success factor was common to all ten of the comparisons, but academic objectives clearly stated and active parental involvement seemed to be most important, followed by a high intensity of treatment (that is, pupils were given many hours in the program), an emphasis on directly attacking pupils' problems, and the use of reading specialists, small groups and individual tutoring. Also important at this level were teacher training and the supervision and training provided for aides. While the patterns are not so marked, it seems that success in compensatory programs at the elementary level largely depends upon:

—academic objectives clearly stated;
—active parental involvement, particularly as motivators;
—individual attention for pupils' learning problems; and
—high intensity of treatment.

In the four secondary school comparisons, the concomitants of failure were fairly obvious: programs failed because they were too "diluted," had very loosely structured objectives, or too wide a range of goals. An academic emphasis was missing from several of the unsuccessful secondary programs. Those that succeeded all had clearly stated academic objectives, often based on individual diagnosis, and incorporated tightly controlled teaching linked to these objectives; small group work was important in two. Successful programs at the secondary level seem to be founded upon:

---

[1]Title I - ESEA: A Review and a Forward Look—1969 Fourth Annual Report, The National Advisory Council on the Education of Disadvantaged Children, pp. 23–24.

—academic objectives clearly stated;
—individualization of instruction; and
—directly relevant instruction.

Far from being dramatic, the results of this study are perhaps not even surprising. In general, the factors consistently identified with successful compensatory education programs and consistently lacking in "unsuccessful" programs might have been advanced on the basis of theories of good management or common sense. But the results are nonetheless of real importance in two directions:

—On the negative side: The analyses repeatedly showed that real compensatory education does not result from services. Any of these elements *can* contribute to success *if* they are carefully integrated into a well-planned program and made relevant to the program's objectives.

4. Programs are better when those who lead them are held accountable for results.

In its most basic sense, holding someone accountable means having him answer for performance. The most impressive gains appear to be associated with those programs or projects in which there was not only a clear statement of what was to be done but who was to be answerable for delays, cost over-runs, standards and accomplishments.

I believe we can generalize this observation about the controlling importance of accountability to its possible use in the basic issues of government and decision making at local, state and federal levels.

Over a whole range of nagging moral, legal and educational problems generated by a society in turmoil and drastic change, school boards and school leaders are caught in the middle of a free-for-all in which courts, states, governmental agencies, unions, citizens groups, students, parents, teachers, rightwingers, leftwingers, and others in varying combinations and alliances fire away at each other. In merely a decade, power to govern in education has been greatly diluted until it is hard to know who is in charge, who has authority and who can be answerable for malfunction. Thus the 110,380 citizens, who as of 1968 sat on 21,704 independent school boards together with their superintendents, presiding over a 40 billion dollar enterprise employing the talent and energies of some 25 percent of our entire population, provide a sitting-duck target and lack the clearly defined authority and tools to deal with the great issues of race, collective bargaining and taxpayers' revolts to name but a few of those thrust upon school officials.

Accountability may be one powerful way to restore stewardship of the school system. Four elements of an accountability process are now described:
1.   Developmental capital via grants management.
2.   Performance contracts via bid to specification (RFP).
3.   The Independent Educational Accomplishment Audit.

4. Management Support Groups for political, social, economic, educational and managerial consultation.

CONCLUSION

Devoted and intelligent men and women are working to serve our children and to improve the quantity and quality of their formal education. They have a lot of which they can be proud. Yet even as we honor their accomplishments we know that the problems we face now and in the future will not yield to the ideas and programs which represent business-as-usual.

Progress and reform are clearly in order. *Progress* is a nice word, but *change* its instigator is not. For change destroys comfort, implies criticism of what *is* and provokes feelings of fear. Change in education means that someone's professional feathers will be ruffled, that pet programs might die and sacred cows placed out to pasture.

Perhaps the most fitting summary is provided by the desperate action of a mayor of a drought-stricken Mexican town. Robert Silverberg in the book *The Challenge of Climate: Man and His Environment* quotes the ultimatum issued by the mayor to the clergy to hold them accountable for results: "If within the peremptory period of eight days from the date of this decree rain does not fall abundantly, no one will go to mass or say prayers. . . . If the drought continues eight days more, the churches and chapels shall be burned, missals, rosaries and other objects of devotion will be destroyed . . . If, finally, in a third period of eight days it shall not rain, all the priests, friars, nuns, and saints, male and female, will be beheaded."

Fortunately, for the clergy, Divine Providence responded to this non-nonsense approach by sending torrential downpours within four days.

The crises in education are not that bad! But the moral is clear: Results are what count, not promises or lamentations.

PROGRAMS IN ACTION

section III

Introduction

It would be a mistake to consider the notion of educational accountability and performance contracting as one concept. Accountability is not new in education; however, it has not until recent years, been defined specifically in terms of student outcomes. Performance contracting is relatively new to education but the movement is definitely underway. This section will attempt to list projects in operation where some form of performance contracting is practiced.

It is important to note that programs in operation at the time of this writing are experimental and limited in scope. Because of the diversity of the programs it is impossible to generalize from any one program to any other program. Evaluation of these programs has not yet been attempted therefore judgements regarding success, continuation and modification remain to be done.

There are a variety of ways in which these programs can vary. There can be differences in: contract terms; sections of the program under contract; types of educational programs; and types of programs utilized by the contractors.

Perhaps the most difficult aspect of the performance contracting idea will come with our attempts to evaluate the outcomes. It will not be sufficient to look only at achievement scores in specific area involved in the contract. The whole field of values and attitudes of students as well, impacts on teachers, school officials, parents, taxpayers and any other group interested in the relationship between the school and the community will have to be examined. Evaluators have already discovered monumental gaps in assessment where traditional techniques have been used. Roger Lennon enumerates some of these problems, under the familiar terms of "validity, reliability, and unit and scalar properties of the measuring intruments." He presents a very convincing argument for the need to develop totally new techniques for assessment. As a case in point, he examined the notion of validity where he says:

> The performance contract begins with a specification of the educational outcomes to be achieved through the contracted interventions; there is strong emphasis on the necessity for detailed enumerations of the behavioral objectives to be achieved. Under these circumstances, one would suppose that identification of appropriate instruments which would validly measure the attainment of these particular objectives would be greatly facilitated. So, indeed, it might - except for the overriding insistence that the results be expressible in units that are thought to be meaningful and comprehensible. This has eventuated, in case of most performance contracts written to date, in a stipulation that the gains be measurable in terms comparable to "normal progress," generally defined as progress in terms of grade equivalents. This requirement has driven the contractors - reluctantly in some instances to adopt one or another of the more widely used achievement series as the instrument for measuring gain, since these are the only series having dependably established normative systems yielding grade - or, age-related measures. But these series are, almost in the nature of things, concerned with a much wider range of content and outcomes than the narrowly defined, more specific ones of the contract interventions, so that they fit between the goals of the interventions and the content or functions measured by the test often leaves much to be desired. A considerable part of the variance in scores on these general achievement tests may be unrelated to the specific goals of the contract program.[1]

Obviously the evaluation of performance contracting and more generally the development of the concepts of accountability rests most assuredly on the ability to secure accurate measurement data. What is being called for is some form of "continuous performance monitoring."

Bearing in mind the obvious primitive state of present day attempts to build accountability into school systems, the subsequent sections of this book will list some projects in operation, contractors involved in performance contracting, description of a useful model and will conclude with a look at schools of the future and educational accountability.

PERFORMANCE CONTRACTORS

Performance contracting by private industry has created some interesting problems for educational publishers. The nature of the type of contracting has created a bonanza for some publishers who possess the education hardware while others do not have material which lend themselves easily to contracting. Both groups of publishers however, face the difficult problem of risking their prestige and profits by offering guarantees. Many of the large

---

[1]Roger T. Lennon. *Accountability and Performance Contracting,* An Address to the American Educational Research Association, New York (February 5, 1971).

educational publishers have held back from performance contracting while others, i.e., Educational Developmental Laboratories and Behavioral Research Laboratory, have taken progressive leadership in the movement.

The willingness or unwillingness to participate in the contract movement is to some extent governed by the state of the technology of how to control instructional management and services on one hand and by the instructional materials on the other. At present, the educational materials which have the greatest application are those which are of a programmed nature and self-instructing teaching machines. The trend toward the greater reliance on self-instructing materials has obviously placed pressure on the more traditional publishers of classroom textbook materials. They are faced with the decision whether the instructional materials most conducive to performance contracting is a trend toward a new way of organizing education or merely another educational fad. Regardless of the outcome, it is perfectly clear that instructional materials will be more carefully scrutinized by educators than ever before.

For the readers information, the following table lists the major performance contractors with basic information concerning their activities.

A MODEL

Inefficient management of the curriculum may be viewed for the failure in increased performance in the skill areas in spite of increased school expenditures. Evaluation of school program management systems indicated that many elements of good management have been ignored by educators. We need to develop a new system and associated skills within the skills areas of the curriculum which will allow management by objectives. In order to accomplish this, we must prepare teachers, administrators and supervisors to (1) specifically state the goals of the curriculum for varying groups of students and the skill elements of the program in particular, (2) state objectives which will contribute to the stated goals, (3) develop strategies based upon differing learning modalities of students and differing educational objectives for accomplishing the objectives, (4) select the strategy which offers the best possibility for improving the student performance (including achievement), (5) develop an organizational plan for implementing the action decided upon, and (6) state clearly and concisely the activities of the program to insure that the personnel involved in augmenting the program are accountable for carrying it out. The approach necessitates wide participation by the faculty, students, and community members in the development while the major emphasis is concerned with the growth and development of each student toward his maximum potential regardless of his experiential background or his evaluated level of achievement. As in all management systems

TABLE 1
PERFORMANCE CONTRACTORS

Contractor	Founded	Contract Officer	Contracts*	Curriculum Area
Alpha Learning Systems 5309 Sequoia Rd. NW Albuquerque, N.M. 87103	1969	Brian Frieder	Hartford, Conn. Grand Rapids, Mich. Taft, Texas	Remedial courses for college students Tutoring program for students at U of Albuquerque
Behavioral Research Laboratory 866 United Nations Plaza New York, N.Y. 10017	1961	George Stern	Gary, Ind. District 4, Phi. Monroe, Mich.	Reading Mathematics
Combined Motivation Education System 6300 River Road Rosemont, Ill. 60018	1970	Charles Welch	Greenville, S.C. Grand Rapids, Mich.	Achievement Motivation
Dorsett Educational System SBox 1226 Norman, Okla. 73069	1962	Stanley Upchurch	Texarkana, Ark.	Reading Mathematics
Educational Developmental Laboratories Huntington, N.Y. 11743	1954 (acquired by McGraw-Hill, Inc. in 1966)	Robert Ruegg	Flint, Mich.	Reading Medina, Ohio
Educational Solution, Inc. 821 Broadway, New York, N.Y. 12204	1968	Eugene Wilson	Boston, Mass. Oakland, Calif.	Reading Mathematics
Learning Foundations, Inc. 824 S. Milledge Ave. Athens, Ga. 30601	1967	Joel Kaye	Hammond, Ind. Duval Co., Fla. District 9, Bronx Savannah, Ga.	Reading Mathematics Language arts

Company	Year	Contact	Locations	Subjects
Learning Research Assoc. 1501 Broadway New York, N.Y 12204.	1968	Lee Brown	Norfolk, Va. Duval Co., la. Jacksonville, Fla.	Reading Mathematics Language arts
Macmillan Educational Service, Inc. 8701 Wilshire Blvd. Beverly Hills, Calif. 90211	1969	Arthur Makhohm	Cajon Valley Elem. School District Cajon Valley, Calif.	Reading Mathematics
New Century Division Meredith Corp. 440 Park Ave. South New York, N.Y. 10302	1969	William Mare	Dallas, Texas Providence, R.I.	Reading Mathematics
Plan Education Centers Little Rock, Ark. 72203	1969	Don Griffith	Witchita, Kansas Clarke County (Athens, Ga.) McNairy County (Selmar) Tenn.	Reading Mathematics
Quality Education Development 1776 K Street Washington, D.C. 20006	1967	C. J. Donnelly	Rockland, Me. Dallas, Texas Anchorage, Alaska	Reading Mathematics
Singer/Graflex Corp. 3750 Monroe Ave. Rochester, N.Y. 14603	1968	John Smingler	Seattle, Wash. McComb, Miss. Portland, Me.	Reading Mathematics
Thiokol Chemical Corp. 3346 Airport Rd. Ogden, Utah 84402	1966	Robert Marquardt	Clairfield Job Corp. Center Dallas Independent School District	Training programs in vocational areas
Westinghouse Learning Corp. 100 Park Ave. New York, N.Y. 10017	1967	Henry K. Steele	Fresno, Calif. Grand Rapids, Mich. Gilroy, Calif.	Reading Mathematics

*Representative - not all inclusive

the product is accountable to those who support the system, in this case the taxpayer.

MANAGEMENT OF THE PROGRAM

In any management program, there must be a system by which activities can be organized to accomplish the established goals. The system presented here is based upon the premise that the structure of the curriculum must be organized in terms that will insure the best educational returns for the monies invested. In order to reach this objective three major elements are essential to the development; (1) statement of direction, (2) objectives, and (3) strategy for accomplishing the goals set.

DIRECTION

A statement of the direction for the curriculum must be broad in nature and define the educational problem which is to be attached. The direction should be stated as goals which represent problem areas as defined by the professional educator and agreed upon by the Board of Education with the community also having input channels into the channels into the decision making process. Once the goals are developed and approved they will provide the necessary guidelines for the development of the structure that will support the initiation of the curriculum change.

It should be mentioned at this point that a number of goals may need to be stated and that the structure of the implementation of each in their specific details necessitate differing organizational patterns. In a model which could be generated it would be necessary to have an overall goal with sub-level goals, stated with increasing specificity, also being indicated. In this way each of the sub-level goals would form a hierarchical supportive structure.

An example of a structure which could support this concept is indicated in Figure 1.

In this particular model, which for illustrative purposes is related to the structures part of the curriculum (skill areas) each of the goals is related to, and supportive of each goal in the hierarchy. Following are some goals which may serve to illustrate the model.

G1–Provide all students with a foundation in the basic skills.

G2–Provide all students with the opportunity to develop skills in reading, mathematics, written and verbal communication.

G3–Provide all students with the opportunity to develop skills in work recognition skills, comprehension and critical reading. (Reading is

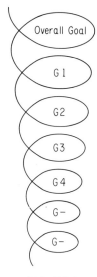

FIGURE 1

used as an example to illustrate only. Other paralled blocks would contain additional skill areas).

G4–Provide all students with the opportunity to develop skills in word recognition.

OBJECTIVES

The objectives of the program are outcomes which can be stated in specific measurable terms at time intervals which lend maximum support to an evaluation of the continuous progress toward the goal. As with the statement of goals, the objectives should also be arranged in a hierarchical order with each successive level contributing to the prerequisite for higher level objectives. This concept is described in Figure 2.

01–Ninety percent of those graduating from high school should be in advanced educational programs or gainfully employed.

02–Eighty percent of those graduating from high school should be able to perform the following tasks (specified by school) in reading, mathematics, writing and speaking.

03–Eighty percent of those graduating from high school should be able to read and understand material used in the tenth grade.

04–Eighty percent of those leaving the primary grades should be able to pass a district-made criterion referenced test in work recognition.

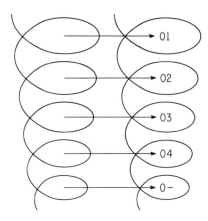

FIGURE 2

It is assumed that measurement of the attainment of the objectives (achievement accountability) is built into the model and that the results are used for constant evaluation and restructuring of the curriculum. As the program develops through the constant ongoing evaluative process it is assumed that the objectives and direction will be modified to correct weaknesses observed and to meet the needs of the changing demands of the society. Accountability can only have meaning for the structuring of the curriculum if it is conceived as a dynamic, progressive and productive force for improvement. Ultra educational conservatism is an anathema to the accountability concept.

STRATEGY

A strategy is a plan designed to accomplish a goal. It is broad in nature and consists of a plan whereby closely related activities, when properly conducted, can yield a vehicle which insures progress toward the objectives.

There is no one plan that is best for the accomplishment of a goal. It is basic however, that an inventory of known alternatives to meet the objectives should be developed. If we take, for example, the objective 03 as desirable a school might elect one or more of the following strategies.

1. An ungraded organization of plan which stresses individual progress along an explicit skill continuum.
2. Departmentalization stressing skill areas.
3. An early intervention program.
4. A strong developmental program in grades k-12 with remedial programs available at every level for students having learning problems.

5. Special skill area laboratories for concentration on specific areas.
6. Reduced class size.
7. Performance contract with industry.
8. Special classes for those who do not reach minimum levels of proficiency.

Any strategy which is finally employed must be guided by the constraints of the system. The section of an appropriate strategy must involve a study of the effects of those factors already in operation and to evaluate how the constraints influence the alternatives.

PROGRAM

The program is an administrative structure designed to achieve a set of objectives. A completed program will describe the activities to be performed, the time period in which they are to be accomplished, the resources available, and the organizational structure. A factor which is often neglected in the formulation of a program, but which must be highly defined as the role and function of the personnel to conduct the program.

Periodic review of the program and the policies and procedures by which it is operating is basic to any management control technique. As in contracting with industry, periodic reviews are necessary by which judgment can be made concerning adequate progress. If the established goals for the program are not met, then a reevaluation and perhaps a reallocation of resources is in order. A reexamination with subsequent changes is often necessary to turn an unsuccessful project into a successful one.

The concept of accountability is in itself accountable only if it allows for a recycling of the management process when difficulties arise. Unless the system has within it the capability to rejuvinate without stagnation the accountability concept is "just another pretty face in the crowd".

AN EXAMPLE OF THE MODEL IN OPERATION

Jackson, Mississippi has initiated a program in one Junior High School which is based upon the model described in the previous section. Grades seven, eight and nine are housed in a very traditional building. The population is 90% black, from lower socio-economic backgrounds.

During the 1970–71 school year the administration and faculty took a hard look at this program and what was happening to the students. The program was departmentalized and class groupings were based on ability. Provisions were made for all students to participate in an elective program which was made up of homemaking, shop, and music.

ANALYSIS OF THE PROBLEM

Problem analysis was based upon the following rather specific manifestation of a program that had little relevance to student needs.
1. Seventy percent of the students were reading below standard norms.
2. Drop out rate was between 25 and 30 percent.
3. Truancy was exceedingly high.
4. Individual student motivation was generally very low.
5. Mathematics skill achievement scores were generally well below standard norms.
6. General discipline problems were numerous.
7. Students felt their day was fragmented and no one teacher got to them well.

The staff at this school requested help. They were not satisfied with the existing program. They were fully aware of the many limitations of this program. It should be noted that the court decisions which resulted in faculty and students being moved from one school to another added another dimension to the schools problems.

THE PILOT PROGRAM

Pilot Program: Under the direction of Superintendent Dr. Brandon Sparkman and Principal Lepolian Gentry, a pilot program was established to try to meet some of the many problems facing the students and staff.

It was decided that the most appropriate approach would be to organize a class of seventh grade students into an inter-disciplinary team-teaching block. Reasons for this decision were:
1. Flexible scheduling could be arranged where the teacher involved could make schedule changes when it seemed appropriate.
2. Four teachers representing mathematics, science, social studies and language arts would get to know 110 students as individuals.
3. Planning time for the four staff members would be built into the program to give them time to discuss student needs and to make the appropriate changes.
4. In designing this pilot program, Principal Gentry and his staff were given permission to involve students in any activity or curriculum plan that teachers, students and parents believed to be worthwhile. Essentially the Jackson Public school curriculum guide was put aside.

This program began operation in January, after the team worked long hours over the Christmas holidays to get organized. Students were randomly selected to avoid the ability grouping. The team had decided that the program would concentrate on two major concepts: (1) teach children reading and mathematics skills, and (2) arrange experiences designed to assure meaning, dignity and success. These experiences would be cooperatively planned by students and teachers. These two concepts formed the basis for what was later termed the structured curriculum and the open-ended curriculum. Mathematics and reading were to be highly structured; the remainder of the curriculum was to have one main function and that was to provide relevant experiences where each student could achieve success in some task. The experiences were designed around problems and concerns that the students were familiar with and interested in pursuing.

Evaluation of the pilot project was sketchy, based primarily on attitude, inventories and instruments designed to determine growth in self image. Achievement scores in reading and mathematics were not significant due primarily to the limited duration of the pilot program.

Significance of the pilot project was that it resulted in the faculty and immediate community's commitment to refine and redesign the program for the 1971–72 school year. Based upon the notion of the two phase instructional program—highly-structured and open-ended—plans have been made and preparation for implementation completed.

A. Structured curriculum:
1. Reading and mathematics laboratories have been designed.
2. Hierarchies of reading and mathematics skills have been prepared.
3. Individual student profiles in reading and mathematics have been designed.
4. Assessment programs for reading and mathematics have been constructed. Assessment will be continuous and based upon time segments of one to two weeks.
5. Materials have been selected and ordered for the laboratories.
6. Diagnosticians have been trained for the laboratories.
7. Jackson State College has agreed to supply student teachers who will work in the laboratories under the direction of the diagnostician.

B. Open-ended curriculum:
1. Teams of teachers are to be organized in cross-discipline teams.
2. Lists of projects, activities, and experiences are being prepared based upon student interest and need.
3. Work study programs and other community based involvement will form the framework for much of this part of the curriculum.
4. Art, music, physical education, dramatics, literature and other fine arts activities will become vital components in this phase of the instructional program.

5. Opportunities for problem solving, discovering, exploring and student managed activities will be offered.

Evaluation

The structured curriculum in reading and mathematics will be evaluated
on a continuous basis and not in terms of grades. Students will evaluate their
own progress and be given evaluation data from the diagnosticians. When
progress isn't being made, recycling will take place, and new strategies
employed. The diagnostician will be responsible for providing continuous
feedback so that if new materials are needed the basis for the claim can be
substantiated. The diagnostician is accountable for this phase of the program.
The Principal and central office will be held responible for requesting or
reallocating and the community for continued financial support.

The open-ended phase of the program will be assessed in a variety of
ways. The goal will be to develop students who have healthy self image and
view themselves as contributing, functioning citizens. The objectives related
to these goals will be determined and evaluated by students and teachers.

Teachers who work in the highly structured curriculum will develop
accountable practices related to their specific tasks. Those teachers who work
in the open-ended curriculum will not confuse their tasks with those of the
staff in the highly structured part of the program. This differentiation assists
in developing educational accountability.

Due to certain limitations of time and financial resources this program
will not be extended throughout the entire school until perhaps the 1972–73
school year.

Much remains to be done. Retraining of faculty, selection of materials
and preparation of experiences are the most immediate needs. Involving the
community has been a part of this project from the beginning, however, this
too needs continuous attention.

If the professional task needs support from outside agencies, this will be
arranged. Perhaps some segments of the structured curriculum will be most
effectively accomplished through contracting with some industry or agency
in the community or for that matter, outside the community. The essential
fact is that the staff is assuming leadership, clearly articulating a program
complete with goals, objectives, assessment plans and strategies and alternate
strategies.

FUTURE OF ACCOUNTABILITY IN THE SCHOOLS

Performance contacting, at least the versions we know today, will very
likely undergo many changes within the next few years. In fact the term may

very well disappear from the educational scene. Educational accountability on the other hand will continue to grow and continue to be a major theme in the practices of public schools. The mere fact that vast amounts of money are being committed to education is a testimonial to the fact that the demand for relating costs to products will become a way of life. Justification for funds will no longer be made in terms of the "process of education", but rather in terms of pupil learning.

What communities, boards of education and schools must do is first accept this mandate; then begin the task of developing accountable practices. Hopefully the approach will be a broad one, not limited to present day standards of performance contracts. The major thrust of accountability today is tied to the rather singular insistence that we "bring children up to" standard" in reading and mathematics. While this notion is essentially sound, indeed, necessary we must realize that this cannot be considered the whole of schooling. Schools will learn how to differentiate tasks and devise appropriate strategies, materials, activities and evaluating designs which means that schools will be capable of accountable practices.

Schools of the future will operate on a "systems" basis. Problem identifications, analysis, and definition will lead toward development of objectives, methods and prototypes which will be evaluated and perhaps lead to a recycling process.

School people will respond enthusiastically to the notions of clearly defined instructional programs, where portions of the program will be highly structured and systematically organized. Yet, major portions of the program will be open-ended, where responses to individual difference will not conform to a prescribed hierarchy of experiences. Evaluation of program outcomes will not focus solely on achievement-gain goals, but will include the entire program and its total impact.

Schools and the communities they represent will be in charge and responsible. The critics of today who fear the "education-industry" complex will have been silenced because schools of the future will not abdicate their professional responsibilities to nonprofessional. Educators will have recognized that the early attempts at performance contracting provided the prototype for professional educators. At the same time educators of the future will have accepted Charles Blashke's notion that performance contracting involving agencies outside the school has appeal as a low-risk approach because of the guarantee or penalty clauses and the fact that failure can be charged to the contracting agency and not the school.

Accountability will be the theme around which educators will change the schools to environments that evoke and maintain openness, excited curiosity, and competence.

CONTRIBUTORS TO SECTION III

The application of accountability to the operation of a real school program is complicated by many questions which demand a reevaluation of educational philosophy if the principle is to be employed. In the introductory article to this section Schiller has organized a presentation around questions and answers most frequently discussed in relation to performance contracting. He states that he is optimistic about performance contracting and the possibility it affords poor children to learn. The article following Schiller's presentation is a description of how performance contracting was actually employed in Gary, Indiana. Mecklinberger and Wilson present the colorful spectrum of educational issues that were involved in the re-examination of school problems which resulted in a contract with Behavioral Research Laboratories.

All of the articles up to this point have indicated the haunting problem of evaluation in accountability. The article from *School Management* and the articles by Millman and Schrag explore the ramifications of how a school system resolves the problem of measurement of achievement. New suggestions for evaluation and reporting student progress are suggested based upon the questions which have been raised because of the accountability concept.

Martin Deutsch et. al. in their article, the final section in this collection, focuses in on the school population that so far has been the primary target of the accountability effort-minority group children. The authors discuss in detail the problems of testing children and suggest ways to take proper compensatory action for educational problems identified.

REFERENCES

1.   Roger T. Lennon. *Accountability and Performance Contracting,* An Address to the American Educational Research Association New York, (February 5, 1971).

Jeffrey Schiller *

Performance Contracting: Some Questions and Answers †

The concept behind performance contracting is deceptively simple: You pay for what you get and only what you get. You aren't concerned with the cost to the supplier to produce what you're buying; you don't care how he produces it, as long as the product meets your quality specifications.

The idea has tremendous inherent appeal to logic. But when the concept is applied to education, it becomes not so simple. Its potential for helping poor children, however, convinced the Office of Economic Opportunity (OEO) to mount an experiment to test its capabilities.

Performance contracting in education first gained national attention when preliminary reports from a project in Texarkana indicated that a private firm was improving the reading and math skills of poor, underachieving students and that the students were staying in school. But the Texarkana experience was not set up as an experiment; it did not include the evaluation design or administrative controls necessary to assess the capabilities of performance contracting in any reliable fashion. Furthermore, the Texarkana experience, even had it included a rigorous evaluation design, would not have indicated whether any results achieved there could be replicated elsewhere.

Thus, the OEO mounted a nationwide test of performance contracting in education in the fall of 1970. The OEO has awarded grants to 18 school districts from Maine to California, and the districts have, in turn, contracted with six private firms to teach their underachieving students reading and math. The contractors' pay is determined solely by their success in improving the students' skills in these two areas.

*Mr. Schiller is director of the Experimental Research Division of OEO's Office of Planning, Research, and Evaluation.
†Reprinted from *American Education,* 7 (May, 1971), pp. 3–5.

The contractors are not even reimbursed for expenses until the students' skill levels improve by an average of one grade level in both subjects. The students' skill levels will have to improve by about 1.6 grade levels (nearly four times the improvement they had been making during a school year) before the contractors will begin to make a profit.

The American Federation of Teachers has strongly opposed both the experiment and the concept itself. The National Education Association initially agreed with the AFT, but it recently modified its stance. It now argues only that no performance contract should be approved unless it includes conditions to protect the teachers' involvement in the education process and their bargaining rights.

There is no question that teachers and school administrators throughout the country are concerned about performance contracting, as is the OEO. To clarify its position and the intent of the experiment, OEO officials have discussed performance contracting with hundreds of educators. Here are some of the questions most frequently asked by educators, with answers based on the most current information gathered by OEO.

Q. You said your interest in performance contracting was sparked by preliminary reports from Texarkana. Yet, weren't the achievement test results there seriously contaminated?

A. At this point, no one can say with any certainty just what effects the Texarkana project did have on achievement. A review alleges that the contractor included the same questions in the classroom material that later appeared on the tests. The contractor has threatened to file a suit against the school district claiming that he did not teach to the tests. So we really don't know what happened there in terms of skill improvement. We do know, however, that only 6.5 percent of those in the project dropped out of school during the year, while 17.8 percent of a comparison group dropped out during the same period.

We feel that the uncertainty surrounding the Texarkana experiences, if anything, underscores the need for a carefully designed national test of performance contracting. It's apparent that performance contracting may become an educational fad, and we feel strongly that school districts should have an indication of the concept's capabilities—and its potential pitfalls—before they leap onto the performance contracting bandwagon.

Q. What about teaching to the test? Since contractors' pay and, in some instances, even teachers' pay is dependent upon their students' performance on tests, how can the temptation to teach to the tests be overcome?

A. We don't know that it can be. That's one of the major reasons for this experiment. We do have an evaluation design that we hope will preclude any possibility of teaching to the tests.

For example, we're not basing pay on the standardized tests alone. We're also using criterion-referenced tests designed to determine how well the student has mastered the particular subject matter to which he has been exposed. The contractors won't begin to make a profit until the students show significant improvement on both the standardized and the criterion-referenced tests.

Second, students are selected on a random basis for one of three standardized tests, and those three were chosen from among eight different tests. Because neither school personnel nor the contractors' staffs are involved in administering or scoring the standardized tests, it would be difficult for them to learn which of the eight tests are being used.

Third, a random sampling of curriculum items from all companies will be run through a computer match with all of the questions on the tests to ensure that the curriculum items and test questions do coincide.

There are a number of other safeguards, but these, I think will give you an idea of the lengths to which we have gone to prevent teaching to the tests. But as I said earlier, we can't say now whether they will work. Equally important, we don't know whether they can or will be replicated by an individual school district entering into a performance contract on its own or whether it will be possible for districts to develop the relatively sophisticated criterion-referenced test.

Q. I'm concerned, too, about the fairness of using tests standardized to the performance of white, middle-class children to judge the performance of minority children from poor socio-economic backgrounds. How do you get around this problem?

A. We certainly agree that it's a problem, but I would like to point out that these children are going to be competing against essentially white, middle-class norms all their lives.

Q. Okay, but is it fair to base a teacher's pay, as some of your contractors are, on the performance of her students? After all, the children come from a variety of backgrounds, and some are just more likely to be able to succeed than others.

A. We've tried to address those issues in the experiment, too. Let me first clarify one thing. In no instance are contractors or teachers rewarded for bringing all students to one certain level—up to grade level, for example. Rather the rewards are based on improvement. The contractor will earn just as much by bringing a ninth-grader from a second-grade to a fourth-grade reading level as he would from bringing another from seventh to ninth.

We have done our best, though, to be sure that there isn't great disparity in ability among the students in the experiment. After retarded and emotionally disturbed children were excluded, the lowest-achieving students in each site were chosen from among all students performing below grade level. Most are at least two grade levels below norm, so one teacher isn't struggling to bring a seventh-grader from fifth-grade to seventh-grade achievement levels while another is being rewarded for increasing a seventh-grader's level from eighth to 10th grade, for example. Further, virtually all the students in the experiment are from the same socioeconomic background; that is, most are poor by the official Federal definition.

Q. In some neighborhoods with high family mobility, a teacher may have a completely different class at the end of the year than she had at the beginning. It doesn't seem right to judge her performance on the same standard as you would a teacher who had no transfers in or out.

A. You're right. It wouldn't be. So we have a formula to adjust payment according to the length of time the student is in class.

Q. Aside from all this, I really question whether it's appropriate to base a teacher's pay, or a private firm's pay for that matter, on the children's performance in just the two areas of reading and math. There's so much more to education than those two skills.

A. Certainly we realize that reading and math are just part of a total education. But without reading and math skills, there aren't very many subjects a student can master, are there? It's painfully evident that these students can't gain from their years in school what you and I consider other important aspects of an education until they have mastered these basic skills.

At the same time, I would like to go into another aspect of this question. One of the things that excites us most about performance contracting is the possibility for talk between teachers, administrators, and school boards while they are drawing up the contract. As the National Education Association has pointed out, learning objectives must be developed with community and professional involvement. I think the process of sorting all this out—deciding just what it is that should be done, how it should done, how to measure the results—quite probably will be fascinating. The potential is even greater when you consider that all those concerned with education—the teachers, the administrators, the school board, and the parents—will be discussing these problems together.

Q. Is it true that you have two sites where there is no private firm involved, where the school boards have contracted with their own teachers?

A. That's right. In Stockton, California, and Mesa, Arizona, the teachers will be paid bonuses in addition to their base pay at the end of the year if their students show at least eight-tenths of a grade level improvement during the program. We've made 80 percent of the maximum funds that the teachers could earn available to them now. The teachers can use these funds in any way they see fit: They may pocket the extra money, or they may use it to purchase incentive rewards for the children or additional instructional materials.

These two sites, however, really aren't a part of the performance contracting experiment, because they were started too late in the school year for any results they achieve to be comparable to the performance of the private firms. The Stockton and Mesa projects are being viewed as a completely separate and independent demonstration.

Q. What is performance contracting really going to mean for me, the teacher? If it works, am I going to find myself replaced by representatives of private firms, teaching machines, and para-professionals?

A. Let me emphasize first that I do not see a massive nationwide im-plementation of performance contracting in the immediate future. We are currently advising educators to wait until after we've seen the results of retention tests in the 1971–72 school year before initiating a performance contract. While we still have some pretty solid indications of the results by the end of the summer, the most crucial aspect of the system, the retention of any gains, won't be evident until the retention tests are analyzed.

Furthermore, before school districts individually begin to undertake performance contracts, they'll need to develop a whole new expertise in the fields of procurement, contract negotiation, and monitoring.

Then there's the turnkey phase, which is the transfer of the problems to the school systems when the contract expires. Quite honestly our office hasn't given a great deal of thought to this. School districts will have open a number of options: Should private firms be brought in only to conduct special training sessions for teachers? Should the firms be asked only to prepare new cur-riculum packages? In other words, just what sort of turnkey effort should take place after the initial pilot period? How should turnkey contracts be written? and what should the performance criteria be? What role will teachers' organi-zations play in future performance contracting projects? These are all ques-tions that will have to be dealt with after we learn whether the concept itself works.

What will happen, I think, is that new instructional systems employing audiovisual devices and paraprofessionals supervised by a teacher will be able to free certified teachers from many of the routine, secretarial duties that now take up so much of a classroom teacher's time. Even more exciting, I think, is the possibility that teachers in inner-city schools may, for the first time, be able to work with an entire class of children who are performing at grade level in reading and math. Can you imagine what you, as a teacher, could do with these youngsters if you didn't have to spend the year on remedial efforts?

I might also add that each of the private firms in the experiment are relying heavily on certified teachers.

Q. Since the experiment is more than half finished, do you have any initial indications of whether performance contracting is, indeed, successful?

A. Obviously nothing that we sense at this time is anything more than an unsupported feeling, since we won't have any data for several more months. But it does seem that, at the elementary level especially, performance contracting is turning youngsters on to learning. There's an unmistakable excitement in the first-, second-, and third-grade classes as the children learn that school can be fun, that they can learn to read and to work their math problems. As some solid indication of this, we are finding a number of students who have been habitual truants or absentees coming regularly to school for the first time. Sometimes they come only for their performance contracting classes, but even at that, they're coming for two class periods a day.

We've also learned a great deal about the administrative complexities of performance contracting. We've had some problems, as any outsider would, mounting a major project in such a short period of time. And, as I implied earlier, the school boards have recognized that they have a great deal yet to learn about administering a performance contract.

On the whole, the OEO is optimistic about the potential of performance contracting to help poor children learn. And, we hope that if we can find a way that is successful in reaching these youngsters, we'll have the key to providing them with the skills and the credentials they need to become self-supporting members of our society. If performance contracting doesn't work, the OEO will continue to seek new alternatives to improving the education of poor children.

James A. Mecklenburger and John A. Wilson *

The Performance Contract in Gary†

Never before, anywhere, has a private corporation contracted with a city school board to manage the entire program of one school—as Behavioral Research Laboratories, Palo Alto, California, have done this year with the School City of Gary, Indiana. (Gary's public schools are called "School City.")

BRL, as consultant to School City, manages Banneker Elementary School, an inner-city school of 850 students. Gary has pledged its average cost per student to BRL; no federal money is involved. BRL guarantees to raise the achievement of Banneker's students; the guarantee states that BRL will return its fee for any child who fails.

In 1971 jargon, BRL is "accountable" for results. This "performance contract" involves more money (over $2,000,000), more responsibility (an entire school), and a longer period of time (four years) than any performance contract yet written in education.

THREE PARTISANS

Gordon McAndrew, Gary's superintendent, once called this project a trial balloon at which everyone can shoot. "It has lost air, but not as much as I thought it would—and the best evidence is that the balloon is still up there," he told us early in January. He predicted that the project will work the kinks out of itself within this first year and operate smoothly thereafter.

I think it's a badly administered and badly run school," Charles Smith, president of the Gary Teachers Union, states. "If I had to make a prediction

*James A. Mecklenburger and John A. Wilson are EPDA Fellows in instructional systems technology at Indiana University.

†Reprinted from *Phi Delta Kappan*, 52 (March, 1971), pp. 406–410, by permission of the authors and Phi Delta Kappan.

right now," he told us in December, "I would predict BRL would not be here for the duration of their contract unless they change the system and they change the administration of the school."

"Banneker School is not being operated in accordance with the State Board of Education rules and regulations," State Superintendent Richard D. Wells stated at the conclusion of several months of investigation. At the January 19 meeting of the state board, a resolution called for Gary to comply with all rules and regulations by February 18, or the Banneker School would automatically be decommissioned.

A BRIEF HISTORY

BRL's *Project Read*— a sequence of programmed textbooks developed by M. W. Sullivan—has been used in Gary in recent years and has shown promise, first in summer remedial programs, then in six schools. Friendship developed over time between BRL and Gary.

"George and I got to talking once," McAndrew told us, referring to George Stern, BRL's president. "This must have been a year ago, and somehow we got to talking about what we thought about this whole 'accountability' notion. I said, kind of facetiously at the beginning, 'Tell you what. We'll contract with you to do this on a school-wide basis, not just reading but the whole shebang. Two conditions: One, it can't cost any more money than we're now spending, and two, you have to take a school as it now exists.' Out of that came a proposal." That was April. By August, in-service training of staff had begun.

Most performance contracts begin, unlike Gary's, with elaborate preparation. A school board prepares a "request for proposals" (RFP) which specifies the board's purposes, standards, funds available, constraints, and preferences for entering then evaluating, then terminating a contract. Frequently a management consultant assists in the preparation; often teachers, parents, and community leaders assist also. Finally, the RFP is published, requesting potential bidders to submit proposals; bids are received and bidders chosen to receive contracts. (BRL was among ten bidders on the Texarkana RFP, for example.) This procedure is commonplace in the defense industry, new to education.

None of these steps occurred in Gary. Despite national efforts to establish RFP's as preconditions for performance contracts[1] only one school board member in Gary even questioned that no bids except BRL's had been sought.

"Why no RFP in Gary?" we asked McAndrew. "I don't know that there

[1]See issues on *Education Turnkey News*, published monthly by Education Turnkey Systems, Inc., Washington, D.C.; or *Every Kid a Winner*, by Leon Lessinger, Simon and Schuster (1971).

were any hard and fast reasons," he said. "I suppose one could argue we should have done that. I knew something about the BRL program, I had some indication of it; I think also in talking with Stern and some of his people, I felt they kind of grabbed the concept as well as I did. For those kinds of reasons, we went that route."

Charles Smith attributes the lack of bids to BRL's merchandising expertise. We surmise deeper reasons also. One can ask, What was the hurry to begin this project? Why not wait a year, plan the project thoroughly?

Impatience to Innovate

Impatience, we sensed in Gary, permeates the city's large minority-group populations and its school board, which has only recently become minority-group dominated. Moreover, desperation characterizes many parents and schoolmen over the failure of many students, particularly nonwhite students, to acquire adequate basic skills. Banneker School, for example, ranked twenty-seventh among 29 elementary schools in achievement test scores by one reckoning; it had only one student in four reaching national norms for reading and mathematics. School City administrators tell us that the school board and the community are zealous believers in test scores, and such scores are hard to swallow.

Impatience and desperation prompted a declaration by the school board in 1970 of a "right to learn" philosophy, which calls for innovative attempts at teaching basic skills. Gary is studded with experiments to achieve better learning of basic skills, including experiments with BRL's *Project Read.* In this setting of impatience and experimentation, the nationwide emphasis on accountability made performance contracting seem irresistible.

Moreover, some insiders judged that if Gary had waited, union and Indiana state education policies would likely have scuttled such a project politically. BRL may be scuttled yet.

McAndrew himself embodies Gary's impatience. "Let's get the bugs and work them out by experience, rather than on paper," he said. "I wasn't interested in developing all kinds of fancy objectives; what I want to know is, can we teach the kids to read and add? And here's a school where 75 percent of them can't. That's the objective."

THE GRAND DESIGN

McAndrew's "trial balloon" may not survive the slings and arrows the Gary Teachers Union, the state of Indiana, some parents, some teachers, and others are hurling. Or it may spring its own leaks and collapse. Survive or not, the grand design of the program—as revealed in BRL's proposal, the contract, press statements by BRL and School City, and in interviews—will remain tantalizing.

To orchestrate its systems approach to schooling, BRL provides a center manager, "systems man," so to speak. Gary provides a learning director, responsible for supervising the academic portion of the system. Five curriculum managers bear responsibility for each of the five curriculum areas. These are language arts, mathematics, science, social studies and foreign language, and enrichment—"enrichment" being arts and crafts, music, drama, and physical education. Seventeen assistant curriculum managers perform the major instruction; 27 learning supervisors recruited from among the parents at Banneker students round out this differentiated staff.

In keeping with Gary's "right to learn" philosophy, the project began with heavy concentration on reading and mathematics, and as performance at Banneker improves, BRL will phase in the other areas.

BRL's *Project Read, Project Math,* and *Project Learn* serve as the cornerstone of teaching materials; BRL has chosen Allyn and Bacon's social studies materials and AAAS science. Inservice training prepares the staff to teach each of these materials.

BRL liberally employs consultants from outside Gary to aid whenever necessary; in fact, several consultants serve full time. As many as 15 consultants at once were present during the two weeks of in-service staff training in August.

Day-to-day evaluation of student progress is built into the teaching materials; frequent evaluation will also be provided by the staff. A "profile" on each student's mastery of a host of skills in reading, mathematics, and other areas is to be updated by the staff monthly and supplied to the child and his parents.

Moreover, two independent firms provide long-range evaluation of each child's progress. One firm, Bernard Donovan's Center for Urban Redevelopment and Education (CURE) from New York, periodically administers the Metropolitan Achievement Test. CURE also monitors the program monthly to see that BRL and Gary both adhere to the terms of the contract. The second firm will audit CURE's findings.

Banneker is designed to be a truly nongraded school, for each child begins at a point where his own knowledge ends and proceeds at his own pace. "Classes" as such disappear in these circumstances, and classrooms become "learning centers." In each center, games and activities daily supplement and reinforce book learning. In practice, children of varied ages share one learning center based on their level of skills; over time children move from center to center as they learn.

An extensive community relations program and an advisory council of famed educators and local persons are promised by BRL.

SOME LEAKS IN THE BALLOON

The letter of the Gary-BRL contract sometimes lacks the grandeur of the design.

For example, advocates say the program "cost no more," but analysis shows that—if successful—it will cost more, for two reasons.

First, roughly $34,000 per year accures to BRL as "extra" income; this is so because Indiana schools determine cost per pupil based on "average daily *attendance*" while BRL is paid based on "active *enrollment.*" If enrollment is 850 students, and daily attendance averages 95 percent of enrollment, BRL receives 5 percent more than a Gary school would; 5 percent means 43 students BRL is paid for that a Gary school would not be.

Second, BRL is paid the average annual cost per pupil in grades one through 12, which is roughly $800. However, in Gary, the average elementary school cost per pupil is less. McAndrew estimated for us that K-6 expenditures average $700; the union says $696. This means Gary pays BRL approximately $85,000 per year more than it would spend in an average elementary school.

Based on these estimates, the program could cost Gary nearly 20 percent more than it spends for an elementary school.

Three qualifications modify this analysis. First, if BRL were only 80 percent successful at raising achievement of every child, BRL would return to Gary roughly 20 percent of its fee. That is, at 80 percent success, it is true that the Banneker program would cost no more. In fact, if BRL were less successful than 80 percent Gary would save on Banneker School. Second, because salaries differ among schools, based on the staff's experience, some elementary schools in Gary may cost $800. Some also may cost less than $700. (McAndrew did not know the cost per pupil at Banneker last year.) Third, this analysis does not criticize School City for deciding to commit more money to one school, which is its perogative; it only questions the many public assertions that this program costs no, more.

When one estimates BRL's costs at Banneker, he begins to doubt that BRL is motivated by profits to be made there, even at $800 per pupil per year. Every observer we interviewed concurred with the conclusion of Otha Porter, Gary's assistant to the superintendent, that "I don't see BRL carrying dollars away from Gary." However, BRL does profit in Gary from the visibility BRL receives nationally (such as from this article), from whatever increased sales this visibility brings to BRL's publications, and—if the Banneker project succeeds—from the subsequent prestige for BRL.

In January *American School Board Journal,* BRL's president, George Stern, reveals that BRL can afford not to make a profit. If one considers the large profit margin that business usually requires in high-risk enterprise, and if one suspects that BRL may not even recoup costs in Gary, he begins to wonder what it would really cost to contract with a corporation that had to make its profit on site. It seems that Gary has gotten a bargain rate; one may look askance at the publicity that says this project can be endlessly duplicated at the Gary price. It might better be thought of as a "loss leader" aimed at the education market.

While BRL is nominally "accountable" for every student, the contract reveals a substantial minority of students for whom no guarantee applies. The annual turnover of students in Banneker School is reported at 5 percent to 7 percent. Because a student must be in the program a full year for either portion of the guarantee to apply, as many as 15 percent of the students of Banneker, over three years, will not qualify. Moreover, even at Banneker some students are already at grade level or above and should remain so without BRL. If these number 25 percent, as is said, the BRL has no effective accountability under the contract for this one-fourth of the school's students.

Most intriguing, there will be a number of students for whom an overwhelming effort would have to be mounted to raise them to grade level—special education students, for example, or simply children years below grade level who do not work well in programmed texts—much more than $800 worth of effort. Would a corporation make this effort, or instead concentrate on the vast majority more likely to succeed? That is, if one is motivated by profit, are there some students too expensive to teach?

School City's contract with BRL makes an intriguing contrast to School City's agreement with the Gary Teachers Union. The latter is precision honed to cover every contingency, while the BRL contract is often sketchy, even incomplete. It reads as if the two parties has agreed more to each other's good intentions than to a program. One wonders how CURE can monitor such a contract.

For example, the "differentiated" staff, from center manager to learning supervisors, consists mostly of the titles of positions; the contract says little about their functions or responsibilities. There shall be teaching in all curriculum areas; but there is no statement of how much instruction, its substance or how anything but reading and math will be evaluated by School City. Who holds propriety rights to materials developed at Banneker? What will the advisory council do? What might happen in the fourth year? When is payment refunded for any sixth graders who fail this year? For all these there are no provisions. Subject to School City's final authority, the contract provided BRL tremendous latitude with few guidelines.

The powerful 120-day withdrawal clause provides that either party may withdraw at will on written notice to the other. If either party withdraws, what happens to the guarantee? No answer. It appears to be a contract based more on good faith than on good business sense.

SLINGS AND ARROWS

One criticism during the first semester was that several provisions of the contract had not been implemented fully, some not at all. Despite the provision for monthly student evaluation on a profile of basic skills, the profile has yet to be issued. One "mini report" was released in December. That report prompted some adverse community reaction, for some parents realized for the first time that their children had studied only reading and math; they feared their children might be getting shortchanged. Apparently, the promised extensive community relations program had not been extensive enough to reach many parents.

Even Superintendent McAndrew became critical of the slow pace with which the three other curriculum areas had been phased into the school; meetings over Christmas vacation resulted in a promise that by second semester these areas would all have begun. In mid-January, Mrs. Sandra Irons, vice-president of the Gary Teachers Union, reported that BRL was still teaching "only reading and math, *all day long!*"

The second evaluator, the so-called auditor, was to be selected by BRL, according to the contract, in September, 1970. It has not yet been named. There never has been an advisory council.

In addition, the Gary Teachers Union (GTU) which represents virtually every teacher in Gary, has some specific grievances. A strike vote, called in September, was rescinded in the face of a threatened court order, and at midwinter, the issues remained in advisory arbitration.

GTU objected to what it saw as three violations of its agreement with School City. One related to class size—the pupil-teacher ratio was said to be greater than 40–1 (850 students, 22 teachers). School City responded first that there are no "classes" as that word is used in the union agreement, and second, that the many paraprofessionals create a ratio of pupils to adults more nearly 20–1.

A second grievance related to a clause in the BRL guarantee; School City agrees to transfer any staff person within 15 days of written notice from BRL; otherwise the guarantee will not be valid. School City responded to the union that certainly the union has no grievance until such a transfer occurs.

The third grievance related to the summary transfer of 14 teachers from Banneker in August. In Gary, teachers are virtually secure within their buildings unless they request transfer, and several provisions of the agreement prescribe procedures for involuntary transfer; these were violated, according to GTU. School City points out that none of the teachers involved filed a grievance, which indicates that the transfers were not involuntary, and that the experimental nature of the program necessitated the transfers.

FUNDAMENTAL ISSUES

Performance contracting in schools, like a crystal dropped into a stream of light, acts as a prism, displaying a colorful spectrum of fundamental educational issues and requiring they be examined anew.

Advocates of the RFP procedure state that fundamental issues are best met in the planning state—there conflicts can be anticipated and resolved before they disrupt a program. In Gary, where much planning was postponed until the program began, only now have major issues surfaced. And they may indeed disrupt the program.

Of What Importance Are Teachers?

The emphasis on performance, guarantee, and evaluation; teachers "replaced" by paraprofessionals, reliance on "teacher-proof" materials; the denial to teachers of "professional" decisions traditionally made by teachers, such as pupil placement, or curriculum decisions—these have prompted many in Gary, not only teachers, to wonder what respect BRL and School City have for teachers. Charles Smith, of the union, echoes a frequently heard sentiment in Gary that BRL would rather have hired "technicians" than teachers.

By some reports, teacher morale throughout Gary has been affected. Rumblings were reported in the *Gary Post Tribune* of December 20 that half the teachers in Banneker are considering or requesting transfer; Smith affirmed this for us in mid-January. Some observers charge that teachers are being made scapegoats for School City's financial inability to pay for needed new programs.

Who Determines What School Shall be Like?

This question lurks behind a standing offer to the union by Gary's school board and superintendent. They propose for the union a project like the one with BRL, "under the same arrangements we've made with the contractor. We'll give them the same fees, the same help, the same control, if they'll agree to the same terms", in the words of Gary school board president Alphonso Holliday. The union is very much interested in implementing better schools, the union will tell you. But not being in the business of publishing and selling materials, the union cannot afford to compete on the same terms as BRL offers. Besides, says Smith, just sit and watch one or two classrooms at Banneker for a few hours, and you won't be so excited about trying to compete with BRL or BRL's terms. Smith deems the board offer not worthy of formal reply.

How Shall We Know Who Has Learned What?

Testing, an issue educators have slipped under the rug of collective guilt for two decades, emerges with a vengeance in a contract like BRL's. For Gary and BRL have agreed to raise test scores, and it is for test scores that BRL is accountable.

The suggestion, to student and community alike, is that standardized achievement tests provide a precise yardstick against which an individual student's learning can be measured. Educators have sold this notion—or allowed school boards and politicians to sell it—for a long time.

But such tests are not that precise. As measuring devices for individual learning, they have more nearly the precision of a fist than a fine yardstick. While these tests yield "scores" that can be treated as if they are precise data, these numbers are very imprecise data. (See "Testing for Accountability," in the December, 1970, NATION'S SCHOOLS, for a fuller treatment of testing problems.) Moreover, many factors besides learning—such as maturation, testing conditions, the timing of the tests, and student attitudes toward a test—can cause scores on standardized tests to improve sufficiently to fulfill a contractor's guarantee.

While a contractor could contract on the basis of specific skills taught, most, including BRL, have not yet done so. In this ill use of testing, contractors may undercut their own future.

Raise the testing question among people involved in performance contracts and they get defensive. For example, McAndrew responded, "In fact, for better or worse or right or wrong, that's the way we do it! We let kids into college based on the SAT, and we let them into graduate school based on the Miller Analogy, and we let them into industry based on all kinds of standardized tests."

Who Wields Authority in Education?

This issue has been especially virulent in Gary, because BRL, as an interloper, makes public school authorities tense. The contract itself does little to clarify the division of authority between BRL and Gary. Between Superintendent McAndrew and BRL's George Stern, this proved tolerable. But facing this issue at Banneker, the division of authority between learning director and center manager became crucial. The learning director, a former principal, and the center manager, not a professional educator, found themselves sharing the kingpin position that Banneker's principal had for years occupied alone. The contract's only guideline was that the learning director manage academic affairs, the center manager manage nonacademic affairs. By January, sensitive feelings had grown into conflict and a host of BRL and Gary referees belatedly rushed in to straighten out the gnarled problem.

By this time, the Indiana School Board, a more powerful referee, decided that neither the contract split of authority nor the true split (according to some observers, the learning director had unwillingly become a figurehead) was legal. A man who performs the administrative duties listed in state regulations must be certified as an administrator. The question of who wields authority jumped, then, to the state level.

The state investigators identified other violations of state rules and regulations. After a series of summertime events as the contract was being written and signed, and subsequently as Gary and BRL, forged ahead on their own regardless of statutes, they communicated to the state superintendent "an attitude of . . . complete contempt" for the state office. State investigators identified six of Banneker's 22 teachers as improperly certified and found that BRL's materials had never been approved by the State Textbook Adoption Commission (and Gary never asked for a waiver of that regulation), that the teacher-pupil ratio at Banneker exceeded legal limits, and that BRL's heavy dose of reading and mathematics violated regulations about time allocation for a well-rounded curriculum.

So on January 19, the General Commission of the Indiana School Board resolved that Gary would comply with all rules and regulations within a month, or the state would decommission the school, thus withdrawing all state money from the Banneker budget.

In the face of the state's resolution, the arbitration with the Gary Teachers Union, some unrest in the community, and several fundamental issues still unresolved, we hesitate to predict (as we write this article January 20) the health of the BRL project as you read this in March.

How to Measure Performance in Your Schools*

For every argument over which of two schools is "better", the stopper goes something like this: "The accomplishments of students at any school depend heavily on the backgrounds and abilities of those students. Since socio-economic and intelligence factors can't be weighted in comparing one school with another, such comparisons are meaningless."

That used to be enough to end the argument. But not any more.

Now, through the methodology of the Yardstick Project—a Cleveland-based, foundation-supported research effort—there *is* a way to isolate the important elements in student backgrounds, so that valid achievement comparisons can be made between various schools.

With information from his own schools' records a superintendent can discover, for example, if certain students in School A are progressing faster than similar students in School B. He can chart the differences in accomplishment by school, classroom, subject, intelligence or socioeconomic position. And, if he finds significant discrepancies in progress between similar groups of pupils in different schools, he has a valid basis for suspecting that something is wrong. The Yardstick data won't tell him the cause of the problem. But it will indicate, with some certainty, *where* it is.

The Yardstick Project organizes data that accumulates in every student's record file—achievement test scores, aptitude test scores, personality inventories and the like—into a configuration that can be used to evaluate the schools, in addition to the students.

The hypothesis: Differences in the achievement growth of a group of pupils in one school, compared to the *growth* of a similar group of pupils in another school, depends less on the backgrounds of the pupils than on the programs offered in the schools themselves.

Yardsticks researchers knew that, if they hoped to design a universal "yardstick," they would have to find the necessary data in records that most schools keep. Standardized achievement tests in reading, mathematics, social studies and other subjects filled the bill perfectly. Administered once a year, they are designed so average pupils will gain one year of achievement for each year in school. And the scores show at a glance the degree of growth (or regression) from year to year.

To determine the yearly value added to pupils' scores in a particular school, it is necessary only to compute the difference between one year's mean score and the next. For example, if fifth graders at School A achieve a 5.5 grade level score on the reading achievement test, and the same group achieved a 4.2 score as fourth graders, then they scored a 1.3 growth in achievement between the fourth and fifth grades. Thus, School A's "value added" for that class for that year is 1.3.

But to compare School A's value-added score to the score of any other school would be meaningless without first limiting the comparison to students of similar intellectual, social and economic assets and liabilities—the "conditioners" of learning. After feeding hundreds of variables into a computer, Yardstick workers determined that the best indicators of these conditioners were (a) the students' IQ's, and (b) their fathers' occupations. Working with these indicators, they verified that achievement levels are closely related to intelligence and background. But they also found that *achievement growth* is not significantly dependent on those factors. It is more dependent on the students' experiences in school.

With this knowledge, Yardstick developed its "growth gauge" during pilot projects in four suburban Cleveland districts. The gauge, a series of charts comparing district-wide and individual school achievement over a period of several years, comprises:

•A chart of overall district achievement growth, grade-by-grade. Administrators can use this chart to trace changes in the achievement scores of different grades as they progressed through the school system. Children who entered or left the system during the years spanned are not included.

•A series of school-by-school charts of student achievement, according to IQ and father's occupation. [See Charts 1 and 2, p. 189. (Source:- The Yardstick Project, Cleveland, Ohio).] Administrators can use their charts to compare the yearly achievement growth of different groups of students—in other words, the value added by their schools. The charts also show if a school is getting different results with different types of students.

CHART 1

MATRIX OF ACHIEVEMENT LEVEL AND GROWTH—
SCHOOL X
Class Entering Third Grade in September, 1961

Father's Occupation	INTELLIGENCE QUOTIENT (IQ)					Average
	1 Over 127	2 119-127	3 112-118	4 102-111	5 Under 102	
1. PROFESSIONALS AND EXECUTIVES	5.4	5.4 2.5	5.7 2.4	4.4 1.4	4.5 2.1	5.8 0.5 2.1
2. MANAGERIAL AND LOWER PROFESSIONAL	5.5 3.0	5.0 2.0	5.0 1.8	5.2 2.0	4.1 1.3	4.9 2.1
3. SKILLED	— —	4.5 1.7	4.6 1.5	5.5 0.3	4.5 1.0	4.8 1.1
4. SEMISKILLED	— —	4.3 0.8	— —	3.9 0.8	4.0 0.7	4.0 1.1
5. UNSKILLED	— —	— —	— —	— —	— —	— ——
AVERAGE	5.4 2.8	5.0 1.9	5.0 1.6	4.6 1.5	4.2 1.1	4.8 2.0

NOTES Average grade equivalent in Grade 3 composite test scores.
       Average growth in grade equivalent; Grades 3 to 5.

CHART 2

MATRIX OF ACHIEVEMENT LEVEL AND GROWTH—
SCHOOL Y
Class Entering Third Grade in September, 1961

Father's Occupation	INTELLIGENCE QUOTIENT (IQ)					Average
	1 Under 127	2 119-127	3 112-118	4 102-111	5 Under 102	
1. PROFESSIONALS AND EXECUTIVES	4.8 4.6	5.4 4.4	— —	5.0 3.0	3.8 2.0	4.6 3.6
2. MANAGERIAL AND LOWER PROFESSIONAL	5.7 2.8	4.7 2.9	5.0 2.5	4.2 2.8	3.9 2.2	4.7 2.8
3. SKILLED	4.8 3.5	4.4 2.3	3.7 3.4	4.7 1.9	3.3 2.2	3.9 2.3
4. SEMISKILLED	— —	— —	— —	3.8 2.4	— —	— —
5. UNSKILLED	— —	— —	— —	— —	— —	— —
AVERAGE	5.5 3.2	4.7 2.9	4.7 2.7	4.4 2.5	3.6 2.2	4.5 2.7

NOTES Average grade equivalent in Grade 3 composite test scores
       Average growth in grade equivalent; Grades 3 to 5.

•A year-by-year chart of the district's student population, according to IQ and father's occupation. From this, schoolmen can trace changes in the socioeconomic makeup of the district's enrollment.

Equipped with Yardstick's growth gauge, a chief administrator can make a number of judgments about his schools. He can see, for instance, which schools consistently give pupils more—or less—value added per year. He can determine the strengths and weaknesses of most of his schools on an individual basis. By revealing major deviations from district norms, the growth gauge points up particular successes or failures in school programs. It does tell them where action is needed.

The growth gauge is an instrument for measuring the output of past and present school district policies and programs. But as useful as it is as an evaluation tool, it is only one-half of the yardstick. The knowledge that your schools are deficient in some areas is practically useless unless you can make plans to bring them up to par. And you can't plan effectively without knowing what implications your plans will have for future budgets and what will be required in terms of physical facilities and staffing. For these problems, the Yardstick Project supplies the other half of the yardstick: The planning model.

The planning model is also constructed from data available in most school files. Simply put, it is a tool for cost-benefit analysis through computer application. It projects planning information in three areas: (1) enrollment by grade and school for as many years into the future as needed; (2) course enrollment and the effect of adding or dropping courses, or switching courses from required to elective; and (3) results of changing school policies (such as class size or teacher load limits), and changing economic conditions (such as inflation).

Through the planning model, a superintendent and board can get answers to most of those "what if" questions that always crop up in planning sessions. The model will project the consequences of juggling class sizes, raising the teacher pay scale, building a new school, or performing a host of alternatives. The advantage, of course, is that the effects of alternate plans can be analyzed without actually trying them, without committing the district and without spending a great deal of time or money.

The application of the Yardstick program as a planning and evaluation tool is being further tested in 24 Ohio districts. The cost, for districts of fewer than 10,000 pupils, is about $5,000, half of which is being underwritten by the Martha Holden Jennings Foundation.

*Jason Millman**

Reporting Student Progress: A Case for a Criterion-Referenced Marking System[†]

Two major trends in the Sixties in education have been increased implementation of individualized instruction[1] and greater emphasis by test specialists on criterion-referenced measurements. My primary purpose in this paper is to indicate how these trends invite a completely different format than that presently used for the reporting of school progress to students and to their parents.

INDIVIDUALIZING INSTRUCTION

Instruction can be individualized in two ways: pacing and branching. Linear programming is an example of individualizing instruction by permitting each student to go through a set of instructional materials at his own rate. Use of self-teaching materials effects differential progress. When individuals are permitted to learn at their own rate, the more able students will complete the instruction and demonstrate competence many times more quickly than the less able students.[2]

*Jason Millman is professor of educational research methodology in the department of education at the New York State College of Agriculture, Cornell University, Ithaca, N.Y., and editor of the *Journal of Educational Measurement.*

†Reprinted from *Phi Delta Kappan,* 52 (December, 1970), pp. 226–230, by permission of the author and Phi Delta Kappan.

[1]For example, the *Health, Education and Welfare News* (November 9, 1969) reports that nearly 50,000 children are learning mathematics mostly on their own with the University of Pittsburgh Individually Prescribed Instruction materials.

[2]Benjamin S. Bloom, "Learning for Mastery." *Evaluation Comment,* 12 (May, 1968, published by the UCLA Center for the Study of Evaluation of Instructional Programs); and Robert Glaser, "Adapting the Elementary School Curriculum to Individual Performance," in *Proceedings of the 1967 Invitational Conference on Testing Problems,* Benjamin Bloom, chairman (Princeton, N.J.: Educational Testing Service, 1967), pp. 3–36.

Providing alternative instructional materials is a second way to individualize instruction. This method may be implemented on a macro level (e.g., students study different elective courses) or on a more micro level (e.g., the particular way a student is taught a unit of instruction depends on his interests and learning style).[3] Of course, individual pacing and providing alternative instructional materials can be combined.

Regardless of how the instruction is individualized, the usual procedures of assessing student progress seem inappropriate. When students in a class are proceeding at their own rate or "doing their own thing" or both, the practice of assigning grades on the basis of the administration of a common achievement test is inapplicable.[4] More appropriate would be a report of an individual's own progress. These points will be elaborated in this article.

Criterion-Referenced Measurement

Since the writings of Ebel and Glaser on the subject[5] there has been increased attention to criterion-referenced measurement, which relates test performance to absolute standards rather than to the performance of others.

> Criterion-referenced measures are those which are used to ascertain an individual's status with respect to some criterion, i.e., performance standard. It is because the individual is compared with some established criterion, rather than other individuals, that these measures are described as criterion-referenced. The meaningfulness of an individual score is not dependent on comparison to others.
> . . . Norm-referenced measures are those which are used to ascertain an individual's performance in relationship to the performance of other individuals on the same measuring device. The meaningfulness of the individual score emerges from the camparison. It is because the individual is compared with some normative group that such measures are described as norm-referenced. Most standardized tests of achievement or intellectual ability can be classified as norm-referenced measures.[6]

[3]See, for example, John C. Flanagan, "Functional Education for the Seventies." *Phi Delta Kappan* (September, 1967), pp. 27–32.

[4]This point was made by Henry M. Brickell, who writes: " . . . If the innovation individualizes instruction in such a way that students begin to move through the same material at variable rates of speed controlled by their mastery of the material, report cards which tell parents about the student's degree of success in learning the content (usually expressed as letter grades indicating class standing) should have been replaced by new report cards which tell parents about the student's rate of progress." From "Appraising the Effects of Innovations in Local Schools," in Ralph W. Tyler, ed., *Educational Evaluation: New Roles, New Means* (Chicago: National Society for the Study of Education, 68th Yearbook, Part II, 1969), pp. 301–302.

[5]Robert L. Ebel, "Content Standard Test Scores." *Educational and Psychological Measurement* (Spring, 1962), pp. 15–25; and Robert Glaser, "Instructional Technology and the Measurement of Learning Outcomes: Some Questions." *American Psychologist* (August, 1963), pp. 519–21.

[6]W. James Popham and T. R. Husek, "Implications of Criterion-Referenced Measurement." *Journal of Educational Measurement* (Spring, 1969), pp. 1–9.

An example of a criterion-referenced test is presented in Figure 3.

Objective: Given a set of objects, the student will be able to identify the longest and/or shortest. (Words to be read aloud to the student.)

1. Put a line through the *shortest* boy.

2. Put a line through the *longer* rope.

FIGURE 3. Examples of a criterion-referenced measurement.

These items were chosen because they constitute a representative set of situations which a student should deal with correctly if he is to demonstrate proficiency in the desired skill. Regardless of how his classmates perform, the student passes the test only if he answers all (or, possibly, nearly all) of the questions correctly. These same items could be part of a norm-referenced test. In such a case, they would have been selected because of their usefulness in discriminating among the students. How well a student does on such a norm-referenced test would be determined by comparing his score with those of his classmates.

A, B, C GRADING IS NORM-REFERENCED

The grading systems which use number or letter scales, as found in the vast majority of schools,[7] are indicators of the comparative performance of

[7]"Reporting Pupil Progress." *Nea Research Bulletin* (October, 1969), pp. 75–76.

students and are devices for *ranking*. Thus, this system is not useful for indicating an individual's progress against performance criteria. Some teachers may object, arguing that their grades *rate* their students' command of course content or degree of fulfillment of predetermined course obejctives. Consider these four arguments against such a position:

1. Teachers who say, "The test scores speak," and "I do not grade on a curve," find themselves using adjustments to make the grade distributions more reasonable. These adjustments take such forms as giving another test, raising marks by some mysterious formula, making the next test easier, and altering grading standards. Naturally, a teacher's increased experience with what students in his school and in his course can do on his examinations reduces the extent of the adjustments necessary to insure that a reasonable curve will result.

2. There is a marked similarity between grade distributions found in high schools and those found in colleges having a different quality of students. If grades were assigned according to standards so that an A, in introductory Physics for example, meant a certain proficiency, then the percentage of students earning an A should be substantially different at the different schools. This is not the case.

3. Perhaps the most convincing evidence to support the claim that A, B, C grading or one, two, three grading is norm-referenced grading is that as the quality of students entering any given college goes up over the years, as attested to by objective test data, the grade distributions of that college remain essentially unchanged.

4. Regardless of what the teacher feels the grade signifies, the students feel they are competing with each other, that it, that the grade is a measure of comparative achievement.

INSTRUCTIONAL GOALS AND MANAGEMENT

A key task of our schools is to maximize the amount of a subject each student has "mastered."[8] Indeed, a reason for having individualized instruction is to maximize achievement by appropriate pacing and provision of instructional materials. The rational management of such an individualized instructional system requires knowing whether each student can perform at

---

[8]See, especially, Bloom, *op. cit.* The ungraded school, an administrative device to facilitate adapting the curriculum and modifying instruction to the individual learner, is said to be based on the assumptions that "up to a certain point a 'slow learner', if taught appropriately and given more time, can learn the same things that more capable students do" (an assumption of the Carroll Model of School Learning which was followed in the Bloom article) and that "up to that certain point all students should learn the same things." Mauritz Johnson, Jr., *Grouping in Graded and Ungraded Schools,* Cornell University Curriculum and Instruction Series, No. 4, pp. 15–16.

some criterion level on measures of the component objectives of the system. Such criterion-referenced measurement characterizes the management of the well-known University of Pittsburgh Individually Prescribed Instruction system.[9]

REPORT CARDS

If criterion-referenced measurement is to serve guidance and monitoring functions for the instructional program, it is a logical next step that such measurement become the basis for communication regarding student progress. Not only could student records contain a listing of skills to be checked as proficiency is demonstrated, but so too could the reports going to the students and their parents.

The essential features of such a report card are: a listing of objectives (most likely abbreviated descriptions of tasks), space to indicate if proficiency has been demonstrated, and a checking system which identifies objectives achieved since the previous report. Since parents, quite reasonably, desire norm-referenced information, some grade designation *might* be included at the lower grades. For high school or junior college courses, skills for which proficiency is usually demonstrated may be differentiated from optional or supplementary skills. A sketch of the kind of report card being suggested is shown in Figure 4.

The number of skills shown on the report card will probably be less than the number used in the school record. For example, before the teacher would check "Understands dollar value of money," he may require identification of coins, converting coins to equivalent amounts of other coin values, counting dollar value of coin sets, and making change.

The report card should probably use objectives stated narrowly enough so that all students will have a chance during a marking period to demonstrate proficiency on tests relative to at least one objective.

The reporting system being suggested should not be confused with various self-marking plans which frequently have been advocated.[10] The mature student, however, may best be able to assess whether proficiency has been demonstrated on objectives covering hard-to-measure student qualities and skills.

---

[9]William W. Cooley and Robert Glaser, "An Information and Management System for Individually Prescribed Instruction," technical report (University of Pittsburgh Learning Research and Development Center, 1968).

[10]See, for example, Peter G. Filene, "Self-Grading: An Experiment in Learning." *Journal of Higher Education* (June, 1969), pp. 451–58; and Ronald J. Burke, "Some Preliminary Data on the Use of Self-Evaluations and Peer Ratings in Assigning University Course Grades." *Journal of Educational Research* (July/August, 1969), pp. 444–48.

MATHEMATICS
Grade Two

Skill	Date
Concepts	
Understands commutative property of addition (e.g., 4+3 = 3+4)	9/27
Understands place value (e.g., 27 = 2 tens + 7 ones)	10/3
Addition	
Supplies missing addend under 10 (e.g., 3+? = 5)	10/8
Adds three single-digit numbers	
Knows combinations 10 through 19	
*Adds two 2-digit numbers without carrying	
*Adds two 2-digit numbers with carrying	
Subtraction	
Knows combinations through 9	10/4
*Supplies missing subtrahend − under 10 (e.g., 6 − ? = 1)	
*Supplies missing minuend − under 10 (e.g., ? − 3 = 4)	
*Knows combinations 10 through 19	
*Subtracts two 2-digit numbers without borrowing	
Measurement	
Reads and draws clocks (up to quarter hour)	
Understands dollar value of money (coins up to $1.00 total)	
Geometry	
Understands symmetry	
Recognizes congruent plan figures − that is, figures which are identical except for orientation	
Graph Reading	
*Knows how to construct simple graphs	
*Knows how to read simple graphs	

*In Jefferson Elementary School, these skills are usually learned toward the end of grade two. Some children who need more than average time to learn mathematics may not show proficiency on tests of these skills until they are in grade three.

FIGURE 4. Report card based on a system of criterion-referenced measurement.

IS THE PLAN FEASIBLE?

It is not reasonable to expect the typical school to itemize, from scratch, a comprehensive set of objectives and to construct related criterion-referenced measures. In the elementary school, students often use workbooks containing exercises which could serve as criterion-referenced tests. The tasks these students are expected to perform are isomorphic to the objectives.

Further, the objectives of many new curricula have already been identified and test items covering these objectives have been provided.[11] More

[11]For example, objectives of the Wisconsin Design for Reading Skill Development, an individualized reading system for the elementary school, are assessed through commercially available criterion-referenced tests. These objectives and tests were developed by the Wisconsin Research and Development Center for Cognitive Learning and are distributed by National Computer Systems, 4401 W. 76th Street, Minneapolis, Minnesota 55435.

frequently the staff in individual school systems is constructing "behaviorally stated" objectives in conjunction with learning packages covering these objectives.[12] Commerical firms are now including tests in their learning packages.[13]

The most ambitious effort in this regard is the Instructional Objectives Exchange, which was created to perform the following functions:

> Serve as a clearinghouse through which the nation's schools can exchange instructional objectives, thereby capitalizing on the developmental efforts of other educators rather than being obliged to commence afresh the development of objectives. Collect and, when necessary, develop measuring techniques suitable for assessing the attainment of the objectives available through the Exchange. Develop properly formulated instructional objectives in important areas where none currently exist, that is, fill the gaps not covered by available objectives.[14]

In connection with an ESEA Title III project, 30,000 items have been produced, accompanied by the objectives they are measuring.[15] Thus, the availability of statements of objectives and criterion-referenced items permits the teacher or school staff to *select* those objectives or items most relevant to their situation rather than to *construct* them.

Even admitting the feasibility of selecting and preparing objectives and tests (a *relatively* fixed, one-time-only expenditure of time), the question of how to operate the system remains.

When instruction is individualized, students must assume an increased responsibility for their own activities. It is reasonable to expect that at least the older students can assume responsibility for self-administering the criterion-referenced tests and, in some cases, scoring them. The teacher need only place a single checkmark (or date) to record the fact that proficiency has been demonstrated. At reporting periods, the teacher merely transfers these checks to the cards.

When considering feasibility, it should be remembered that a school system need not convert to the criterion-referenced reporting system in all subject areas at once. A school system, or an individual school or teacher, may choose to utilize the criterion-referenced reporting system first in subject areas where the defining and measuring of objectives is easiest. These areas would include mathematics and those vocationally oriented courses in which a large segment of the objectives involves performance skills.

---

[12]See, for example, three articles on An Educational System for the 70's, *Phi Delta Kappan* (December, 1969), pp. 199–210.

[13]For example, Individual Mathematics Programme Kits, Rigby Ltd., Australian Council for Educational Research, Frederick St., Hawthorne, Victoria 3122 Australia; and Individual Mathematics: Drill and Practice Kits, L. W. Singer Company, Westminster, Md.

[14]W. James Popham, *Instructional Objectives Exchange* (Los Angeles: UCLA Graduate School of Education, no date), p. 1.

[15]Evaluation for Individual Instruction, Downers Grove School District 99, 1400 West Maple Ave., Downers Grove, Ill. 60515.

ADVANTAGES

The emphasis on proficiency forces the school staff to focus on both instructional process and outcomes rather than on process alone and to view formal education "as an enterprise which is designed to *change* human beings so that they are better, wiser, more efficient."[16] The instructional means are judged by the ends achieved. In these days when decentralization brings parents closer to the schools, when parents demand more information, when school bond issues are being rejected because of ignorance about the school's benefit as well as for financial reasons, and when accountability is in fashion, the staffs of our schools would be well advised to demonstrate that the modifications they wish to promote do occur.

The report card format suggested in this paper permits a degree of communication and accountability to the parent not possible with other systems of reporting. Every student will be shown to be learning, and both the parent and student will know better what has been learned and what can now be done.

Besides change of focus, other advantages of a criterion-referenced system have been listed elsewhere.[17] These include improved student attitudes where the less wholesome competition for grades gives way to competition (frequently within oneself) to acquire proficiencies in much the same way that a scout earns his badges.

LIMITATIONS

Objections have been raised against requiring that objectives be stated in behavioral terms and also against criterion-referenced measurement. There is the danger that objectives involving hard-to-measure qualities like appreciations and attitudes may be slighted. If such objectives are taken seriously by the school staff, then it has a responsibility to provide experiences for developing the desired qualities. It is then possible to list on a criterion-referenced report card "expressible objectives,"[18] meaning that certain tasks or encounters are to be experienced. To take an example, *to visit a slum area* may be an objective (more appropriately, a learning activity) which is satisfied when the visit is actually made. Nevertheless, school staff should give thought both to the intended changes in appreciation, understanding, and so forth, in the learners which lie behind the selection of the

[16]W. James Popham, "Focus on Outcomes: A Guiding Theme of ES '70 Schools." *Phi Delta Kappan* (December, 1969), p. 208.

[17]William Clark Trow, "On Marks, Norms, and Proficiency Scores." *Phi Delta Kappan* (December, 1966), pp. 171–73.

[18]Elliott W. Eisner, "Instructional and Expressive ELducational Objectives: Their Formulation and Use in Curriculum," in Robert E. Stake, series ed., *American Educational Research Association Monograph Series on Curriculum Evaluations* (Chicago: Rand McNally, 1969), pp. 1–31.

activity and to the criteria for determining whether these changes did take place.

Other objectives which are in danger of being slighted involve the ability to retain and transfer what is learned. To ascertain if skills are retained, the students could be given the criterion-referenced tests at a later date. To record the results of such testing, an extra column of blanks could be provided on the report card or perhaps only on the form used by the staff for monitoring.

The nature of the desired transfer skills needs to be identified. Once this is done, construction of appropriate criterion-referenced tests will often be straightforward.[19] It is safe to predict that sizable proportions of students will not be able to demonstrate proficiency on "transfer" tests until key elements of the new task have been specifically taught.

In terms of sheer number of words written, criterion-referenced tests have not received as much criticism as has the requirement that objectives be stated in behavioral terms.[20] There are however, at least two very difficult problems associated with criterion-referenced testing: specifying the universe of tasks and determining proficiency standards. Both of these difficulties remind us that the wording of the objective is perhaps less important than the selection of tasks and criteria.[21]

As Loevinger has pointed out in another context,[22] one cannot define a universe of possible test items (tasks) sample randomly from them except in some unusually restrictive situations. The second difficulty arises from the fact that the choice of a proficiency standard is, to a large extent, arbitrary. Whether a student's performance is good enough to permit him to commence instruction in new skills is, in the final analysis, a matter of judgment.

These very real difficulties are not limited to criterion-referenced tests. To insure that norm-referenced tests have content validity, the universe of relevant content must be defined. Further, in determining who gets a satisfactory score (for example, on an achievement test used to assign grades), one

[19]Of course, it will be infeasible or virtually impossible to measure whether certain skills transfer to "real life." If such transfer skills are part of the instructional objectives, reasonable efforts should be made during instruction to simulate these real life experiences. Compromises will then have to be made concerning what will count as evidence that these transfer skills have been acquired.

[20]It is not my position that objectives need to be stated in behavioral terms and, indeed, the objectives shown in Figure 2 are not. Rather, I am arguing that what counts as evidence that the objectives have been met should be made explicit by the items constituting the criterion-reference tests.

[21]There is the added question of college admissions. The school records will, under the system being proposed, contain information about how much a student has achieved—what he can and cannot do—rather than whether he earned higher grades than his classmates. This record, together with aptitude scores, letters of reference, the application form, and other items, should permit a sound basis for making admission decisions, especially in those institutions moving closer to an open enrollment policy.

[22]Jane Loevinger, "Person and Population as Psychometric Concepts," *Psychological Review* (March, 1965), pp. 143–55.

cannot escape the fact that these decisions also involve judgment and are often quite arbitrary.

Some things can be done to deal partially with these problems. Criterion tasks should be constructed which sample a great range of situations and methods covered by the objective. For example, in Figure 3, note that the longest object is not always the largest, nor does it span the most distance horizontally. It was a conscious decision to include in the item universe only comparisons among pictures of objects of the same class and to exclude items which required reading and fine perceptual discriminations.

The question of what proportion of correct responses is needed to demonstrate proficiency is not an easy one to answer. Perfect or near-perfect performance should be required if (a) the objective is worded such that near mastery is expected, (b) the skills are deemed important for future learning, (c) items are the objective type (thus increasing the likelihood of successful guessing), and (d) the test is short and thus likely to be unreliable. Less stringent cutoffs might be employed if any of the above four conditions are relaxed. Certainly, there is no good reason why the same cutoff score should be used on every test.

Many, but by no means all, of the problems involved in using a system of criterion-referenced testing will be minimized with increased experience with this mode of assessing school progress. The more refractory of these problems are inherent in any measurement system. But when a school staff is committed to changing students, to helping them grow and learn and feel, and to focusing on outcomes, then reporting school progress using a criterion-referenced measurement system not only follows logically, but there is, in fact, no viable alternative.

Peter Schrag *

A New Standard of Accomplishment[†]

Anyone who looks back over the last five years in American education must be struck by the realization that many of the things we all knew for certain in 1960 or 1962 are just not so. I think almost any writer who indulged his anger at the obvious failures of American schools must, by now, have become a more chastened man, not because the failures don't exist but because the solutions are elusive and because some of our best intentions are turning into social mistakes.

One major fact—a new consciousness of the crucial place of education —underlines nearly everything that has happened in American education in the past decade. The old rhetoric about the importance of learning has been reinforced with economic and social statistics and with data on employment and unemployment. When there were other options, the farm, the shop, the apprenticeship, book learning may have been considered sissy stuff. Now the book is a prime weapon in the arsenal of the toughest economic competitors in America. The results of this new awareness are manifest in two divergent thrusts to reform education. The first of these is the national movement toward the development of new curricula, the improvement of teachers' salaries, and the intellectual upgrading of schools. Much of this has taken place and continues to take place in middle-class schools that are fired by parental ambitions, by pressure for college admission, and by a national passion to upgrade the pool of manpower in the name of defense and economic growth.

In hundreds of schools the rhetoric of good education, if not the practice, has shifted from content to process, from the presentation of ingestion of data

*Peter Schrag, associate education editor of *Saturday Review,* former director of publication and assistant secretary of Amherst College. His books include *Village School Downtown* and *Voices in the Classroom.*

†Reprinted by permission from the February 1968 issue of the *Wilson Library Bulletin.* Copyright © 1968 by The H. W. Wilson Company.

to some sort of Socratic questioning and inductive thought. The new courses in history, physics, biology, mathematics, chemistry, and the social sciences, the infusion of linguistics into the teaching of English—all of these things are shifting the focus from the accumulation of formulas, facts, and conclusions to the stimulation, hopefully, of styles of thought, of trying to make students understand how historians or physicists operate, of the power of the various disciplines and of their limitations. Some of these changes, like many other innovation (team teaching, nongraded classes, etc.), still seem rather perfunctory in actual practice. Teachers trained to use textbooks sometimes make Socrates sound like the weekly quiz, and most of the curriculum developers are rediscovering the importance of teacher training, the significance of making a curriculum relevant to the interests of students, and the importance of student participation in the learning process. Thus the trail that led away from the excesses of progressive education a decade ago is bringing even the most tough-minded educators back to a new confrontation with John Dewey. The basic change, at any rate, was to make the schools of the middle class intellectually more rigorous and more demanding, and thereby to make the definition and the requirements of good education even more remote for the disadvantaged. Every curricular improvement in the better schools makes access to "good education" even more difficult for those who are unprepared for it.

The second thrust, stimulated by the civil rights movement, is toward "Equality of Educational Opportunity." No one is certain what that phrase means or whether indeed it can have a meaning. Historically it merely suggested that all children were to have access to similar educational resources, the same books and teachers, the same financing, the same treatment from the schools. Where a child failed, it was his responsibility: he failed because he was not sufficiently intelligent or too lazy, not because the school was considered to have failed him. The big change of the last decade reflects the growing rejection of that old conception of democratic education and the assignment of positive responsibility to the school for the education of all children, no matter how apparently unwilling or unable they may appear. Five years ago the solutions seemed relatively simply; essentially they amounted to a combination of "cultural enrichment" and integration. Children who were labeled disadvantaged could be stimulated through intensive programs of preschool education which would give them the language, the stories, the "experience" that teachers took for granted among their middle-class peers, and they would thereby achieve education parity as they went through school. Integration, which would guarantee them the same teachers and facilities and exposure to other children, would take care of the rest. Part of the difficulty of combining integration with enrichment and "compensatory education" is that they were always in some measure antithetical. If certain children required special attention or programs, it would be difficult, at least at first, to integrate them with others. At the same time, compensatory education always carried with it a tone of condescension.

We will never know what the real possibilities of those solutions are because they were never seriously tried. The general outcome of the integration battles of the early 1960's seems to have been more segregation, not less, while the chasm between the schools of privilege and the schools of poverty has become wider, more pronounced, and more insurmountable. America clearly has two school systems, one for the middle class and one for the poor. In each, the teachers, the students, the community, and the general atmosphere—the way business is done—are internally consistent. Where the community is affluent, the schools are likely to be newer, the teachers better paid, the dropout rates lower, the pathology less apparent. Where the community is poor, there is a prior assumption that there will be trouble, that children will fail, that teachers are hostile. Both of these conclusions are loaded with exceptions. The suburban schools can sometimes be vicious, empty, and intellectually shabby places; there are exciting classes in the ghetto. Nonetheless, the generalizations usually hold.

The fact that educational performance is so closely linked with social and economic background raises a much more disturbing issue: do schools make any significant difference? All of us can talk about experiences with exciting teachers and can recount moments in our own lives and in those of others who someone or something in a school made a substantial difference in a person's life, where new ideas and new possibilities were suddenly discovered. Yet we often talk about these moments as we would talk of miracles that help justify an otherwise perfunctory faith that is constantly battered by the tests of everyday experience. Formal schooling has its healers, but it also becomes more and more apparent as a great destroyer, a device that bruises and demoralizes children and that selects and rejects them not according to a presumably fair sampling of abilities but according to race and social background.

As formal education becomes more crucial to economic and social success, as it becomes the one available avenue of entry into the cultural mainstream, so also it becomes the major instrument of rejection and denial. Each day there are fewer alternatives, and each day educational selection becomes more ruthless as a determinant of economic acceptability. Education has now become the most effective way for an advantaged family to endow its children, to provide them with the privilege that birth, wealth, and family standing no longer supply. The conventional assets of economic and social privilege are converted into academic assets for later reconversion into new economic assets. The disadvantaged who lack economic and social power have nothing to convert, and it is unlikely that a class whose privilege depends on academic inequality will willingly open the gates to a whole new group of competitors.

The phrase "Equality of Educational Opportunity," which is the title of the so-called Coleman Report, a 737-page, federally financed study of educational inequities in the United States, is a philosophical and political "black-box" that has not yet been opened. Does equality mean equal inputs or equal results? Does successful education for the children of the ghetto demand the making of middle-class suburbanites? Is there a way of educating a Negro child without forcing him to deny his own background and his own cultural style? What is it that the culture of the ghetto can offer the mainstream, if anything, and how do we make use of it? The failures of school integration, as most of us know, have stimulated pressure for ghetto control of community schools, demands for more black teachers, Negro history, and a locally directed educational effort aimed at asserting parental power and price in relationship to the educational process. Given the rigidity of many city school administrations (where the neighborhood school is like a colonial outpost), there may, at this point, be few political alternatives if ghetto parents want better education. Nonetheless, the more local schools become detached, the more difficult it will be to achieve any genuine integration.

In New York and other cities there are now serious proposals for decentralizing schools and giving local communities substantial control over them. Many people who feel overwhelmed by the educational failures of the inner cities feel that no other possibility is now open, and that segregated education is preferable to no education at all. And yet as long-run solution decentralization may rest on a romantic Populist myth. What we seem to be doing is giving responsibility for the most difficult and heretofore insoluble social problems to those who, at least on the face of it, have the fewest resources and the least experience for dealing with them, simply because they are the "people." We seem to believe that good intentions with a small share of political power will enable people in the ghetto to accomplish what no one else has been able to do. I think I share with many others a personal ambivalence about the possibilities of decentralization and community power. It may well be on the one hand that the pride and morale, as well as the adult education of a community, will be stimulated by a sense of control. It may also be that at least another generation of children will be miseducated while their parents battle over politics, jobs, and appropriations, and while they begin to work out the incredibly difficult problems of operating an urban school. The most persuasive rationale for community control may well be community education and the regeneration of a sense of participation. The prime beneficiaries of decentralization, at least at first, may not be children but parents. In trying to operate schools and determine their policies, they may learn a great deal indeed.

The alternative to decentralization is probably a great deal more radical and expensive. What it suggests, essentially, is that where the culture of poverty (either black or white) is inconsistent with middle-class aspirations, where the debilitating effects of broken homes and dangerous streets impede effective learning, there the school must become a total agency with sufficient resources, rewards, and influence to attract children away, even if that means that they must reject their parents and their background. Such a school represents the closest thing we have yet seen to an educational "final solution" in which the school offers three meals a day, a full range of jobs and social activities, and possibly even residential arrangements, all of it designed to wean children away from the lives they normally lead.

The most likely possibility, of course, is that neither of these approaches will be carried very far, that, at best, we will begin to take some hesitant steps toward the implementation of a little of each. (Ultimately, pragmatic, locally devised approaches, rather than some national "solution" may be more effective. The techniques and ideas that may work in one community will not necessarily be useful in another. The problems of learning in New York may be the same as those in Chicago, but political attitudes and conditions are likely to be sufficiently different to demand a different set of solutions.) The national commitment to any kind of educational equality, like the commitment to integration, is far more rhetorical than real, while our economic and psychological dependency on inequality is overwhelming. What I am suggesting here is not simply the apparent need for an economic lower class which will do the menial jobs and the dirty work: the labor of such people, given the technology, is less and less necessary. What may be necessary (and I don't wish to sound too cynical) is a national visible lower class, a class of failures, that will give the often empty, conventional success more meaning.

And yet, even if we disregard such sinister reflections, we are still confronted with the essential problem of our educational structure. If integration has any meaning in education indeed if education is to have any substantial social value, it must also include the relationship of school and community, the transfer from school to job and back again, and the recognition that education is not solely and perhaps not even primarily the possession of the schools. Racial integration makes very little sense as long as we conceive of education in terms of diplomas, ranks, grades, failures, and boxes: boxes for the middle class, boxes for blacks, boxes for whites, boxes for adults, boxes for people who are out of school, boxes for college admission, boxes for dropouts. In this sense integration and real education are nearly synonymous, and they have only incidentally any connection with the issue of race. Ultimately the question is whether we are really courageous enough to provide a sufficiently broad spectrum of educational opportunities, and not to worry about who's in and who's out and where he happens to live. Are we prepared to regard our communities as total educational instruments where all comers are welcome? In the structure of the American school establishment, segregation, repression, competition, and failure are all essential parts, and until we are ready to stop selecting people out, almost any conception of good education is going to drag behind it some form of segregation and inequality. The successful owe part of their achievements to this system; success is partly defined by failure, and on the dark side of opportunity lies an equal measure of rejection. The test of this society will lie in the extent of which it can define its progress in terms that include the lives of its less fortunate citizens. We need a new standard of accomplishment.

Guidelines for Testing Minority Group Children*

INTRODUCTION

American educators have long recognized that they can best guide the development of intellect and character of the children in their charge if they take the time to understand these children thoroughly and sympathetically. This is particularly true with respect to the socially and culturally disadvantaged child.

Educators must realize that they hold positions of considerable responsibility and power. If they apply their services and skills wisely they can help minority group children to overcome their early disadvantages, to live more constructively, and to contribute more fully to American society.

Educational and psychological tests may help in the attainment of these goals if they are used carefully and intelligently. Persons who have a genuine commitment to democratic processes and who have a deep respect for the individual, will certainly seek to use educational and psychological tests with minority group children in ways that will enable these children to attain the full promise that America holds out to all its children.

Educational and psychological tests are among the most widely used and most useful tools of teachers, educational supervisors, school administrators, guidance workers, and counselors. As is the case with many professional tools, however, special training and diagnostic sensitivity are required for the intelligent and responsible use of these instruments. That is why most col-

*Prepared by a Work Group of the Society for the Psychological Study of Social Issues (Division 9 of the American Psychological Association), Martin Deutsch, Joshua A. Fishman, *Chairman,* Leonard Kogan, Robert North, and Martin Whiteman. Reprinted from the *Journal of Social Issues,* Vol. XX, Supplement No. 2 (1964), pp. 129–145, by permission of the authors and editor.

leges and universities offer courses in educational and psychological testing. It is also the reason for the growing number of books and brochures designed to acquaint educators and their associates with the principles and procedures of proper test selection, use and interpretation.[1]

Responsible educational authorities recognize that it is as unwise to put tests in the hands of untrained and unskilled personnel as it is to permit the automobile or any highly technical and powerful tool to be handled by individuals who are untrained in its use and unaware of the damage that it can cause if improperly used.

The necessity for caution is doubly merited when educational and psychological tests are administered to members of minority groups. Unfortunately, there is no single and readily available reference source to which test users can turn in order to become more fully acquainted with the requirements and cautions to be observed in such cases. The purpose of this committee's effort is to provide an introduction to the many considerations germane to selection, use and interpretation of educational and psychological tests with minority group children, as well as to refer educators and their associates to other more technical discussions of various aspects of the same topic.

The term "minority group" as we are using it here is not primarily a quantitative designation. Rather it is a status designation referring to cultural or social disadvantage. Since many Negro, Indian, lower-class white, and immigrant children have not had most of the usual middle-class opportunities to grow up in home, neighborhood, and school environments that might enable them to utilize their ability and personality potentials fully, they are at a disadvantage in school and in after-school and out-of-school situations as well. It is because of these disadvantages, reflecting environmental deprivations and experimental atypicalites, that certain children may be referred to as minority group children.

The following discussion is based in part on some of the technical recommendations developed for various kinds of tests by committees of the American Psychological Association, the American Educational Research Association, and the National Council on Measurement in Education (1954, 1955). Our contribution is directed toward specifying the particular considerations that must be kept in mind when professional educators and those who work with them use educational and psychological tests with minority group children.

CRITICAL ISSUES IN TESTING MINORITY GROUPS

Standardized tests currently in use present three principal difficulties when they are used with disadvantaged minority groups: 1) they may not

---

[1]See for example, Katz (1958), Froelich and Hoyt (1959), Cronbach (1960), Anastasi (1961), Thorndike and Hagen (1961).

provide reliable differentiation in the range of the minority group's scores, 2) their predictive validity for minority groups may be quite different from that for the standardization and validation groups, and 3) the validity of their interpretation is strongly dependent upon an adequate understanding of the social and cultural background of the group in question.

I. Reliability of Differentiation

In the literature of educational and psychological testing, relatively little attention has been given to the possible dependence of test reliability upon subcultural differences. It is considered essential for a test publisher to describe the reliability sample (the reference group upon which reliability statements are based) in terms of factors such as age, sex, and grade level composition, and there is a growing tendency on the part of test publishers to report subgroup reliabilities. But to the best of our knowledge, none of the test manuals for the widely used tests give separate reliability data for specific minority groups. Institutions that use tests regularly and routinely for particular minority groups would do well to make their own reliability studies in order to determine whether the tests are reliable enough when used with these groups.

Reliability Affected by Spread of Scores

In addition to being dependent on test length and the specific procedure used for estimating reliability (e.d., split-half or retest), the reliability coefficient for a particular test is strongly affected by the spread of test scores in the group for which the reliability is established. In general, the greater the spread of scores in the reliability sample, the higher the reliability coefficient. Consequently, if the tester attempts to make differentiations within a group which is more homogeneous than the reference or norm group for which reliability is reported, the actual effectiveness of the test will be found to be lower than the reported reliability coefficient appears to promise. For many tests, there is abundant evidence that children from the lower socio-economic levels commonly associated with minority group status tend to have a smaller spread of scores than do children from middle-income families, and such restriction in the distribution of scores tends to lower reliability so far as differentiation of measurement with such groups is concerned.[2]

Characteristics of Minority Group Children that Affect Test Performance

Most of the evidence relating to the contention that the majority of educational and psychological tests tend to be more unreliable, i.e., more characterized by what is technically called "error variance," for minority group children, is indirect, being based on studies of social class and socio-

---

[2]See Anastasi (1958) and Tyler (1956).

economic differences rather than on minority group performance *per se.* Nevertheless, the particular kinds of minority groups that we have in mind are closely associated with the lower levels of socio-economic status. The results of studies by Warner, Davis, Deutsch, Deutsch and Brown, Havighurst, Hollingshead, Sears, Maccoby, and many others are cases in point. Many of these studies are discussed by Anastasi (1958), Tyler (1956) and Deutsch (1960).

For children who come from lower socio-economic levels, what characteristics may be expected to affect test performance in general, and the accuracy or precision of test results in particular? The list of reported characteristics is long, and it is not always consistent from one investigation to another. But, at least, it may be hypothesized that in contrast to the middle-class child the lower-class child will tend to be less verbal, more fearful of strangers, less self-confident, less motivated toward scholastic and academic achievement, less competitive in the intellectual realm, more "irritable," less conforming to middle-class norms of behavior and conduct, more apt to be bilingual, less exposed to intellectually stimulating materials in the home, less varied in recreational outlets, less knowledgeable about the world outside his immediate neighborhood, and more likely to attend inferior schools.

Some Examples

Can it be doubted that such characteristics—even if only some of them apply to each "deprived" minority group—will indeed be reflected in test-taking and test performance? Obviously, the primary effect will be shown in terms of test validity for such children. In many cases, however, the lowering of test validity may be indirectly a result of lowered test reliability. This would be particularly true if such characteristics interfere with the consistency of performance from test to retest for a single examiner, or for different examiners. Consider the following examples and probable results.

Example: A Negro child has had little contact with white adults other than as distant and punitive authority figures.

Probable Result: Such a child might have difficulty in gaining rapport with a white examiner or reacting without emotional upset to his close presence. Even in an individual testing situation, he might not respond other than with monosyllables, failing to give adequate answers even when he knows them. The examiner, reacting in terms of his own stereotypes, might also lower the reliability and validity of the test results by assuming that the child's performance will naturally be inferior, and by revealing this attitude to the child.

Example: Children from a particular minority group are given little reason to believe that doing well in the school situation will affect their chance for attaining better jobs and higher income later in life.

Probable Result: Such children will see little purpose in schooling, dislike school, and will reject anything associated with school. In taking tests, their primary objective is to get through as rapidly as possible and escape from what for them might be an uncomfortable situation. Their test performance might, therefore, be characterized by a much greater amount of guessing, skipping, and random responses that is shown by the middle-class child who never doubts the importance of the test, wants to please his teacher and parents, and tries his best.

Special Norms Often Needed

When the national norms do not provide adequate differentiation at the lower end of the aptitude or ability scale, special norms, established locally, are often useful. For instance, if a substantial number of underpriviledged or foreign-background pupils in a school or school district rank in the lowest five percent on the national norms, local norms might serve to provide a special scale within this range. If the score distribution with the first few percentiles of the national norms is mainly a function of chance factors, however, a lower level of the test or an easier type of test is needed for accurate measurement of the low-scoring children.

Responsibilities of Test Users

The sensitive test user should be alert to reliability considerations in regard to the particular group involved and the intended use of the tests. In assessing reports on test reliability provided by test manuals and other sources, he will not be satisfied with high reliability coefficients alone. He will consider not only the size of the reliability samples, but also the nature and composition of the samples and the procedures used to estimate reliability. He will try to determine whether the standard error of measurement varies with score levels, and whether his testing conditions are similar to those of the reliability samples. He will ask whether the evidence on reliability is relevant to the persons and purposes with which he is concerned. He will know that high reliability does not guarantee validity of the measures for the purpose in hand, but he will realize that low reliability may destroy validity.

The examiner should be well aware that test results are characteristically influenced by cultural and subcultural differentials and that the performance of underpriviledged minority group children is often handicapped by what should be test-extraneous preconditions and response patterns. He should not necessarily assume that the child from a minority group family will be as test-sophisticated and motivated to do his best as are the majority of environment-rich middle-class children.

If the examiner finds—and this will be typical—that the reliability sample does not provide him with information about the reliability of the test for the kind of children he is testing he should urge that the test results not be taken at face value in connection with critical decisions concerning the children. Very often, careful examination of responses to individual test items will indicate to him that the apparent performance of the child is not adequately reflecting the child's actual competence or personality because of certain subcultural group factors.

II. Predictive Validity

Of course, if an individual's test scores were to be used only to describe his relative standing with respect to a specified norm group, the fact that the individual had a minority-group background would not be important. It is when an explanation of his standing is attempted, or when long-range predictions enter the picture (as they usually do), that background factors become important.

For example, no inequity is necessarily involved if a culturally disadvantaged child is simple reported to have an IQ of 84 and a percentile rank of 16 on the national norms for a certain intelligence test. However, if this is interpreted as meaning that the child ranks or will rank no higher in learning ability than does a middle-class, native born American child of the same IQ, the interpretation might well be erroneous.

Factors Impairing Test Validity

Three kinds of factors may impair a test's predictive validity. First, there are test-related factors—factors or conditions that affect the test scores but which may have relatively little relation to the criterion. Such factors may include test-taking skills, anxiety, motivation, speed, understanding of test instructions, degree of item or format novelty, examiner-examinee rapport, and other general or specific abilities that underlie test performance but which are irrelevant to the criterion. Examples of the operation of such factors are found in the literature describing the problems of white examiners testing Negro Children (Dreger and Miller, 1960), of American Indian children taking unfamiliar, timed tests (Klineberg, 1935), and of children of certain disadvantaged groups being exposed for the first time to test-taking procedures (Haggard, 1954).

It should be noted that some test-related factors may not be prejudicial to disadvantaged groups. For example, test-taking anxiety of a disruptive nature (Sarason et al., 1960) may be more prevalent in some middle-class groups than in lower-class groups. In general, however, the bias attributable to test-related factors accrues to the detriment of the culturally disadvantaged groups.

The problem of making valid predictions for minority group children is faced by the Boys' Club of New York in its Educational Program,[3] which is designed to give promising boys from tenement districts opportunities to overcome their environmental handicaps through scholarships to outstanding schools and colleges. Although the majority of the boys currently enrolled in this program had mediocre aptitude and achievement test scores up to the time they were given scholarships, practically all of the boys have achieved creditable academic success at challenging secondary boarding schools and colleges. In this program, normative scores on the Otis Quick-Scoring Mental Ability Test and the Stanford Achievement Test are used for screening purposes, but they are regarded as minimal estimates of the boys abilities. The Wechsler Intelligence Scale for Children (WISC) is frequently used in this program to supplement the group tests. The boys typically score 5 to 10 points higher on the WISC than on the Otis, probably because the WISC gives less weight to educational and language factors.

Interest and Personality Inventory Scores

When standardized interest inventories are used, special caution should be observed in making normative interpretations of the scores of culturally disadvantaged individuals. When a child has not had opportunities to gain satisfaction or rewards from certain pursuits, he is not likely to show interest in these areas. For example, adolescent children in a particular slum neighborhood might rank consistently low in scientific, literary, musical, and artistic interests on the Kuder Perference Record if their home and school environments fail to stimulate them in these areas. With improved cultural opportunities, these children might rapidly develop interests in vocations or avocations related to these areas.

Scores on personality inventories may also have very different significance for minority group members than for the population in general (Auld, 1952). Whenever the inventory items tap areas such as home or social adjustment, motivation, religious beliefs, or social customs, the appropriateness of the national norms for minority groups should be questioned. Local norms for the various minority groups involved might again be very much in order here.

Predicting Complex Criteria

A second class of factors contributing to low predictive validity is associated with the complexity of criteria. Criteria generally represent "real

[3]Information about this program is obtainable from The Boys Club of New York, 287 East 10th Street, New York, N.Y.

life" indices of adjustment or achievement and therefore they commonly sample more complex and more variegated behaviors than do the tests. An obvious example is the criterion of school grades. Grades are likely to reflect motivation, classroom behavior, personal appearance, and study habits, as well as intelligence and achievement. Even if a test measured scholastic aptitude sensitively and accurately, its validity for predicting school marks would be attenuated because of the contribution of many other factors to the criterion. It is important, therefore, to recognize the influence of other factors, not measured by the tests, which may contribute to criterion success. Since disadvantaged groups tend to fare poorly on ability and achievement tests (Anastasi, 1958; Tyler, 1956; Masland, Sarason, and Gladwin, 1958; Eels et. al., 1951; Haggard, 1954), there is particular merit in exploring the background, personality, and motivation of members of such groups for compensatory factors, untapped by the tests, which may be related to criterion performance.

In some instances, such as in making scholarship awards on a statewide or national basis, test scores are used rigidly for screening or cut-off purposes to satisfy demands for objectivity and "impartiality." The culturally disadvantaged child (quite possibly a "diamond-in-the-rough") is often the victim of this automatic and autocratic system. Recourse lies in providing opportunities where the hurdles are less standardized and where a more individualized evaluation of his qualifications for meeting the criterion may prove to be fairer for him.

For example, the following characteristics that may be typical of minority group children who have above-average ability or talent are among those cited by DeHaan and Kough (1956), who have been working with the North Central Association Project on Guidance and Motivation of Superior and Talented Secondary School Students:

They learn rapidly, but not necessarily those lessons assigned in school.
They reason soundly, think clearly, recognize relationships, comprehend meanings, and may or may not come to conclusions expected by the teacher.
They are able to influence others to work toward desirable or undesirable goals.

Effects of Intervening Events on Predictions

A third set of contributors to low criterion validity is related to the nature of intervening events and contingencies. This class of conditions is particularly important when the criterion measure is obtained considerably later than the testing—when predictive rather than concurrent validity is at stake. If the time interval between the test administration and the criterial assessment is lengthy, a host of situational, motivational, and maturational changes may occur in the interim. An illness, an inspiring teacher, a shift in aspiration level or in direction of interest, remedial training, an economic misfortune, an emotional crisis, a growth spurt or retrogression in the abilities sampled by the test—any of these changes intervening between the testing and the point or points of criterion assessment may decrease the predictive power of the test.

One of the more consistent findings in research with disadvantaged children is the decline in academic aptitude and achievement test scores of such children with time (Masland, Sarason, and Gladwin, 1958). The decline is, of course, in relation to the performance of advantaged groups or of the general population. It is plausible to assume that this decline represents the cumulative effects of diminished opportunities and decreasing motivation for acquiring academic knowledge and skills. When such cumulative effects are not taken into consideration, the predictive power of academic aptitude and achievement tests is impaired. If it were known in advance that certain individuals or groups would be exposed to deleterious environmental conditions, and if allowances could be made for such contingencies in connection with predictions, the test's criterion validity could be improved.

Looking in another direction, the normative interpretation of the test results cannot reveal how much the status of underprivileged individuals might be changed if their environmental opportunities and incentives for learning and acquiring skills were to be improved significantly. In the case of the Boy's Club boys mentioned above, estimates of academic growth potential are made on the basis of knowledge of the educational and cultural limitations of the boys' home and neighborhood environment, observational appraisals of the boys' behavior in club activities, and knowledge of the enhanced educational and motivational opportunities that can be offered to the boys in selected college preparatory schools. With this information available, the normative interpretation of the boys' scores on standardized tests can be tempered with experienced judgment, and better estimates of the boys' academic potential can thus be made.

In situations where minority group members are likely to have to continue competing with others under much the same cultural handicaps that they have faced in the past, normative interpretation of their aptitude and achievement test scores will probably yield a fairly dependable basis for short-term predictive purposes. When special guidance or training is offered to help such individuals overcome their handicaps, however, achievement beyond the normative expectancies may well be obtained, and predictions should be based on expectancies derived specifically from the local situations. In this connection, it should be recognized that attempts to appraise human "potential" without defining the milieu in which it will be given an opportunity to materialize are as futile as attempts to specify the horsepower of an engine without knowing how it will be energized.

"Culture Fair" and "Unfair"—in the Test and in Society

The fact that a test differentiates between culturally disadvantaged and advantaged groups does not necessarily mean that the test is invalid. "Culturally unfair" tests may be valid predictors of culturally unfair but nevertheless highly important criteria. Educational attainment, to the degree that it reflects social inequities rather than intrinsic merit, might be considered culturally unfair. However, a test must share this bias to qualify as a valid predictor. Making a test culture fair may decrease its bias, but may also eliminate its criterion validity. The remedy may lie in the elimination of unequal learning opportunities, which may remove the bias in the criterion as well as in the test. This becomes more a matter of social policy and amelioration rather than a psychometric problem, however.

The situation is quite different for a test that differentiates between disadvantaged and advantaged groups even *more* sharply than does the criterion. The extreme case would be a test that discriminated between disadvantaged and advantaged groups but did not have any validity for the desired criterion. An example of this would be an academic aptitude test that called for the identification of objects, where this task would be particularly difficult for disadvantaged children but would not be a valid predictor of academic achievement. Here, one could justifiably speak of a true "test bias." The test would be spuriously responsive to factors associated with cultural disadvantage but unrelated to the criterion. Such a test would not only be useless for predicting academic achievement, but would be stigmatizing as well.

While certain aptitude and ability tests may have excellent criterion validity for some purposes, even the best of them are unlikely to reflect the true *capacity for development* of underprivileged children. For, to the extent that these tests measure factors that are related to academic success, they must tap abilities that have been molded by the cultural setting. Furthermore, the test content, the mode of communication involved in responding to test items, and the motivation needed for making the responses are intrinsically dependent upon the cultural context.

Elixir of "Culture-Fair" Tests

The elixir of the "culture-fair" or "culture-free" test has been pursued through attempts to minimize the educational loading of test content and to reduce the premium on speed of response. However, these efforts have usually resulted in tests that have low validities for academic prediction purposes and little power to uncover hidden potentialities of children who do poorly on the common run of academic aptitude and achievement tests.

In spite of their typical cultural bias, standardized tests should not be sold short as a means for making objective assessments of the traits of minority-group children. Many bright non-conforming pupils, with backgrounds different from those of their teachers, make favorable showings on achievement tests, in contrast to their low classroom marks. These are very often children whose cultural handicaps are most evident in their overt social and interpersonal behavior. Without the intervention of standarized tests, many such children would be stigmatized by the adverse subjective ratings of teachers who tend to reward conformist behavior of middle-class character.

III. The Validity of Test Interpretation

The most important consideration of all is one that applies to the use of tests in general—namely, that test results should be interpreted by competently trained and knowledgeable persons wherever important issues or decisions are at stake. Here, an analogy may be drawn from medical case history information that is entered on a child's record. Certain features of this record, such as the contagious-disease history, constitute factual data that are easily understood by school staff members who have not had medical training. But other aspects of the medical record, as well as the constellation of factors that contribute to the child's general state of health, are not readily interpretable by persons outside the medical profession. Consequently, the judgment of a doctor is customarily sought when an overall evaluation of the child's physical condition is needed for important diagnostic or predictive purposes. So, too, the psychological and educational test records of children should be interpreted by competently trained professional personnel when the test results are to be used as a basis for decisions that are likely to have a major influence on the child's future.

There are several sources of error in test interpretation stemming from a lack of recognition of the special features of culturally disadvantaged groups. One of these may be called the "deviation error." By this is meant the tendency to infer maladjustment or personality difficulty from responses which are deviant from the viewpoint of a majority culture, but which may be typical of a minority group. The results of a test might accurately reflect a child's performance or quality of ideation, but still the results should be interpreted in the light of the child's particular circumstance in life and the range of his experiences. For example, a minister's son whose test responses indicate that he sees all women as prostitutes and a prostitute's son whose test responses give the same indication may both be accurately characterized in one sense by the test. The two boys may or may not be equally disturbed, however. Clinically, a safer inference might be that the minister's son is the one who is more likely to be seriously disturbed by fantasies involving sex and women.

There is evidence to indicate that members of a tribe that has experienced periodic famines would be likely to give an inordinate number of food responses on the Rorschach. So too might dieting Palm Beach matrons, but their underlying anxiety patterns would be quite different than those of the tribesmen. Or, to take still another example, the verbalized self-concept of the son of an unemployed immigrant might have to be interpreted very differently from that of a similar verbalization of a boy from a comfortable, middle-class, native-American home.

A performance IQ that is high in relation to the individual's verbal IQ on the Wechsler scales may signify psychopathic tendencies but it also may signify a poverty of educational experience. Perceiving drunken males beating up women on the Thematic Apperception Test may imply a projection of idiosyncratic fantasy or wish, but it may also imply a background of rather realistic observation and experience common to some minority group children.

For children in certain situations, test responses indicating a low degree of motivation or an over-submissive self-image are realistic reflections of their life conditions. If these children were to give responses more typical of the general population they might well be regarded as sub-group deviants. In short, whether test responses reflect secondary defenses against anxiety or are the direct result of a socialization process has profound diagnostic import so that knowledge of the social and cultural background of the individual becomes quite significant.

What Does the Test Really Measure

A second type of error, from the view point of construct and content validity,[4] might be called the "simple determinant error." The error consists in thinking of the test content as reflecting some absolute or pure trait, process, factor, or construct, irrespective of the conditions of measurement or of the population being studied. Thus, a fifth-grade achievement test may measure arithmetical knowledge in a middle-class neighborhood where most children are reading up to grade level, but the same test, with the same content, may be strongly affected by a reading comprehension factor in a lower-class school and therefore may be measuring something quite different than what appears to be indicated by the test scores.

Generally, the test-taking motivation present in a middle-class group allows the responses to test content to reflect the differences in intelligence, achievement, or whatever the test is designed to measure. On the other hand in a population where test success has much less reward-value and where degree of test-taking effort is much more variable from individual to individual, the test content may tap motivation as well as the trait purportedly being measured.

Caution and knowledge are necessary for undertaking and taking into

[4]For a discussion of various types of test validity, see Anastasi (1961), Cronbach (1960), Guilford (1954), Thorndike and Hagen (1961), Lindquist (1950).

account testing conditions and test-taking behavior when test results are being interpreted for children from varying backgrounds. A child coming from a particular cultural subgroup might have very little motivation to do well in most test situations, but under certain conditions or with special kinds of materials he might have a relatively high level of motivation. As a result, considerable variability might be evident in his test scores from one situation to another, and his scores might be difficult to reconcile and interpret.

How a question is asked is undoubtedly another important factor to consider in interpreting test results. A child might be able to recognize an object, but not be able to name it. Or, he might be able to identify a geometric figure, but not be able to reproduce it. Thus, different results might be obtained in a test depending upon whether the child is asked to point to the triangle in a set of geometric figures or whether he is required to draw a triangle.

Response Sets May Affect Test Results

In attitude or personality questionnaires, response sets[5] such as the tendency to agree indiscriminately with items, or to give socially desirable responses, may contribute error variance from the view point of the content or behavior it is desired to sample. To the extent that such sets discriminate between socially advantaged and disadvantaged groups, the target content area may be confounded by specific test format. Thus, a scale of authorization may be found to differentiate among social classes, but if the scale is so keyed that a high score on authoritarianism is obtained from agreement with items, the social class differences may be more reflective of an agreement set rather than an authoritarian tendency. If authoritarian content is logically distinct from agreement content, these two sources of test variance should be kept distinct either through statistical control, by a change in the item format, or by having more than one approach to measurement of the trait in question.

From the standpoint of content validity, there is a third type of error. This may be termed the "incompleteness of content coverage" error. This refers to a circumscribed sampling of the content areas in a particular domain. In the area of intelligence, for instance, Guilford (1954) has identified many factors besides the "primary mental abilities" of Thurstone and certainly more than is implied in the unitary concept of intelligence reflected by a single IQ score. As Dreger and Miller (1960) point out, differences in intellectual functioning among various groups cannot be clearly defined or understood until all components of a particular content area have been systematically measured.

Familiarity with the cultural and social background of minority-group children not only helps to avoid under-evaluating the test performance of

[5]For a discussion of this and related concepts, see Anastasi (1961), Cronbach (1960).

some children, but also helps to prevent over-evaluating the performance of others. For example, children who have been trained in certain religious observances involving particular vocabularies and objects, or those who have been encouraged to develop particular skills because of their cultural orientations, might conceivably score "spuriously" high on some tests or on particular items. In other words, any special overlap between the subgroup value-system of the child and the performances tapped by the test is likely to be an important determinant of the outcome of the test.

Failure Barriers May Be Encountered

Failure inducing barriers are often set up for the minority-group child in a testing situation by requiring him to solve problems with unfamiliar tools, or by asking him to use tools in a manner that is too advanced for him. To draw an analogy, if a medical student were handed a scalpel to lance a wound, and if the student were to do the lancing properly but were to fail to sterilize the instrument first, how should he be scored for his accomplishment? If he had never heard of sterilization, should his skillful performance with the instrument nevertheless be given a "zero" score? Similarly, if a child from a disadvantaged social group shows a considerable degree of verbal facility in oral communication with his peers but does very poorly on tests that stress academic vocabulary, can he justifiably be ranked low in verbal aptitude?

In a broad sense, most intelligence test items tap abilities involving language and symbol systems, although opportunities for developing these abilities vary considerably from one social group to another. One might reasonably expect that a child living in a community that minimizes language skills—or, as depicted by Bernstein (1960), a community that uses a language form that is highly concrete—will earn a score that has a meaning very different from that of the score of a child in a community where language skills are highly developed and replete with abstract symbolism. It is important, therefore, to interpret test results in relation to the range of situations and behaviors found in the environments of specific minority groups.

Some Suggested Remedies

While this analysis of the problems involved in the use and interpretation of tests for minority group children may lead to considerable uneasiness and skepticism about the value of the results for such children, it also points up potential ways of improving the situation. For example, one of these ways might consist of measuring separate skills first, gradually building up to more and more complex items and tests which require the exercise of more than one basic skill at a time. With enough effort and ingenuity, a sizable universe of items might be developed by this procedure. Special attention should also be given to the selection or development of items and tests that maximize criterial differentiations and minimize irrelevant discriminations. If a test is likely to be biased against certain types of minority groups, or if its validity for minority groups has not been ascertained, a distinct *caveat* to that effect should appear in the manual for the test.

Furthermore, we should depart from too narrow a conception of the purpose and function of testing. We should re-emphasize the concept of the test as an integral component of teaching and training whereby a floor of communication and understanding is established and *learning* capabilities are measured in repeated and cyclical fashion.

Finally, we should think in terms of making more use of everyday behavior as evidence of the coping abilities and competence of children who do not come from the cultural mainstream. Conventional tests may be fair predictors of academic success in a narrow sense, but when children are being selected for special aid programs or when academic prediction is not the primary concern, other kinds of behavioral evidence are commonly needed to modulate the results and implications of standardized tests.

CONCLUSION

Tests are among the most important evaluative and prognostic tools that educators have at their disposal. How unfortunate, then, that these tools are often used so routinely and mechanically that some educators have stopped *thinking* about their limitations and their benefits. Since the minority group child is so often handicapped in many ways these test scores may have meanings different from those of non-minority children, even when they are numerically the same. The task of the conscientious educator is to ponder what lies behind the test scores. Rather than accepting test scores as indicating fixed levels of either performance or potential, educators should plan remedial activities which will free the child from as many of his handicaps as possible. Good schools will employ well qualified persons to use good tests as one means of accomplishing this task.

In testing the minority group child it is sometimes appropriate to compare his performance with that of advantaged children to determine the magnitude of the deprivation to be overcome. At other times it is appropriate to compare his test performance with that of other disadvantaged children —to determine his relative deprivation in comparison with others who have also been denied good homes, good neighborhoods, good diets, good schools, and good teachers. In most instances it is especially appropriate to compare the child's test performance with his previous test performance. Utilizing the individual child as his own control and using the test norms principally as "bench marks," we are best able to gauge the success of our efforts to move the minority group child forward on the long, hard, road of overcoming the deficiencies which have been forced upon him. Many comparisons depend upon tests, but they also depend upon *our* intelligence, our good will, and our sense of responsibility to make the proper comparison at the proper time and to undertake proper remedial and compensatory action as a result. The misuse of tests with minority group children or in any situation, is a serious breach of professional ethics. Their proper use is a sign of professional and personal maturity.

REFERENCES

1. American Educational Research Association and National Committee on Measurements Used in Education. *Technical Recommendations for Achievement Tests* (Washington, D. C.; National Educational Association, 1955).
2. American Psychological Association, "Technical Recommendations For Psychological Tests and Diagnostic Techniques." *Psychol. Bull.,* 51, No. 2, (1954).
3. A. Anastasi. *Psychological Testing,* 2d ed., (New York: Macmillan, 1961).
4. ——— *Differential Psychology,* 3d ed. (New York: Macmillan, 1958).
5. F. Auld, Jr., "Influence of Social Class on Personality Test Responses." *Psychol. Bull.,* 49 (1952), pp. 318–332.
6. B. Bernstein, "Aspects of Language and Learning in the Genesis of the Social Process." *J. Child Psychol. Psychiat.,* 1 (1961) pp. 313–324.
7. ———"Language and Social class." *Brit. J. Social,* II 1960 pp. 271–276.
8. L. Cronbach. *Essentials of Psychological Testing,* 2d ed. (New York: Harper, 1960).
9. R. DeHaan, and J. Kough, "Teacher's Guidance Handbook: Identifying Students with Special Needs." Vol. I Secondary School Edition (Chicago: Science Research Associates, 1956).
10. M. Deutsch. *Minority Group and Class Status as Related to Social and Personality Factors in Scholastic Achievement.* Monograph No. 2 (Ithaca, New York: The Society for Applied Anthropology, 1960).
11. ———"The Disadvantaged Child and the Learning Process: Some Social Psychological and Developmental Considerations." In H. Passow, ed., *Education in Depressed Areas* (New York: Teachers College Press, 1963).
12. M. Deutsch and B. Brown, "Some Data on Social Influences in Negro-White Intelligence Differences." *J. Social Issues,* XX, No. 2, pp. 24–35.
13. R. Dreger and K. Miller, "Comparative Psychological Studies of Negroes and Whites in the United States." *Psychol. Bull.,* 57 (1960), pp. 361–402.
14. K. Eells et al. *Intelligence and Cultural Differences* (Chicago: University of Chicago Press, 1951).
15. J. A. Fishman and P. I. Clifford, "What Can Mass Testing Programs Do for-and-to the Pursuit of Excellence in American Education?" *Harvard Educ. Rev.,* 34 (1964), pp. 63–79.
16. C. Froehlich and K. Hoyt. *Guidance Testing,* 3d ed. (Chicago: Science Research Associates, 1959).
17. J. Guilford. *Psychometric Methods,* 2d ed. (New York: McGraw-Hill, 1954).
18. E. Haggard, "Social Status and Intelligence: an Experimental Study of Certain

Cultural Determinants of Measured Intelligence." *Genet. Psychol. Monogr.*, 49 (1954), pp. 141–186.

19. O. Klineberg. *Race Differences* (New York: Harper, 1935).
20. M. Katz. *Selecting an Achievement Test: Principles and Procedures* (Princeton, N.J.: Educational Testing Service, 1958).
21. E. Lindquist, ed. *Educational Measurement* (Washington, D.C.: American Council of Education, 1950).
22. R. Masland, S. Sarason, and T. Gladwin. *Mental Subnormality* (New York: Basic Books, 1958).
23. S. Sarason, et al. *Anxiety in Elementary School Children* (New York: Wiley, 1960).
24. R. Thorndike and E. Hagen. *Measurement and Evaluation in Psychology and Education*, 2d ed. (New York: Wiley, 1961).
25. L. Tyler. *The Psychology of Individual Differences*, 2d ed. (New York: Appleton-Century-Crofts, 1956).

GLOSSARY OF TERMS

Criterion. A standard that provides a basis for evaluating the validity of a test.

Cultural bias. Propensity of a test to reflect favorable or unfavorable effects of certain types of cultural backgrounds.

Culture-fair test. A test yielding results that are not culturally biased.

Culture-free test. A test yielding results that are not influenced in any way by cultural background factors.

Error variance. The portion of the variance of test scores that is related to the unreliability of the test.

Educational loading. Weighing of a test's content with factors specifically related to formal education.

Norms. Statistics that depict the test performance of specific groups. Grade, age, and percentile are the most common type of norms.

Normative scores. Scores derived from the test's norms.

Reliability. The degree of consistency, stability, or dependability of measurement afforded by a test.

Reliability coefficient. A correlation statistic reflecting a test's consistency or stability of measurement.

Standard deviation. A statistic used to depict the dispersion of a group of scores.

Standard error of measurement. An estimate of the standard deviation of a
   person's scores that would result from repeated testing with the same or
   a similar test, ruling out the effects of practice, learning, or fatigue.

Validity. The extent to which a test measures the trait for which it is designed,
   or for which it is being used, rather than some other trait.

Index

Ability grouping, 5
Accomplishment; *see also* Achievement
  new standard for, 201–206
Accountability; *see also* Responsibility
  as achievement, 107
  administrators in, 69–70
  center of, 103
  charter of, 54–56
  central committee for, 55
  comparisons among districts in, 92–93
  concept of, 77–78
  criterion problem in, 51–52
  curricular reform and, 73–76
  defined, 4, 50
  of district administrators, 87–88
  evaluation of results against objectives in, 8, 56, 71
  experimental verification of approach in, 93–95
  failure of, 50–52
  four elements in, 153–154
  future of, 168–169
  vs. humanism, 5
  for instructional growth, 45
  instruments of, 59
  intercorrelation in, 93
  intervention and, 56–58
  level of, 103
  liabilities in, 68–69
  measures of, 51
  "modes of proof" in, 75
  omitted variables in, 94
  performance contracting and, 157, 165–168
  potential problems in, 93
  of principal, 103
  principal's reaction to, 106
  proposed approach to, 82–83

Accountability (*continued*)
  for public schools, 77–98
  purpose, goals, and objectives of, 54
  reasons for, 3–5
  responsibility assignment in, 84
  results vs. objectives in, 56
  of school administrators, 86–87
  socioeconomic status and, 93
  subject matter in, 68–72
  teacher-pupil relationships in, 25–26
  teachers and, 69, 84
  trend toward, 9–10
Accountability interview, 59–60
Accountability measurement
  personnel assignment and selection in, 96–97
  personnel incentives and compensation in, 97
  potential uses of, 96–98
  program evaluation and research in, 97–98
  proposed methodology for, 88–93
  replication in, 95–96
  validity in, 95–96
Accountability programs, 157–222
  background of, 51
  children's reaction to, 108
  educators' responsibility in, 71–72
  for elementary schools, 99–108
  failure of, 50–52
  management of, 162
  model of, 165–168
  parents and, 106–107
  pilot project in, 166–167
  problems of, 101–102
  public participation in, 112–113
  requirements for, 52
  teacher needs in, 58–60

225